PRAISE FO[...]

sensitive

"Offering a deft mixture of science reporting, manifesto, and advice, Granneman and Sólo make an urgent case for harnessing the power of the sensitive individual in an increasingly noisy world."

—CAL NEWPORT, *New York Times* bestselling author of *Digital Minimalism* and *Deep Work*

"Granneman and Sólo's engaging and science-backed gem of a book is equal parts revelation, validation, and celebration. An absolute must-read for everyone who experiences this world with wholehearted deep feeling, conscience, and empathy."

—ELLEN HENDRIKSEN, PhD, author of *How to Be Yourself*

"A well-organized, thoughtful look at sensitivity by the devoted creators of a popular, information-rich online community for sensitive people." —JUDITH ORLOFF, MD, author of *The Empath's Survival Guide*

"Who wins human flourishing wins the future. In gardens of the overlooked and underrated, smart leaders will discover amazing talents: introverts, late bloomers, and now the highly sensitive. Granneman and Sólo's book expands our horizons. It is a victory for humanity."

—RICH KARLGAARD, author of *Late Bloomers*

"Granneman and Sólo, creators of Highly Sensitive Refuge online community for sensitive people, skillfully explore the misunderstood trait. The authors' argument is cogent and accessible, and they make clear ways readers can harness the trait without ignoring its challenges. This will empower readers to reframe their sensitivity as a strength."

—*Publishers Weekly*

Also by Jenn Granneman

The Secret Lives of Introverts

sensitive

sensitive

....

THE HIDDEN POWER
of the HIGHLY SENSITIVE PERSON in a
LOUD, FAST, TOO-MUCH WORLD

Jenn Granneman and Andre Sólo

HARMONY

NEW YORK

For anyone who is softer inside than they let on

contents

Introduction

It starts with a boy and a girl. They've never met, but their stories begin the same. They're from the Midwest, with blue-collar parents and not enough money. Neither of their families knows what to make of them. They're different from other kids, you see, and it's starting to show.

Sometimes the boy seems normal enough. He follows the rules in kindergarten. He's polite to his teachers, and kind to the other kids, but when recess rolls around, he shrinks. Something about the playground is too much for him. Instead of joining for kickball, or tag, or king of the jungle gym, he runs away. He flees from the screaming and laughing and hides in the only place he can find: an old storm sewer pipe.

At first, the teachers don't even notice, because he always slinks back at the end-of-recess bell. But one day he takes a kickball with him so he won't be alone. It might be cute under different circumstances, but there are never enough balls to go around, and the other kids complain when they see him run off with it. That's when the teachers find him, and the concern starts. His parents don't understand: Why do you hide in a sewer pipe? What do you *do* in there? His answer—that it's quiet—doesn't help. He'll need to learn to play with the other kids, they tell him, no matter how loud or overstimulating it is.

The girl, on the other hand, doesn't run away. In fact, she seems to have a knack for reading people. She becomes the ringleader of her group of friends, sensing easily what each kid wants or what will make them happy. Soon, she organizes them to pull off neighborhood events: a family carnival, complete with games and prizes, or a particularly elaborate haunted house for Halloween. These events take weeks of effort, and she's perfectly at home refining every detail. Yet when the big day comes, she's not out in the middle of the action, howling at the puppet show or running from game to game. Instead, she stays on the edges. There are just too many people, too many emotions, too much laughing and shouting and winning and losing. Her own carnival overwhelms her.

It's not the only time she gets overstimulated. She has to modify her clothes, cutting off straps so the fabric doesn't rub her skin (when she was a baby, her mom recalls, they had to cut the feet off her footed sleepers, too). In the summer, she's excited to go to a week-long camp, but her mom has to drive her home early; she can't sleep in a crowded bunk, let alone one crackling with the feelings and intrigues of a dozen little girls. These reactions surprise and disappoint people, and their reactions in turn surprise and disappoint the girl. For her parents, her behavior is a cause of worry: what if she can't handle the real world? Still, her mom does her best to encourage her, and her dad reminds her she has to say things out loud rather than just thinking them in her head. But she has a *lot* of thoughts—libraries of them—and people rarely understand them. She is called many things, sometimes even sensitive, but it's not always a good thing. It's something to be fixed.

No one calls the boy sensitive. They do call him gifted when he reads and writes above his grade level, and he eventually gets permission to spend lunch hours in the school library—it frees him from the roar of the lunchroom, and it's less alarming than a drainpipe. His peers have other words for him. They call him weird. Or that worst-of-all word, *wuss*. It doesn't help that he can never hide his big feelings, that he sometimes cries at school, and that he breaks down when he sees bullying—even if he's not the victim.

But as he grows older, he increasingly is. The other boys have little respect for the dreamy kid who prefers a walk in a forest over a football game, who writes novels instead of coming to parties. And he has no interest in vying for their approval. It costs him: He gets shoved in hallways and mocked at lunch, and gym class may as well be a firing squad. He is seen as so soft, so weak that an older girl becomes his biggest bully, laughing as she writes obscenities on his shirt with a marker. He cannot admit any of this to his parents, least of all his dad, who told him the way to handle a bully is to punch the person in the face. The boy has never punched anyone.

Both the girl and the boy, in their separate lives, start to feel as if there is no one else like them in the world. And both seek a way out. For the girl, the solution is to withdraw. By high school, each day overwhelms her, and she comes home so fatigued that she hides in her room from her friends. She often stays home sick, and though her parents are nice about it, she wonders if they worry about her. For the boy, the way out is to learn to act tough. It's to say he doesn't care about anyone—as if he could take them all on. The attitude fits him about as well as a grown-up's army helmet. Nor does it have the intended effect: Rather than coming to respect him, the other kids avoid him completely.

Soon the boy is skipping school and hanging out with a clique of stoner artists—people who feel as deeply as he does, who don't judge his way of seeing the world. The girl finds acceptance in an abusive church. The church members don't think she's weird, they assure her. They think she has miracle powers, even a special purpose, as long as she does everything they say.

What no one says is, You're perfectly normal. You're sensitive. And if you learn how to use this gift, you can do incredible things.

The Missing Personality Trait

In common usage, *sensitive* can mean a person has *big emotions*—crying for joy, bursting with warmth, wilting from critique. It can also be *physical;* you may be sensitive to temperature or fragrance or sound. A growing body of scientific evidence tells us that these two types of sensitive are real and that they are in fact the same. Physical and emotional sensitivity are so closely linked that if you take Tylenol to numb a headache, research shows you will score lower on an empathy test until the medication wears off.

Sensitivity is an essential human trait, and one that is tied to some of our species' best qualities. But as we'll see, it is still not widely understood by the public, despite being well studied by the scientific community. These days, thanks to advances in technology, scientists can reliably test how sensitive a person is. They can spot differences in the brains of sensitive people on functional magnetic resonance imaging (fMRI) scans, and they can accurately identify the behavior of sensitive people in scientific studies, including the powerful advantages that come with being sensitive. Yet most people—perhaps your boss, your parents, or your spouse—do not think of sensitivity in this way, as a real, measurable personality trait.

More to the point, sensitivity is often seen as a bad thing. We discourage it in our kids ("stop crying!" or "shake it off!"), and we weaponize it against adults ("you're overreacting" or "you're being too sensitive"). We hope this book will change that. We envision a world where the word *sensitive* is commonplace in our everyday conversations, so that a person can say "I'm very sensitive" at a job interview or on a first date and receive an approving smile. This is a tall order, but it's not impossible. *Introverted* was once a dirty word, too, but today there's nothing unusual about introducing oneself in this way. We want to create a world where the same is true of sensitivity. We believe that normalizing this deeply human quality will finally allow sensitive people to thrive—and when they do, society will benefit from their unique gifts.

Over the last decade, we've been privy to many conversations in which someone learns for the first time what sensitivity really is. When they do, something that was previously missing clicks into place. They have an aha moment about who they are and why they do the things they do—or they finally understand their child, coworker, or spouse in a different way. Thus, we believe that sensitivity is often the missing personality trait. It is missing from our daily conversations and from our awareness as a society. It's missing from our schools, workplaces, politics, institutions, families, and relationships.

This missing knowledge matters. It's what makes sensitive people hide who they are, like our boy, or feel so out of place, like our girl. Perhaps this knowledge has been missing from your life, too. If so, we hope you find comfort in these pages and gain a deeper understanding of yourself.

Who This Book Is For

This book is written for three types of people. The first is the reader who already knows they are sensitive, and perhaps even identifies as a *highly sensitive person*. If this is you, we hope everything in this book will be of value to you and that you will learn something new. We have drawn on the most recent research, across many disciplines, to offer you the tools you need to harness your tremendous gifts and to protect yourself from overstimulation. More than that, we aim to help you do the crucial work of flipping the conversation about being sensitive. You will learn how to thrive in an often overbearing world, how to change shame-based patterns, and how to step up when needed as a leader (even if you don't feel like one). In the end, we hope you will feel empowered to advocate for a better, more sensitive age in our increasingly loud and cruel world.

The second is the person who may never have thought of themselves as sensitive but who is starting to wonder. Perhaps you've always known you're different in how you think and react to situations. Perhaps you have a deep sensitivity on the inside that you do not always show on the outside. Or perhaps you are simply starting to recognize a part of yourself in what we've described. If this is you, we hope our book will give you some answers. You may even find a sense of peace in learning that others have shared struggles much like your own and that you are not alone in what you've experienced. In the end, it may feel good to call yourself a sensitive person. There is power in words, names, and labels, as sensitive people already know. Often, when we give something a name, it helps us make sense of it and embrace and nurture it in a healthy way.

The third type of person is our treasured guest. It's the reader who was handed this book by a friend, a spouse, a child, or an employee. If this is you, someone in your life knows that they are sensitive, and they want you to understand them. This is a sign of trust. It may mean they've been cautious sharing their sensitivity up until now, worrying that others would see it as a weakness. Or it may mean they have struggled to put it into words. Either way, this person is probably hoping that as you read, you will come to understand their experiences and needs—and accept them as valid. They are asking you to be on their side.

What's in This Book

The first half of this book will give you a clear picture of what it really means to be sensitive and what strengths sensitive people bring to the world. It will also help you see which parts of sensitivity you relate to and determine for yourself if you are a sensitive person. We'll get into the science behind sensitivity and the five mighty gifts that all sensitive people are born with. We'll also look at the cost of those gifts—overstimulation—and how sensitive people can overcome that cost and thrive. Finally, we'll zoom in on one of the most misunderstood gifts of all, empathy, and how to transform it from a source of hurt to a world-changing strength.

The second half of this book will get into the specifics: How, exactly, does a sensitive person thrive in life—and how are their needs different from those of less-sensitive people? We'll look at sensitive people in love and friendship, raising a sensitive child, building a meaningful career, and the powerful traits of sensitive leaders, who are often the most effective leaders of all. Finally, we'll paint a picture of what comes next: how we can stop hiding our sensitivity and start valuing it. Despite living in a loud, fast, and too-much world—one that is increasingly harsh and divided—we believe there has never been a better time to be sensitive. In fact, our world's biggest challenges are sensitive people's greatest opportunities to shine. We believe they are the leaders, healers, and visionaries that our world needs the most right now, if only we can recognize their strengths.

Sensitive Is Strong

None of this is easy, as our boy and our girl discovered. As adults, both found only half the solution. The boy built an independent lifestyle that let his mind roam free, riding a bicycle across Mexico and sleeping under the stars while he wrote books. It was a meaningful way to live, and he didn't have to worry about overstimulation. But he still denied he was sensitive and hid his powerful emotions.

The girl knew very well that she was sensitive and led with her heart in all things, but she struggled to build a life that worked for her. She burned through a series of relationships and careers that she had hoped would fill her life with meaning—journalism, marketing, and teaching—but each bombarded her sensitive mind until she came home in a fog. She could feel herself burning out—again.

And then they met.

A curious thing happened. The girl taught the boy what it means to be sensitive, and he finally stopped hiding his feelings. The boy taught the girl how to live a different life, one where she no longer spent every waking minute worn out. Soon they joined forces. They began to work together, they founded a website together, and bit by bit, they each built a happy sensitive life.

And they became the authors of this book.

Those little kids were us. Jenn got out of the harmful church and made a life in which her strength came from inside, not from the approval of others. Andre retired his bicycle—temporarily, he insists—and he learned to take pride in his sensitive mind. And, together, we created Sensitive Refuge, the world's largest website for sensitive people. We are sensitive, and we are proud of it.

Our story is just one of many, many ways that sensitive can be strong. Every sensitive person gets to choose their own path. But there's one step that we all have to take, and it's the hardest of all: to stop seeing sensitivity as a flaw and to start seeing it as a gift.

chapter 1

Sensitivity:
Stigma or Superpower?

I can't stand chaos. I hate loud environments.
Art makes me cry. No, I'm not crazy; I'm a textbook
example of a highly sensitive person.

—Anne Marie Crosthwaite

The year was 1903. Picasso danced at the Moulin Rouge, electric lights burned at all-night clubs, and Europe's cities thundered into a new era. Streetcars rushed commuters down buggy-packed streets, telegraphs connected faraway places, and breaking news crossed continents in minutes. Technology charmed its way into people's homes, too, with phonographs squawking out music on demand for parties. The songs may have been a prelude to an evening at the picture house—or they may have covered up the sound of streets being ripped up to install modern sewers. Even the countryside was abuzz, with farmers using mechanized equipment for the first time. Life was changing, and progress, it was believed, was good.

The German city of Dresden wasn't about to be left behind. Its leaders wanted to show off their own steps forward and crib achievements from other cities. Votes were held, committees were formed, and a citywide expo was announced, complete with a series of public lectures. One of the speakers was the early sociologist Georg Simmel. Although little known today, Simmel was influential in his time. He was one of the first people to apply a scientific approach to human interaction, and his work tackled every part of modern life, from the role of money in human happiness to why people flirt. If city officials hoped he would praise progress, however, they were badly mistaken. Simmel took the podium and promptly threw out the topic he'd been given. He wasn't there to talk about the glories of modern life. He was there to discuss its effect on the human soul.

Innovation, he suggested, had not just given us more efficiency; it gave us a world that taxed the human brain and its ability to keep up. He described a nonstop stream of "external and internal stimuli" in a loud, fast, overscheduled world. Far ahead of his time, he suggested that people have a limited amount of "mental energy"—something we now know to be more or less true—and that a highly stimulating environment consumes far more of it. One side of our psyche, the side built around achievement and work, may be able to keep up, he explained, but our spiritual and emotional side was absolutely spent. Humanity, Simmel was saying, was too sensitive for such a life.

Of particular concern to Simmel was how people coped. Unable to react meaningfully to every new piece of information, overstimulated citizens were apt to become "blasé" or, simply put, apathetic. They learned to suppress their feelings, to treat one another transactionally, to care less. After all, they had to. They heard terrible news from around the world daily, like the eruption of Mount Pelée, which killed twenty-eight thousand people in minutes, or the horrors of British concentration camps in Africa. Meanwhile, they tripped over homeless people and tuned out strangers packed tightly in the streetcar. How could they possibly extend empathy, or even simple acknowledgment, to everyone they met? Instead, they closed off their hearts out of necessity. Their demanding outer world had devoured their inner world and, with it, their ability to connect.

Simmel warned that by living under such overload, we face "being levelled down and swallowed up." As you might expect, his words were initially met with scorn. But once published, they became his most-talked-about essay. The piece spread quickly because it put to words something that many people secretly felt: The world had become too fast, too loud, too much.

That was more than 120 years ago, when much of life still moved at the speed of the horse and buggy. It was before the invention of the internet, the smartphone, and social media. Today, life is even busier, as we work long hours, care for our children or aging parents with little support, and squeeze friendships into text threads between errands. No wonder we are stressed, burned out, and anxious. Even the world itself is objectively more overstimulating than in Simmel's day. By some estimates, we are now exposed to more information each day than a person living in the Renaissance encountered in their entire lifetime: As of 2020, we produce 2,500,000,000,000,000,000 bytes of data *per day*. At that rate, roughly 90 percent of all the data in human history has been created in the last five years. Every scrap of this data, in theory, is aimed at someone's brain.

The human animal is not designed for such unlimited input. Rather, our brain is a sensitive instrument. Researchers who study that instrument now agree that, just as Simmel warned, it can only process so much. Push its limit, and everyone, no matter their personality or how tough they are, eventually hits overload. Their reactions start to slow, their decisions suffer, they become irate or exhausted, and if they keep pushing, they burn out. This is the reality of being an intelligent and emotional species: Like an overworked engine, our big brain eventually needs time to cool off. Humanity really is, as Simmel knew, a sensitive creature.

What Simmel did not know, however, is that not everyone is sensitive to the same degree. In fact, there is one group of people who are wired to be more physically and emotionally responsive than others. These people—the sensitive people—feel our too-much world very deeply.

The Stigma of Being Sensitive

Although you are reading this book, you may not want to be called sensitive, let alone *highly* sensitive. To many people, *sensitive* is a dirty word. It sounds like a weak spot, a guilty admission, or, worse, an insult. In common usage, *sensitive* can mean many things, and most of them are based in shame:

- When we call someone sensitive, what we really mean is they can't take a joke, are easily offended, cry too much, get their feelings hurt too easily, or can't handle feedback or criticism.
- When we refer to ourselves as sensitive, what we often mean is we have a habit of overreacting.
- Sensitivity is associated with softness and femininity; in general, men especially do not want to be seen as sensitive.
- A sensitive subject is one that is likely to offend, hurt, anger, or embarrass the listeners.
- Likewise, the word *sensitive* is often paired with an intensifier: Don't be *too* sensitive; why are you *so* sensitive?

In light of these definitions, it makes sense why you might bristle at being called sensitive. Case in point: As we wrote this book, curious friends and family asked us what our book was about. "Highly sensitive people," we'd reply. Occasionally, people would get excited because they knew what this term meant. "That's me!" they'd tell us enthusiastically. "You're describing me." But the vast majority of the time, people had the wrong idea of what we were talking about, and their misconceptions about sensitivity became clear. Some thought we were writing a book about how our society has become too politically correct. Others thought we were giving advice on how to be less easily offended (the word *snowflake* came up more than once).

Another time, we asked a friend who is an author to read an early draft of our book and give us feedback on it. While reading, she realized that she herself is a sensitive person and that the man she is dating fits the sensitive description as well. For her, this revelation was deeply affirming. Yet when she broached the topic with her boyfriend, he got defensive. "If someone called me sensitive," he retorted, "I'd be really offended."

Sensitivity, then, as a dimension of human personality, has gained an unfortunate reputation: It has wrongly become associated with weakness. It's seen as a defect that must be fixed. Just type the word *sensitive* into Google, and you'll see what we mean: As of December 2021, the top three related searches were "suspicious," "embarrassed," and "inferior." Or, type the phrase "I'm too sensitive," and you'll find articles with titles like "I'm Too Sensitive. How Can I Toughen Up?" and "How to Stop Being So Sensitive." Because of the misconceptions around sensitivity, even sensitive people themselves have internalized a sense of shame about who they are. For years, we have run an online community for sensitive people called Sensitive Refuge. Although there is growing awareness around the topic, readers still frequently ask us, "How do I stop being so sensitive?"

The answer, of course, is *not* to stop being sensitive—because, in reality, these shame-based definitions are not what sensitive means at all.

What Being Sensitive Really Means

It began with a simple observation about babies: Some were upset by new sights and smells, while others remained unfazed. In his lab in the 1980s, psychologist Jerome Kagan and his team performed a series of tests on about five hundred babies. They dangled Winnie the Pooh mobiles before them, held cotton swabs dipped in diluted alcohol to their noses, and projected a face onto a screen that seemed to speak in an eerie synthetic voice. Some babies hardly reacted at all, remaining calm throughout the entire forty-five-minute session. Others moved constantly, kicking, thrashing, arching their backs, and even crying. Kagan labeled these babies "high reactive," while the others were "low reactive" or fell somewhere in the middle. The high-reactive babies, it seemed, were more sensitive to their environment and had probably had this trait since birth. But would this temperament stay with them for life?

Today, we know that it does. Kagan and his associates followed many of the babies into adulthood. Those high-reactive infants, now in their thirties and forties, have become high-reactive adults. They still have big reactions—they confess to getting nervous in crowds, overthinking things, and worrying about the future. But they also work hard and excel in many ways. Most earned high grades in school, built good careers, and made friends just as easily as anyone else did; many were thriving. And many described how they had built confidence and calm in their lives while still preserving their sensitivity.

While Kagan associated this temperament with fearfulness and worry, connecting it to the amygdala (the "fear center" of the brain), today we know it's a healthy trait. Dozens of researchers have confirmed this finding—most notably Elaine Aron, arguably the founder of the field of sensitivity research. (In fact, the fearfulness that Kagan observed in some of those high-reactive kids largely went away by adulthood.) Today, the same trait Kagan studied is known by many names:

highly sensitive people (HSPs), sensory processing sensitivity, biological sensitivity to context, differential susceptibility, or even "orchids and dandelions," with sensitive people being the orchids. The experts behind each of these terms agree they all refer to the same trait, however. And, recently, there has been a move to bring these theories together under a single umbrella term: *environmental sensitivity.* We take our cue from these researchers and will refer to the trait as environmental sensitivity, or just sensitivity for short.

No matter what you call it, sensitivity is defined as the ability to perceive, process, and respond deeply to one's environment. This ability happens at two levels: (1) perceiving information from the senses and (2) thinking about that information thoroughly or finding many connections between it and other memories, knowledge, or ideas. People who are sensitive do more of both. They naturally pick up more information from their environment, process it more deeply, and are ultimately more shaped by it. Much of this deep processing happens unconsciously, and many sensitive people aren't even aware that they do it. This process applies to everything a sensitive person takes in.

However, we prefer a simpler definition: If you're sensitive, everything affects you more, but you do more with it.

In fact, a better word for *sensitive* might be *responsive.* If you are a sensitive person, your body and mind respond more to the world around you. You respond more to heartbreak, pain, and loss, but you also respond more to beauty, new ideas, and joy. You go deep where others only skim the surface. You keep thinking when others have given up and moved on to something else.

Not Just Artists and Geniuses

Sensitivity, then, is a normal part of life. All humans—and even animals—are sensitive to their environment to some degree. There are times when all of us cry, get our feelings hurt, and feel overwhelmed by stressful events, and there are times when all of us reflect deeply, marvel at beauty, and pore over a subject that fascinates us. But some individuals are fundamentally more responsive to their surroundings and experiences than others are. These are the highly sensitive people.

Like other traits, sensitivity is a continuum, and everyone falls somewhere along it, from low to average to high sensitivity. All three categories are considered normal, healthy traits. And sensitive people are not alone: Recent research suggests that highly sensitive individuals make up approximately 30 percent of the population. (Another 30 percent are low sensitive while the remaining 40 percent fall somewhere in between.) Being sensitive, in other words, isn't some rare fluke, reserved only for artists and geniuses. It's about one out of every three people in every city, workplace, and school. Sensitivity is also equally common among men and women. Men may be *told* not to be sensitive, but that doesn't change the fact that they are.

In Their Own Words: What Does Being Sensitive Mean to You?

"I am sensitive, and I spent most of my life believing I was flawed because no one else I knew was quite like me. Now I see my sensitivity as a blessing. I have a very rich and imaginative inner life. I've never been bored. I feel sorry for some of my friends who live their lives on the surface, never experiencing the deep, inner attunement to nature, the arts, and the universe in all its magnificent splendor. They do not ask the big questions about life and death. They talk about what they watched on TV or where they're going next Sunday." —Sally

"To some people, the word *sensitive* has the connotation of being touchy or weak. But it can be a great asset to be emotionally in touch with what others are feeling as well as what you are feeling. I view being sensitive as a way of being respectful and kind to yourself and others. It's a special and important awareness that not everyone has." –Todd

"As a guy, toxic masculinity meant that being labeled sensitive was akin to being labeled effeminate, moody, or touchy. In reality, I was none of those things. I was hyper-aware of my own self and feelings, and I knew those other labels were not true—but I had no idea what it was until I happened upon some literature about HSPs [highly sensitive people]." –Dave

"I used to view the word *sensitive* as a negative thing because my dad would tell me, 'You are too sensitive.' Now I see the word in a different light. I feel good about being sensitive, and I now know that it is a positive thing in this world that can be so cold. Overall, I would not trade my sensitivity if I could. I love how deeply I can appreciate all that is around me." –Renee

"I used to think of sensitivity as a weakness because my family of origin and my ex-husband constantly told me that I needed to grow up or grow a thicker skin and that I was overreacting. I was constantly put down for it. But now that they're out of my life, I'm focusing on it as a strength, and I'm actually back in grad school getting a second master's degree to change careers and become a therapist. Now I'm going to use my sensitivity to help others." –Jeannie

Are You a Sensitive Person?

Maybe you can taste the oak in a chardonnay before anyone else at a dinner party. Maybe you become pleasantly overwhelmed by

Beethoven's Ninth Symphony, or you tear up while watching pet rescue videos. Or maybe the constant click-clack of someone typing nearby makes it impossible to concentrate. These can all be signs of heightened sensitivity—and many of us are more sensitive than we realize.

So, here is a checklist of the most common characteristics of sensitive people. The more boxes you check, the more sensitive you are. You don't need to check every box—or relate to every point in this book—to be considered a sensitive person. Remember, sensitivity is a continuum, and everyone will fall somewhere along it.

Also, keep in mind that your life experiences will influence how your sensitivity is expressed. For example, if you were taught to set healthy boundaries from a young age, you may have never struggled with people pleasing or conflict avoidance as some sensitive people do. Other aspects of your personality will also make a difference in how closely you relate to the following statements. For example, if you consider yourself more of an extrovert than an introvert, you may need less downtime than an introverted sensitive person needs.

Which of the following statements are true for you?

- ☐ In general, you tend to pause before acting, giving your brain time to do its work.
- ☐ You notice subtle details, like the slight difference in shade between brushstrokes on a painting or a microexpression that quickly vanishes from your coworker's face.
- ☐ You feel strong emotions. You have a hard time shaking intense emotions like anger or worry.
- ☐ You have a lot of empathy, even toward strangers or people you only hear about in the news. You easily put yourself in other people's shoes.
- ☐ Other people's moods really affect you. You easily absorb emotions from others, taking on their feelings as if they were your own.

☐ You feel stressed and fatigued in loud, busy environments, like a crowded shopping mall, concert, or restaurant.

☐ You need plenty of downtime to maintain your energy levels. You often find yourself withdrawing from other people so you can calm your senses and process your thoughts.

☐ You read people well and can infer, with surprising accuracy, what they are thinking or feeling.

☐ You have a hard time watching violent or scary movies or witnessing any kind of cruelty toward animals or humans.

☐ You hate feeling rushed and prefer to do things carefully.

☐ You're a perfectionist.

☐ You struggle to perform at your best under pressure, such as when your boss is evaluating your work or you are participating in a competition.

☐ Sometimes your environment is your enemy. A chair with a hard back, lights that are too bright, and music that is too loud can make it feel impossible to relax or focus.

☐ You startle easily at sudden noises, like when someone sneaks up on you.

☐ You're a seeker. You think deeply about life and ask why things are the way they are. You may have always wondered why other people aren't as captivated by the mysteries of human nature and the universe as you are.

☐ Your clothing really matters. Scratchy fabrics or restrictive clothing—like pants with a tight waistband—can throw off your day.

☐ You seem to have a lower pain tolerance than other people.

☐ Your inner world is alive and present. You've been described as imaginative and creative.

☐ You have vivid dreams (and nightmares).

☐ You seem to have a harder time adjusting to change than other people.

☐ You've been called shy, picky, intense, dramatic, too sensitive, or high maintenance.

☐ You've also been called conscientious, thoughtful, wise, insightful, passionate, or perceptive.

☐ You read a room well.

☐ You are sensitive to changes in your diet and blood sugar levels. If you haven't eaten in a while, you might get "hangry" (hungry + angry).

☐ For you, a little caffeine or alcohol goes a long way.

☐ You cry easily.

☐ You desire harmony in your relationships, so conflict can be very distressing for you, perhaps even making you feel physically ill. As a result, you may people-please or go to great lengths to avoid disagreements.

☐ You desire depth and emotional intensity in your relationships. Transactional or surface-level connections aren't enough for you.

☐ Your mind moves quickly. Thus, you often feel out of sync with other people, and this feeling can be profoundly lonely.

☐ Words really matter to you. You can't easily brush off hurtful or critical words.

☐ You are self-reflective, knowing your strengths and weaknesses well.

☐ You are deeply moved by art and beauty, whether it's a song, a painting, or just the way the sunlight hits the autumn leaves.

Or, consider the following simple self-assessment about what is easy for you versus what is challenging for you. If you relate to most of these statements, you are likely a sensitive person.

It's easy for me to . . .	It's challenging for me to . . .
• read people's moods or intentions.	• deal with strong emotions from other people, especially anger, stress, or disappointment.
• do slow, careful work to high standards.	• work fast under pressure or scrutiny.
• notice details that others ignore.	
• seek holistic solutions that benefit the group.	• prioritize my own needs.
	• ignore intrusive scents, textures, or noises.
• find beauty and meaning in the everyday world.	• endure overly busy or active environments.
• make art, be creative, or deliver unique insights.	
	• spend time in ugly or harsh settings.
• empathize with others, especially when they are hurt.	• watch or read depictions of violence.

Perhaps you are realizing for the first time in your life that you are a sensitive person. If so, welcome to the club; you are not alone. In fact, you're in good company: Many of history's greatest scholars, artists, leaders, and movement builders have been sensitive. Without the sensitive mind, the world would not have:

- The theory of evolution
- Germ theory
- *West Side Story*
- The theme music from *Star Wars*
- The end of apartheid
- Studio Ghibli
- Maya Angelou's *I Know Why the Caged Bird Sings*
- Netflix
- Maslow's hierarchy of needs
- Klimt's *The Kiss*

- The Declaration of Independence
- The first non-fungible token (NFT)
- Mary Shelley's *Frankenstein*
- *Mister Rogers' Neighborhood**

The most important thing to know is you're not broken or wrong because you're sensitive. The truth is, you have a superpower—one that the human species has relied on for millions of years.

An Evolutionary Advantage

More than just being normal, sensitivity is a good thing. In fact, scientists believe it's an evolutionary advantage, one that helps organisms survive in a variety of environments. For evidence, you need only look at how many species have developed the trait: The list stands at more than one hundred, including cats, dogs, fish, birds, rodents, insects, and numerous primates. What's more, researchers have found that sensitivity has evolved multiple times in separate primate lineages—a strong sign that it has survival and social benefits. Just following around rhesus macaques shows those benefits in action. One study found that sensitive macaques who had caring mothers grew to be precocious, clever individuals who were resilient to stress. They frequently became leaders in their monkey troop. Sensitivity can be seen all across the animal kingdom. Maybe you've witnessed a particularly cunning squirrel outsmart your attempts to keep it off your bird feeder, or you've had

---

* Charles Darwin, Girolamo Fracastoro, Jerome Robbins, John Williams, Nelson Mandela, Hayao Miyazaki, Maya Angelou, Reed Hastings, Abraham Maslow, Gustav Klimt, Thomas Jefferson (warts and all), Kevin McCoy, Mary Wollstonecraft Shelley, and Fred McFeely Rogers. We cannot know for certain whether all of these individuals would consider themselves sensitive, but all of them—based on interviews, biographies, or their own words—exhibit traits common to highly sensitive people.

an exceptionally smart pet. (One of Jenn's cats, Mattie, who we think was highly sensitive, learned to open cabinet doors.)

Among early humans, the advantage may have been even more vital—and it still is today. After all, the ability to see patterns and notice key details means that sensitive people are often good at predicting events; they have strong intuition. This connection between intuition and sensitivity is measurable: In one study, sensitive people outperformed others at a gambling game. Another study, using a computer simulation of natural selection, showed that sensitive individuals came out ahead of less-sensitive individuals over time. Effectively, they spent more time studying their options and comparing them to past results, and this discernment earned them more resources over time—more than enough to offset the extra time and energy they spent.

Thus, researchers theorize, sensitive people probably increase the survival odds of the whole human species. When you see and hear what others miss, you are better able to avoid predators and threats, or to find resources. When you learn well from your mistakes, you don't make them twice and you help others avoid pitfalls, too. And when you read others well—including what they don't say—you're better equipped to form alliances and help people cooperate.

On the tundra or in the jungle, then, sensitivity is an advantage. Sensitive people may once have been our weather predictors, spiritual advisers, and trackers. Take that same trait and apply it to a teacher, a stock market trader, or a CEO, and you can see how sensitive people are still built to thrive today—even if society doesn't think so.

Our World Needs Sensitive People and Their Superpowers

The nurse didn't like to complain, but she couldn't shake the feeling that something was wrong. Her latest patient, a middle-aged woman, was recovering from heart valve surgery. She told her story in Ted Zeff's book *The Power of Sensitivity* but wished to remain anonymous. So, let's call her Anne. Anne was a Canadian nurse with over twenty years of experience working in critical care. "Although I'm the type of nurse that thrives on the excitement of the high-paced intensive care unit, on my days off, I lay on the couch watching movies to recover from all the overstimulation," she said. "My colleagues tease me, since my downtime is so different from most of their 'adrenaline seeking' behavior."

Until this point, Anne's patient had been recovering well, and the doctor thought no further care was needed. It would have been easy for Anne to sign her off her list and let the surgical team manage her instead. But something in her gut kept stopping her from doing that. Each time Anne checked on her, the patient seemed a little worse. For one, the patient only felt comfortable lying on her right side, which was unusual.

Anne had recently learned that she was a sensitive person, so she had come to work that day acutely aware of her superpowers. Taking a break in her office to process the events of the day, she wondered, "If [the patient's] body was trying to tell me something, what would it be? . . . And why am I so worried about her?" Perhaps, as a sensitive person, she was picking up on things that other people on her team couldn't see yet. Usually, at the end of her shift, she felt peaceful, as if she could go home knowing that she had helped someone. But today, she didn't feel that way.

Anne thought about what would happen if she contradicted the doctors. Nurses who step out of line are reprimanded or retrained—or sometimes even fired. Even if the worst didn't happen, Anne didn't want to offend or upset her colleagues, because she knew that strained relationships could compromise patient care. To top it all off, she admitted, she was a little afraid of the lead surgeon, who was overseeing her patient's case.

Despite her fear, Anne knew what she needed to do—speak up. "I knew that I might be her only chance for survival," she said. When one doctor dismissed her concerns, she didn't give up; she went to someone else. He believed her, and he asked if he should scan the patient's heart with a portable ultrasound machine to see if fluid was accumulating around it. Anne said yes, even though it meant performing the procedure without the surgeon's consent, an action she hated to take. But the test immediately validated her intuition—the patient had a large blood clot in her heart. Her heart was mere minutes away from stopping.

The patient was rushed into surgery, and the clot was removed. Thanks to Anne, she made a full recovery. Later, Anne was told that if she hadn't done what she did, the patient would have died. "I felt honored that I could use my HSP gifts to help her," she said. "I now know that my keen observation skills and inner strength helped me see the situation from many levels." And if she could do it all again, she would not be so afraid of the reaction from the surgical team. She "would just kindly, but forcefully, explain my concerns, knowing I could make myself heard." As word of her intervention got around, Anne became the hero of the unit.

Anne is just one person whose sensitivity gives her an advantage on the job. Her story shows that sensitivity isn't just a personal superpower—it's a trait that evolved to benefit the whole human species. If you or your loved one were sick, Anne is exactly the kind of nurse you would want on your side. Sensitivity might just save your life.

The Deep-Processing Sensitive Brain

So how do sensitive people like Anne do it? What gives them their superpowers? The answer lies in how the human brain works.

To a neuron, all kinds of input, from the roar of a cargo train to a smile on a loved one's face, are just data points to be processed. Some brains—those of sensitive people—process more deeply and at greater length than others. A brain can be a bored teenager working a part-time job and missing half of what goes on around it, or it can be a lawyer poring over every detail of a case. Sensitive brains are the lawyers, and like a top lawyer, they don't take time off. They are wired to go deep.

Science backs these differences up. In 2010, Jadzia Jagiellowicz and her team used functional magnetic resonance imaging (fMRI) to peek inside the brains of sensitive people. They looked at both highly sensitive and less sensitive people while showing them black-and-white images of natural scenes, like a house with a fence around it or hay bales in a field. Then the images were changed in some way and shown to the participants again. Sometimes the changes were major, like the addition of a post to the fence, and sometimes they were minor, like slightly enlarging one of the hay bales.

You might think you know where this is going. But if you were going to guess that the most sensitive people spotted the differences quicker than the less-sensitive people did, you'd be wrong. Instead, the most sensitive people took slightly *longer* to notice the changes—in particular, the minor ones. They took longer probably because, according to the researchers, "they are attending more closely to the subtle details of that scene." (If you scour those spot-the-difference images shared on social media and you spend a good amount of time doing it, you might be a sensitive person.)

When the scientists reviewed the brain scans, they noticed another difference. The highly sensitive people showed significantly greater activation in key areas of the brain related to visual processing and evaluating complexities and details rather than just superficial traits. Specifically, highly sensitive people had more activity in the medial and posterior parietal regions and the temporal and left occipitotemporal regions. These differences remained even when the researchers controlled for other traits, like neuroticism and introversion. In other words, it was the trait of sensitivity—not something else—that made them process more deeply.

And this deep processing didn't stop after the experience was over—

the sensitive mind kept going. We know this because Bianca Acevedo, a neuroscientist at the University of California, studied the sensitive brain at rest. To do so, Acevedo and her team scanned the brains of sensitive people while they performed an empathy task: They looked at images and descriptions of happy, sad, or neutral events, then saw the faces of their significant other and strangers making the emotion that corresponded with the event. Between viewing the photos, they were asked to count backward by seven from a large number "to wash away the effects of experiencing any kind of emotion," Acevedo explains. They were also asked to describe how they felt after viewing each photo and, finally, were told to relax while their brains were scanned.

The researchers found that even after the emotional event was over—and even after washing away the resulting emotions—the brains of sensitive people were still processing the event deeply. This depth of processing, Acevedo explains, "is a cardinal feature of high sensitivity." So if you regularly find yourself reflecting on something—an idea, an event, or an experience—long after others have moved on, you might be a sensitive person.

High Intelligence Meets High Empathy

These brain differences show why physical and emotional sensitivity are essentially the same trait: The sensitive mind spends more time processing *everything*, whether it's a bright overhead light, a child's smile, or a new scientific theory. In turn, sensitivity shows itself in different ways: a deep, thoughtful intelligence and a profound, empathetic awareness of people. If you relate to one of these sides more than the other, that doesn't mean you're not sensitive; many sensitive people do lean in one direction. But you have the capability for both.

In fact, the deep processing that a sensitive mind does is so valuable that sensitivity is often linked to brilliance. Linda Silverman, the director of the Gifted Development Center in Denver, says that most gifted individuals are highly sensitive—especially gifted people who rank within the top 1 or 2 percent in terms of intelligence. "My clinical research, spanning more than 42 years, with over 6,500 children assessed with individual intelligence scales at the Gifted Development Center, suggests that there is a correlation between giftedness and sensitivity," she tells us. "The higher an individual's IQ, the more likely the person is to fit the characteristics of an HSP."

Research on successful musicians supports these findings. Psychologist Jennifer O. Grimes studied performers at Ozzfest, of all places, which is one of the largest and wildest heavy-metal festivals in the United States. She found that behind the scenes, these rockers were often sensitive and withdrawn, the opposite of their flamboyant stage personas. This pattern isn't found just in the arts, though. To be sensitive means to think deeply in *any* situation, so high sensitivity leads to innovation in science and good leadership in business. The more sensitive a person is, the more connections they see—connections that others tend to miss. The fact that they can also be warm and empathetic only sweetens the deal.

What Sensitivity Is Not

Just as important as understanding what sensitivity *is,* is knowing what it is *not.* The trait of sensitivity is not the same as introversion, autism, sensory processing disorder, or trauma.

It's easy to see how introversion and sensitivity are mistaken for each other. Recently, introversion has become less stigmatized, thanks in part to Susan Cain's groundbreaking book *Quiet.* Sensitivity, however, is still highly stigmatized, despite the tendency of introverts and sensitive people to share some characteristics, like needing regular downtime, thinking deeply, and having a vivid inner world. (Some experts, including Aron, believe that Cain was actually writing more about highly sensitive people than introverts.) It makes sense that if you are more sensitive to your environment, you may prefer to spend less time around people as a way to reduce stimulation.

Yet there are some key differences between introverts and sensitive people. Introversion describes a social orientation: a person who prefers the company of small groups and enjoys spending time alone. Sensitivity, on the other hand, describes an orientation toward one's environment. Therefore, we could say that introverts are primarily fatigued by socializing, while sensitive people are fatigued by highly stimulating environments, whether they involve socializing or not. In fact, Aron estimates that about 30 percent of sensitive people are extroverts, while 70 percent are introverts. So, you can be an extroverted sensitive person who is outwardly expressive and thrives on relationships, or you can be an introverted sensitive person who cherishes solitude and quiet. (In other words, there's no wrong way to do sensitivity.)

Likewise, autistic people and sensitive people may share some characteristics, such as the tendency to avoid certain smells, foods, or textures, or to be overwhelmed by certain stimuli. However, according to Acevedo's research, there are differences in the brains of autistic people and sensitive people. For one, the autistic and sensitive brains are almost opposites in terms of how they process emotional and social cues. Specifically, the sensitive brain shows higher-than-typical levels of activity in areas related to calmness, hormonal balance, self-control, and self-reflective thinking. The autistic brain, on the other hand, is less active in regions related to calmness, emotion, and sociability. You can see this in the way that individuals with autism may have to learn strategies to interpret social cues, whereas sensitive people read others almost effortlessly—more easily, in fact, than less-sensitive people do.

Sensory processing disorder is sometimes confused with sensitivity because both conditions involve sensitivity to stimuli. However, sensory processing disorder occurs when the brain has trouble receiving and responding to information from the senses. For example, a child with this disorder may overrespond to stimuli and scream when touched, or the child might underrespond to stimuli and play roughly on the playground. Although some sensory discomfort is a characteristic of sensitivity, it does not impair day-to-day functioning the way sensory processing disorder does. Nor is sensory discomfort the only characteristic of sensitivity. Rather, sensitivity means having unusually deep or elaborate mental processing.

Trauma is anything that is too intense for the nervous system to process in the moment. Severe situations like abuse, food scarcity, or violence may cause trauma, but so can experiences like losing a cherished relationship (or pet), becoming ill, or being bullied. Experiencing trauma fundamentally changes the nervous system, leaving the survivor in a state of hypervigilance and hyperarousal. Sensitive people, too, can easily enter a state of hyperarousal, because of their deep mental processing. We call this experience overstimulation, which we discuss in more detail in Chapter 4. Experts agree that sensitive people may be more easily traumatized than others because they are more responsive to *all* stimuli, including stimulation that is traumatic. However, trauma and sensitivity are not inherently the same thing; again, Acevedo found differences in the brains of sensitive people and those with post-traumatic stress disorder (PTSD).

A final note: Just as a person can be both tall and left-handed, it's possible to be sensitive and experience another trait, condition, or disorder alongside sensitivity. For example, you can be a sensitive person and have PTSD (or depression, anxiety, sensory processing disorder, etc.). But sensitivity in and of itself is not a disorder. You cannot be "diagnosed" as a highly sensitive person, and sensitivity does not require treatment, although sensitive people will benefit from learning strategies to deal with overstimulation and emotional regulation. Some people are even starting to consider sensitivity a form of neurodiversity. The theory of neurodiversity says that brain differences should not be considered deficits; rather, they are healthy variations on the spectrum of normal human traits. Sensitive people perceive the world differently and have different needs than less-sensitive people do. Sensitivity isn't substandard or deficient. It helps our species thrive.

The Toughness Myth

As you consider whether you are a sensitive person—or whether someone you know is—keep in mind that sensitive people don't always look like sensitive people. A sensitive person might look like a man who feels out of sync with the dating game because of his uncommon desire for emotional depth and intensity in romantic relationships. Or a new mother who wonders why she can't handle the demands of parenthood the way that other mothers seemingly can. A sensitive person might look like an employee who feels distressed by the competitive nature of her work environment or by the unethical behavior of her boss. Another sensitive person might look like a soldier whose intuition keeps his whole unit safe. Or a scientist whose nagging questions lead her to an important medical breakthrough.

In other words, sensitive people aren't always easy to spot. In many cultures, society requires that we hide our sensitivity. We call this attitude the Toughness Myth. The Toughness Myth tells us:

- Sensitivity is a flaw.
- Only the strong survive.
- Being emotional is a sign of weakness.
- Empathy will get you taken advantage of.
- The more you can endure, the better.
- It's shameful to rest or ask for help.

As a result, many sensitive people downplay or deny their sensitivity. They may put on a mask to appear like the majority, even though they have known from a young age that they stand out. They go to another exhausting party or take on another demanding work project, even though their bodies are begging for rest. They pretend they are not moved deeply by a beautiful song or a poignant movie. They may cry, yes, but in the privacy of their own home, away from intrusive stares.

Sensitive males, especially, are targets of the Toughness Myth. In many cultures, they are taught from a young age that boys don't cry and that being a real man means pushing through physical and emotional pain. Fábio Augusto Cunha is a sensitive man who lives in Brazil, a country known for its culture of machismo, which equates manliness with courage, strength, and power—and sometimes even violence. "For my entire life, I've always felt out of place and had trouble fitting into the traditional way that men 'should' behave," Cunha writes on our site Sensitive Refuge. "I could never fit into the competitive discourse among men. It was like others didn't feel what I felt, like they didn't see the world the way my sensitive soul saw it. In many phases of my life, but especially when I was a teenager, I forced myself to adapt. I had a group of male friends and I'd try to be 'tough' like them. But when I was alone, that's when I really found myself and my sensitive nature through books, songs, and dramatic movies I watched, almost in secret, like I had a hidden identity."

Women, too, are targets of the Toughness Myth, but in a different way, such as when they are brushed off for being "too emotional." Writer, director, and producer Nell Scovell, the creator of *Sabrina the Teenage Witch,* encountered this myth when she took her first TV writing job. "I thought if my male colleagues didn't notice that I was a (whisper) woman, they'd let me stick around," she writes in an essay. So for three decades, she tamped down her emotions at work: "I shrugged off disappointment. I laughed off harassment. When a male boss explained to me why it made sense for him to take credit for work I'd done, the smile on my face did not give away the screaming in my head."

Indeed, Scovell says that men—the people who are supposedly tougher—were given a very different standard, one that allowed for plenty of fragility as long as it was masked with rage. After one tough meeting with the network, for example, a male colleague stomped into the room, yelled a curse word, and threw his script across the table. "It struck me that anger is an emotion too," she writes. "But nobody thought he was 'hysterical.' When a man storms out of the room, he's passionate. When a woman storms out, she's unstable and unprofessional."

Individuals who are marginalized by society, such as people of color or those who are LGBTQ+, may face a double issue when it comes to the Toughness Myth. Having already suffered discrimination and harmful stereotypes, they may resist being seen as sensitive. The term *sensitive* may feel as though it narrows their identity even more, when their identity is already under scrutiny because of the color of their skin or their sexuality. But for many, embracing their sensitivity can feel empowering. Michael Parise, who wrote about being highly sensitive for the LGBT Relationship Network, explains it this way: "Understanding my HSP traits has helped me from feeling like a victim or judging myself and others. It has also freed me to be the gay man I am, without attributing unnecessary baggage to my sexuality."

Black people in particular often say they are expected to project an image of mental toughness and strength, one that is free of emotion, to cope with the stress of racism. Sensitive Refuge contributor Raneisha Price is a sensitive Black woman who has had this experience. She recalls being called a racial slur when she was growing up in a mostly white town in Kentucky. Instead of helping her make sense of the situation—her "unquenchable thirst to know more"—her dad insisted that she remain confident and not let her emotions show (and that she hit back with the equivalent of "kiss my Black ass"). "Being raised a Black woman, you are taught that strong isn't what you have to be, it is what you are. Period," she writes. "So many times—too many to count—

what I felt like on the inside didn't mirror who I was told I was 'supposed to' be." As a result, Price felt as if something was wrong with her. "If I retreated to my room for the 'me time' that sensitive-me craved—the alone time that all HSPs need to process their thoughts and feelings—I was labeled as 'funny-acting' and 'moody,' or mocked as having an undiagnosed psychological problem." It wasn't until her late thirties, when an exceptional therapist helped her embrace her sensitivity, that Price finally believed she no longer needed to hide it.

This constant pressure to hide sensitivity means it remains largely invisible to the world. We routinely laud the accomplishments of sensitive souls—life-changing musical albums, world-changing civil rights movements, and so on—even while we try to quash sensitivity itself. It's good to be kind, but don't be a bleeding heart; it's good to be creative, but stop being so weird about it. Express your feelings, but not so much that anyone must take them seriously. The Toughness Myth, in other words, robs us of something. It leads to harmful choices about our well-being, our work-life balance, how we allow ourselves to be treated, and how we treat one another. Perhaps, as Simmel warned, when we try to tough out an overwhelming world, we really do lose our compassion.

So maybe it's time to try something new.

The Sensitive Way

Let's turn back to that lecture in Dresden. Simmel spoke of a world where urban citizens were so bombarded with sensory input that they became apathetic. More than a hundred years later, the bombardment has only gotten worse. If you're a sensitive person, you feel this too-much world deeply. You feel it as you look for love or raise your children or go to work. You feel the highs higher and the lows lower, and you easily become overstimulated in the kind of environment that Simmel described.

As a result, sensitive people show us a different approach. You might call their viewpoint the Sensitive Way. The Sensitive Way is the belief, deep down, that quality of life is more valuable than raw achievement, that human connection is more satisfying than dominating others, and that your life is more meaningful when you spend time reflecting on your experiences and leading with your heart. In contrast to the Toughness Myth, the Sensitive Way tells us:

- Everyone has limits (and that's a good thing).
- Success comes from working together.
- Compassion pays off.
- We can learn a lot from our emotions.
- We do bigger, better things when we take care of ourselves.
- Calm can be as beautiful as action.

What would happen if we started listening to the Sensitive Way instead of the Toughness Myth? What would happen if sensitive voices began to speak out? If we stopped hiding our sensitivity and started to embrace it? After all, the city officials of Dresden never asked Simmel to speak on how modern life affects the soul. He did it without permission. It took a daring yet contemplative voice to point out what all of us secretly know: that economic progress is good, but progress in human happiness is better.

In this way, your sensitivity can be a gift to the world—even though, at times, it may feel like a curse. In this book, we will celebrate the exceptional strengths that you as a sensitive person have access to, as well as give you tools to lessen and overcome the challenges you face. Our hope is that, through this journey, you will come to see your sensitivity as a good thing. (As we, the authors, have come to see ours.)

That journey starts with understanding what makes you sensitive in the first place—and the surprising advantage that comes with it.

chapter 2

The Sensitive Boost Effect

I think that your entire life is a process of sorting out
some of those early messages that you got.

—Bruce Springsteen

When Bruce Springsteen plays a show, he explodes onto the stage. A true rock legend, he's lost no steam in his seventies, putting on performances that one critic describes as "barn-burning, bombs-dropping, ceiling-cracking, ozone-splitting, three-hour mega-extravaganza concerts." It's this energy that has earned him the title "The Boss" and holds his fans rapt. Many of them have blue-collar roots like those of Springsteen himself. To them, he's emblematic of a tough, hardworking, rebellious American spirit that offers—to quote one of his songs—"no surrender." His fans might call him many things, but "sensitive" probably wouldn't top the list.

Those same fans might be surprised if they met Springsteen off-stage. As a boy, he was "a pretty sensitive kid and quite neurotic, filled with a lot of anxiety," he told an interviewer. He howled in fear during thunderstorms and ran to his baby sister's side to take care of her whenever she cried. A self-described "mama's boy," Springsteen was sometimes so nervous that he chewed his knuckles and blinked "hundreds of times a minute," he reveals in his memoir, *Born to Run*. His shyness and sensitivity didn't always endear him to his classmates, either. Springsteen writes that he quickly became "an unintentional rebel, an outcast weirdo misfit sissy boy . . . alienating, alienated and socially homeless." That was at seven years old.

Springsteen's father, Douglas, who would go on to inspire several of his son's most notable songs, didn't like this sensitive streak. Built like an ox, he was a working man who prized strength, toughness, and the ability to fight. According to Springsteen's memoir, his father's disapproval took the form of a distant aloofness from Bruce, plus nightly alcohol-fueled bouts of chewing him out. (Douglas Springsteen would later be diagnosed with paranoid schizophrenia.) One of the few times he showed any fatherly pride was the day Bruce caught him drunkenly screaming at Bruce's mom. Frightened for his mother—who Bruce adored—he came up behind his dad with a baseball bat and cracked it across his shoulders. The elder Springsteen spun around with rage in his eyes, but rather than exploding, he began to laugh. It became one of his favorite stories to tell: Maybe his boy was tough after all.

Springsteen's experiences are far from unique. As children, many sensitive people are seen as broken. Parents want to fix them or toughen them up—as do coworkers, friends, and even romantic partners later in life. These efforts are misguided not only because sensitivity is a strength but because they simply don't work. Case in point: As Douglas Springsteen found out, all the yelling in the world didn't make his kid less sensitive. That's because, whether you're a rock-and-roll power-house or not, your sensitivity is dyed into who you are.

So, what makes you sensitive in the first place? And how does your sensitivity help you in life? Scientists don't have all the answers about what causes sensitivity, but thanks to new advances in technology, they've discovered some important clues.

It's in Your Genes

When the short version of the serotonin transporter (*SERT*) gene was discovered in the 1990s, it was believed to cause depression. Or rather, since depression is more complex than any one gene can explain, it was believed to increase one's *risk* of depression. The evidence for this connection seemed solid: Multiple studies showed that people with this version of the gene were more likely to react to hard times by becoming either depressed or anxious. And that made sense. The short *SERT* gene variant—which has a shorter section of genetic code in one region than the long variant does—affects serotonin production, and serotonin plays a major role in regulating our mood, well-being, and happiness. Consequently, many researchers accepted the link between the short *SERT* gene and depression as fact. But this conclusion didn't sit well with Joan Chiao. As a neuroscientist, Chiao had come across data that suggested that people of East Asian descent—like herself—were much more likely to carry this gene variant. Nearly twice as likely, in fact, compared to white Westerners. But Chiao had spent much of her life among Asians and Asian Americans, and they didn't seem any more depressed than anyone else. Of course, as a scientist, Chiao didn't take her personal experiences as proof. She decided to investigate: Are depression rates higher in areas such as East Asia, where lots of people have the gene?

Getting the answer wasn't easy. Chiao had to pull together scores of studies, plus data from the World Health Organization, feeding it all into a pair of maps that she published in a 2010 article. One map showed areas where the gene is most common; the other showed areas with the most depression. If it really was the "depression gene," Chiao reasoned, the two maps should look roughly identical. But they didn't. In fact, if you place them side by side, the maps are *opposites* in some ways. East Asia—a place where many people have the gene—barely lights up on the depression map. Yet the United States and parts of Europe—places where people have only a moderate chance of having the gene—glow bright red with depression.

Going by the maps alone, you'd be forgiven for thinking the gene makes certain people depression-proof (it doesn't). Hesitant, Chiao went through other possibilities, like whether depression is overdiagnosed in the West and underdiagnosed in Asia. (It might be, but probably not enough to account for the dramatic difference.) None of her leads bore out, however. So what was going on? Why weren't people with the depression gene getting, well, *depressed*?

For Some, Social Support Goes Further

Chiao wasn't the only scientist asking this question, and some researchers were finding clues. One study, for example, found that people with the short *SERT* gene who had survived a traumatic experience (in this case, a hurricane) were at no higher risk of getting depressed than were people with the long *SERT* gene—if they believed they had good social support. If they lacked that social support, then they were at 4.5 times greater risk of getting depressed. Another study, this one looking at teenagers in foster care, found something similar. The teens with the short *SERT* gene were no more likely to get depressed as long as they had a reliable adult mentor in their life. Only if they lacked a mentor was their risk of depression higher.

Slowly, a new picture emerged. As Chiao compared the maps, she realized that the short gene was more common in places with collectivist cultures, like East Asian countries. Maybe, in these places, certain features of the culture—like long-lasting relationships and family closeness—provide more social support, helping insulate against depression.

Contrast this with individualistic cultures—like the United States—where relationships tend to be more fluid and more easily replaced. In fact, maybe those with the short variant get even more out of whatever kind of social support they receive. Other studies have found, for example, that people with the short *SERT* gene can more easily read, react to, and predict other people's emotions compared to people with the long variant. They may also evaluate risk more accurately and be more creative and empathetic. Later, two other scientists, Baldwin Way and Matthew Lieberman, came to a similar conclusion in 2010. In their study, they gave the short *SERT* variant a new name: the *social sensitivity gene*.

A Modern Approach to Genes

Today, scientists no longer look for a single candidate gene like *SERT* to explain human characteristics. Most heritable traits—even those as seemingly straightforward as height and skin color—are controlled by many genes, not just one. (It's the reason we aren't the exact same height as one parent or have their exact skin color.) Using robotic arms to drip DNA samples onto tiny, chemically reactive trays, researchers can now scan the entire genome of a person, checking for millions of gene variants at once. If this process is repeated across a large-enough sample size—drawn from DNA databases like those you use to check your ancestry—researchers can identify thousands of gene variants involved in a single trait. None of these genes are enough, on their own, to turn a trait on or off, but they all contribute to it in some way. Thus, sensitivity—and most other traits—can be seen as a pattern that emerges across a person's entire genome. The more your genome matches the pattern, the more sensitive you are.

Currently, this work is still in progress for sensitivity, and the pattern hasn't been fully identified. However, the *SERT* gene is probably one of the genes involved in the pattern. Researchers now call *SERT* a *plasticity gene* because it appears to make people more open to their environment, allowing it to shape them more. Other plasticity genes include *MAOA, DRD4,* and others involved in the dopamine system, the brain's reward center. This finding may suggest that sensitive people don't just experience the world differently but that they want different things out of life, too.

Ultimately, the trait of responsivity is what might explain the link to depression. Obviously, if you have a stronger response to the events in your life, negative events may take a higher toll on you. Losing your job or an important relationship, for example, could then make you more at risk of depression than someone else would be. But responsiveness also helps explain why the link isn't always there. What happens, for example, when a person with plasticity genes receives support, encouragement, and affirmation? They still have a strong response to their circumstances, but this time it's positive—it gives them an advantage that other people don't receive. We call this advantage the *Sensitive Boost Effect.* This boost allows sensitive people to springboard far beyond others when they are given basic support. It makes sense, then, that these individuals are at *low* risk of depression because they are insulated by the powerful positive effect of their environment in a way that others are not.

In other words, the more sensitive you are, the more you get out of any experience, good or bad—largely because of your genes.

The Three Types of Sensitivity

The fact that sensitivity isn't determined by just one gene helps explain why no two sensitive people are exactly alike. So far, researchers have identified three main ways that people differ in their sensitivity.

Low sensory threshold: You are sensitive to information you take in through your senses, such as sights, smells, sounds, and textures. Or as we like to say, you are a *super sensor.* This type of sensitivity determines, on the one hand, how attuned you are to your environment and, on the other, how quickly you become overstimulated. You might have a low sensory threshold if any of these tendencies apply to you:

- You feel tired or are quickly overwhelmed in crowded or busy places.
- You have strong reactions to small amounts of caffeine, alcohol, medication, or other substances.
- You feel very bothered by loud noises (like alarm bells or shouting), scratchy or uncomfortable textures (like a wool sweater), or bright lights.
- You are sensitive to slight changes in temperature, such as when a room is a little too warm or cold.

Ease of excitation: You easily respond to emotional stimuli, both from inside yourself and from others. You are a *super feeler.* This type of sensitivity often comes with an innate ability to read people, but it also means you may stress over details or struggle more with painful emotions. You might be sensitive in this way if you experience these behaviors or feelings:

- You easily absorb other people's moods and emotions.
- You need lots of downtime to calm your nervous system and recharge your energy.
- You feel stressed or frazzled when you have a lot to do in a short amount of time.
- You get hangry (hungry + angry) easily.
- You're very sensitive to physical pain (you have a low pain tolerance).
- You try hard to avoid making mistakes (because mistakes cause you to feel a strong sense of embarrassment or shame).
- You jump easily (you have a high startle reflex).

Aesthetic sensitivity: You pay close attention to details in your surroundings, especially artistic details. You are an *aesthete,* someone who has a special appreciation of art and beauty. Signs you might have high aesthetic sensitivity include:

- You are deeply moved by music, poetry, artwork, novels, movies, TV shows, and plays—or a nicely decorated room or a striking scene in nature.
- You have a strong appreciation for delicate scents or tastes (like those of a fine wine).
- You notice small details that others miss.
- You know what needs to be changed to improve an uncomfortable environment (like turning down the thermostat or softening the light).
- You have a rich, imaginative inner world.

If you're a sensitive person, you may be very responsive in all three of these ways, or you may be more responsive in only one or two ways. Michael Pluess, a behavioral scientist at Queen Mary University of London and one of the leading sensitivity researchers in the world, points out that in addition to these three types of sensitivity, some of us are simply wired to respond more to negative experiences (a bad day, a loss, a trauma, etc.), while some of us respond more to positive experiences (e.g., watching an inspirational movie or getting a compliment from our boss). These differences in sensitivity are caused, in part, by variations in our genes. In their chapter in *The Highly Sensitive Brain,* researchers Corina U. Greven and Judith R. Homberg put it this way: "Sensitivity may be thought of as multifaceted and highly flexible, being both affected by variation in genes and life experiences, including childhood environments."

This bring us to the next cause of sensitivity: your childhood environment, including the first one you ever experienced—your mother's womb.

What the Children of the Survivors of 9/11 Teach Us

On the morning of September 11, 2001, tens of thousands of people were going about their lives in the area around the World Trade Center. About seventeen hundred of these people were pregnant women, according to Annie Murphy Paul, author of *Origins: How the Nine Months Before Birth Shape the Rest of Our Lives.* When the planes hit and the Twin Towers fell, these women were swept up in the chaos. Some fought for their lives to escape the towers before the structures collapsed. Others witnessed the horror from neighboring buildings. About half the women would go on to develop PTSD, as was common among 9/11 survivors. Long after the terror of the day had ended, their bodies were convinced they remained in danger, even though they were safe. They suffered panic attacks and nightmares. They jumped at the smallest hint of a threat.

That same morning, about fifteen miles away, Rachel Yehuda was arriving for work at the Bronx Veterans Affairs Medical Center. After finding a TV and watching as the atrocities unfolded, Yehuda began to wonder about the long-term effects of 9/11 on the survivors. A PTSD researcher, she had spent her career working with Holocaust survivors and Vietnam War veterans. In 1993, she opened the world's first psychiatric clinic committed to treating Holocaust survivors. She expected an influx of phone calls from those who had experienced Nazi cruelty directly, but what happened surprised her. Instead, she got more calls from the survivors' grown children than from the survivors—by a ratio of about five to one. "Many of these members of the second generation had symptoms of PTSD," Yehuda told Paul in her book. They described the same nightmares, the same anxiety, and even the same hypervigilance as their parents, even though they had not lived particularly traumatic lives.

At the time, the theory was that children of trauma survivors were scarred by hearing their parents' stories and seeing their struggles. In turn, this experience made them more fearful, more anxious, more attuned to the ever-present dangers of the world. But Yehuda had a different idea. In the years that followed, she went on to coauthor several studies that examined how trauma affects survivors' children. She found that babies of 9/11 survivors had levels of cortisol similar to those of their mothers. Cortisol levels are a key predictor of who will develop PTSD and who won't—and the effect was strongest if 9/11 had occurred in the third trimester of the pregnancy. A later study added another twist: Children were more likely to develop PTSD if their moms—but not their dads—also had PTSD.

What was going on? Since these kids were too young to have heard and understood their moms' terrifying stories of 9/11, the typical explanation didn't hold up. And because the effect was strongest when the trauma happened in the third trimester, it wasn't as simple as the babies inheriting genes that increased their risk of PTSD. Could a mother's experience of trauma pass on to her baby even before that baby was born?

Messages from Our Ancestors

Yehuda had stumbled on what scientists now call *epigenetics*, the relatively new study of how our experiences change the way our genes work. And it's not just our own experiences that affect gene expression—it's the experiences of our ancestors, too. Put simply, epigenetic markers turn certain genes on or off, allowing a species to respond quickly to its environment. Not all these changes are permanent, and the markers don't actually alter your DNA code.

Imagine your genes are a library. Each book contains the instructions to make you who you are. Epigenetics helps choose which books are read and which books are left on the shelf. Traumatic events—like war, the Holocaust, or 9/11—can change the way your genes are read, or expressed, but normal, everyday things can change them, too. Things like diet, exercise, and aging can alter how our genes work. Epigenetics also helps explain why some people are sensitive.

Evidence for epigenetics comes from a recent study on prairie voles, a small brown animal that looks like a mouse. In this study, conducted by Jay Belsky and others, some pregnant voles were placed in a stressful situation (they shared a cage with an aggressive vole), while others were not. Then, their babies were given to adoptive parents. Half of those parents were known to be good caregivers; for prairie voles, good caregiving means lots of nursing, licking, and grooming. The other half were given to negligent parents. When the voles had grown into adults, the scientists evaluated how anxious they were.

The results left no doubt in the scientists' minds. The voles whose mothers were stressed and who were then adopted by good parents were the *least* anxious of all the animals—even compared with the voles whose mothers weren't stressed. The voles that were prenatally stressed and then adopted by bad parents were the *most* stressed of all the animals. The other voles that were not prenatally stressed fell somewhere in between, and it made no difference to their level of anxiety whether they had good or bad parents.

At first glance, these results may seem like no big deal, but they are actually groundbreaking. Until that point, scientists had only focused on the downsides of prenatal stress, like the trauma passed to future generations after 9/11. But just as astronomers can be blinded by a single mote of dust, social science can be clouded by simple human bias. Sometimes, this bias is forgivable; as one developmental researcher told us, no one asks you to study their kid when everything is going fine. Thus, the early work on sensitivity focused on those who were struggling. Belsky, along with Pluess, saw it differently. Similar to the SERT gene, maybe prenatal stress somehow enhances plasticity, sending babies a "message" before they are born. "Pay attention!" the stress might signal to the child. "It's a wild world out there." This message primes them to be more responsive to their environment after birth, making them better able to deal with a fluctuating world than children who had less prenatal stress—the *Sensitive Boost Effect*.

The Other Half of the Story

In the great debate between nature and nurture, the popular answer is, "It's both." But this observation applies especially well to sensitive people, because their genetic pattern makes them more responsive to nurture. Astonishingly, scientists have been able to put an exact number on the split: Your genes are about 47 percent responsible for how sensitive you are. The other 53 percent comes from what scientists call *environmental influences*. (Pluess figured this out by studying pairs of twins who had the same genes but who scored differently on sensitivity.) As a result, influences like your family, your school, and your community can make you more sensitive—and they might matter more than they would for other traits.

In particular, researchers believe that our experiences in the first few years of life are especially important, although they don't know exactly which experiences make us more or less sensitive. "This is one of the important questions still to be explored," Pluess told us in an interview.

One hint comes from a recent U.S. study by Zhi Li and her colleagues, who looked at how children's sensitivity levels changed over one year. In a lab decorated to look like a living room, kids solved puzzles, played games, and, in one case, had their patience tested with treats they were told to wait to eat. The team was looking for signs of sensitivity, such as creativity, deep thinking, and persistence on challenging tasks. The researchers even did some peculiar things to see how the kids would react. In one experiment, a stranger wearing a black plastic bag entered the room, hung out for ninety seconds, and then left without saying anything or even looking at the child. The aim was to see if the sensitive children would be more afraid than the less-sensitive children (they weren't). In another experiment, Li and her colleagues pretended to hurt their head or knee, yelling in pain. They were testing whether the sensitive kids would show more empathy (they did). All the kids in the experiment were about three years old in the first session and returned at about four years old for the second, and most of the experiments were repeated.

The investigators were trained to look for subtle reactions. They knew that sensitive kids tend to be more open to forming positive relationships with others but also tend to be more reserved when going about it. So, Li's team looked for small signs, such as the child's desire to please the experimenters by being polite and following directions carefully. They also expected that the sensitive kids would monitor their own performance and reflect on feedback before making decisions. And, the investigators thought, the sensitive kids would be more cautious in general and work harder to control their emotions and impulses.

Li also wanted to get a glimpse of the children's home life. Was their household unpredictable and chaotic, or was it safe-feeling and stable? Were their parents kind, attentive, and fair, or were they harsh, impatient, and disapproving—yelling when the children made a mistake or acted up? To assess this environment, the investigators watched as the mothers talked to their child about a recent time when the child misbehaved. They also evaluated the kids for cognitive functioning and any behavioral problems, like depression, attention issues, and aggression.

After the last experiment was finally completed and the numbers were crunched, the scientists noticed an interesting pattern: a U-shaped graph. The kids who lived in the most extreme environments—either very supportive or negligent—remained at a consistent level of heightened sensitivity from one year to the next. The kids who had neutral or middle-of-the-road environments—not exceptionally supportive but not necessarily negligent, either—actually *decreased* in their level of sensitivity. And just as in the prairie vole study, the sensitive kids raised in supportive environments benefited the most out of all the children, showing the best cognitive functioning and the fewest behavioral problems.

Why? Scientists aren't entirely sure, but they think it has something to do with what makes sense, in terms of energy usage, for the body. A sensitive person's brain works hard, and sensitive people may spend more time on tasks, using more energy. In supportive environments, children probably benefit from becoming sensitive despite this energy cost because their sensitivity allows them to learn better and thrive— they make the most of their exceptional environment. Sadly, in harsh environments, children also probably benefit from sensitivity, which helps them stay vigilant to threats and evaluate situations carefully before proceeding. It also helps them comply with requests from their caretakers, who may be unpredictable, insensitive to their needs, or harsh in their discipline.

Then there are children raised in neutral environments. They probably don't become as sensitive because sensitivity wouldn't benefit them as much. Sensitivity is a waste of their energy, because they have few threats to defend against and few enriching experiences to learn from. As any sensitive adult can tell you, being highly responsive to your environment can be an exhausting and energy-consuming process and not one to embark on lightly.

So, here we have another clue to what causes sensitivity. In your early years of life, if you were raised in a harsh environment, you may have become more sensitive as a means of survival. If, however, you were raised in a very supportive environment, you may have become more sensitive so that you could soak up every last drop of benefit.

The Power of Vantage Sensitivity

But how much do these early life experiences really matter? For example, if you didn't inherit much of the genetic pattern for sensitivity but your parents fought a lot when you were a child, are you now a highly sensitive adult? Not necessarily. On the other hand, if you *did* inherit the genes for sensitivity but you were raised in a neutral environment, did that environment cancel out your genes? Probably not. It seems that early life experiences add to your sensitivity, but the genetic pattern must first be there. Returning to the study of young children, the kids who already scored high for sensitivity didn't change nearly as much as the other kids over the year, probably because their genes had already made them sensitive. It was the children who started off lower in sensitivity who increased their sensitivity the most in extreme environments, because they were adapting to their surroundings.

As Pluess told us, if sensitivity were simply a trauma response, it would be fairly rare—but it's not. To the contrary, sensitive people are everywhere—about 30 percent of the population—and many of them come from average childhoods. To Pluess, that meant one thing: Sensitivity must offer a bigger advantage than scientists first realized.

Reviewing the data, he thought he knew what that advantage was. What if the swing could go higher than researchers first thought? What if sensitive people were actually poised to rocket past others, if given the right conditions, even later in life? Pluess called this idea *vantage sensitivity,* the theory that high sensitivity is an adaptive trait that maximizes the benefit of any form of support.

To test this theory, Pluess led a depression study of his own, this one not based on the *SERT* gene but based on how people score for sensitivity itself. Importantly, his study looked at teenagers who were well past the early childhood development stage. Not only were they older, but the teens lived in one of the most economically deprived neighborhoods in England. Statistically, they were less likely to have stable households, putting these teens at high risk of depression. But if vantage sensitivity were correct, the most sensitive teens should be the ones most able to overcome it.

For the study, all the teens were given an antidepression program. This program lasted about four months and taught the teens techniques to recognize and become resilient to their depression symptoms. They were assessed for depression at several points before, during, and after the program, to measure how much it was helping them. The results were stunning. For the teens as a whole, the program seemed to have very little impact—until their scores on a sensitivity test were taken into account. It turns out that the less-sensitive teens got almost no benefit out of the program, whereas for sensitive teens, the program was a massive win: They overcame their depression both during the program and for at least one year after it ended, when researchers stopped checking in. The teens' success seemed to thumb the nose at earlier models. Here were kids who had been handed perhaps the toughest childhood environment, and their sensitivity wasn't just helping them survive; it was springboarding them past their peers.

These results have been repeated with sensitive people of other ages and in different circumstances. Sensitive adults on the verge of divorce are more likely to save their marriage if given a relationship intervention. Sensitive kids given quality care go on to develop better social skills and earn better grades than do less-sensitive kids with the same care—and even score higher for altruistic behavior. Meanwhile, therapists report that sensitive people of all ages seem to make more progress and get more out of sessions. By adulthood, sensitive people can even end up being more resilient to stress than less-sensitive people are—the opposite of what most of us would expect. Sensitive people, it appears, are not hothouse orchids who wither in anything but the most perfect conditions. Rather, they are akin to succulents: No drop of nourishment escapes them, and they continue to absorb it until they swell with lovely blossoms.

Sensitive People Are Built for Supergrowth

The reason this advantage goes unrecognized—by people like Bruce Springsteen's father and, for a long time, by many social scientists—is partly because it's counterintuitive. How could the people who are most easily stressed also be the ones who pull ahead of the pack? It's also an issue of language. We have plenty of words to describe someone who is more vulnerable to bad stuff or—getting warmer—someone who's more protected from it. What do you call someone who gets an extra benefit from good stuff? Belsky, who conducted the prairie vole study and mentored Pluess, went so far as to ask colleagues who spoke eight languages if they had a word for it. The closest anyone could come up with was *lucky*.

That's why Belsky and Pluess coined *vantage sensitivity*, and it's why we offer the less technical term, the *Sensitive Boost Effect*. Sensitive people get a bigger boost from the same things that help anyone: a mentor, a healthy home, a positive group of friends. This boost allows them to do more and go further if they are given a nudge in the right direction. Sensitive people are built for *supergrowth*.

Both halves of the sensitivity equation are reminiscent of Springsteen's upbringing. On the one hand, growing up with an angry and disapproving father is exactly the kind of trauma we know increases sensitivity. (In a sense, his father's attempts to toughen him up may have made his son more sensitive.) Springsteen's mother, Adele, was different. Working as a legal secretary, she was the breadwinner of the family and a stabilizing force in young Bruce's otherwise chaotic life. According to Bruce, Adele was kind, compassionate, and considerate of other people's feelings. She was also encouraging. When he thought he could become a rock star, for example, his mother scraped together the money to rent his first guitar. That early attempt was a false start—he actually gave up music until he found a better mentor a few years later—but that's exactly the kind of unflinching support that makes sensitivity pay off the most.

Our Past Doesn't Have to Hold Us Back

Over a career spanning six decades, Bruce Springsteen has won an Academy Award, a Tony Award, twenty Grammy Awards, and more. *Rolling Stone* declared his 2009 Super Bowl halftime show one of the greatest of all time. He's in the Rock & Roll Hall of Fame, and he's one of the world's most famous and highest-paid musicians. His father, Douglas, lived to see him rise to fame. Eventually, Bruce found out that he and his father had more in common than he thought. Douglas might have been a bull on the surface, but inside, "he harbored a gentleness, timidity, shyness and a dreamy insecurity." His father, he saw, was also sensitive; he just hid it. These were all the things that young Bruce "wore on the outside. . . . It was 'soft.' And he hated 'soft.' Of course, he'd been brought up 'soft.' A mama's boy, just like me," he writes in his memoir. While Douglas buried his sensitivity under beer and fistfights, Bruce embraced it, and it took him to great heights.

Despite his extraordinary success, one question still haunts him: Who is he? After all these years, he still doesn't know. Bruce Springsteen, he says, is "a creation," something that remains "liquid." He tells *Esquire*, "You're in search of things like everybody else. Identity is a slippery thing no matter how long you've been at it." More to the point, why is he the way he is? And will DNA always rule his life?

Like Springsteen, you may have asked the same questions about yourself. Why are you the way you are? Is it DNA? Your life experiences? The answer, we now know, is both.

But there's another answer. Springsteen shows us that we aren't locked into the past experiences that we had no control over. You may have had an average childhood or even suffered abuse. But now you have your own power to shape who you want to become—even more power than less-sensitive people have—thanks to the *Sensitive Boost Effect*. Springsteen has utilized this power well. After two mental health crises in his thirties and sixties, he turned to therapy and self-analysis. As he discovered, his childhood set him on one course, but his sensitivity allowed him to change it. In other words, his sensitivity was a gift.

chapter 3

The Five Gifts of Sensitivity

Being gifted doesn't mean you've been given
something. It means, you have something to give.

—Iain S. Thomas

By the time Jane Goodall sat down for her 2014 interview with PBS,
she was already an icon. Holding a plush chimpanzee and stroking its
fur, Goodall was one of the biggest names in biology: a woman who
had not only done decades of groundbreaking research but also bridged
the gap between biology and public imagination. She was the first person to showcase the incredibly humanlike behavior—and emotions—of
chimpanzees, erasing the line that once stood between humanity and
"soulless" animals. If you've ever seen Koko the gorilla communicate
with sign language, it's in part because of Goodall. And if you've ever

thought it makes perfect sense that humans could have evolved from primates, it is, again, in part because of Goodall.

But if you ask Goodall what allowed her to do such groundbreaking work, she won't say it was her academic training. She started out having never attended college, simply showing up in Africa and following the instructions of a professor she'd contacted. Nor was she fueled by a particular passion for chimps—at least not at first. While she had grown up idolizing characters like Mowgli from *The Jungle Book* and even had a stuffed toy chimpanzee named Jubilee, she chose to study chimps because she had asked her mentor where she could make the most difference. That mentor, the anthropologist Louis Leakey, believed that chimpanzees could shed light on human nature, and Goodall took his suggestion to heart.

Without formal training, then, what allowed Goodall to excel? It was her personality, specifically, the warm, sympathetic way in which she viewed her subjects, the chimps. In those days, other scientists gave animals numbers; Goodall gave them names. "I was told you have to give them numbers because you've got to be objective as a scientist," Goodall said in her interview. "And, you mustn't empathize with your subject. And I feel this is where science has gone wrong." Other scientists remained apart, as detached observers; Goodall earned the chimps' trust and walked among them.

The result was spectacular. What looked like unintelligent nesting behavior from a distance, for example, looked to Goodall more like human quirks up close. One nesting female chimp named Mrs. Maggs gingerly tested the branches of a treetop before deciding to settle in. Goodall wrote that people checked hotel beds the same way. Would it be too hard, too soft, too lumpy? Should they request a different room?

Goodall even came to understand chimpanzee humor. One day, when she was walking along the edge of a cliff, a male chimp came charging out of the brush directly at her. Any other biologist might have braced to avoid being shoved over and recorded the event as an attack. Goodall, however, knew that this male was a trickster. She feigned alarm and the chimp stopped short, both of them "laughing" in their respective ways. (Chimp laughter sounds like screechy breathing to our ears.) The chimp repeated the prank a total of four times, much like a kindergartener who tells a favorite joke over and over. He never once touched Goodall.

Lacking a book of procedures, Goodall simply did what came naturally to her—which, thankfully, was empathy. Another untrained observer might have defaulted to identifying the chimps by physical descriptors or lived in fear of the next attack. Some people, without training, might have even tried to control the chimps by force, becoming one of the horror stories of the history of science. But Goodall's personality had a different default: Stay warm and open, take time to understand what people (and animals) are feeling, and treat everyone, including chimps, the way you'd like to be treated yourself. "Empathy is really important," she said. "Only when our clever brain and our human heart work together in harmony can we achieve our true potential."

Despite its success, to say her approach met resistance is an understatement. At the time, anthropomorphizing animals in any way—even just by giving them names—was forbidden and could end a scientist's career. It was considered a massive bias to assume that any animal, no matter what their behavior looked like, might verge on sharing the same inner feelings that people have. To dare to speak of the opposite bias—that biologists might be overlooking the very real emotions of animals—was effectively unpublishable. Even today, respected researchers who are the heirs of Goodall's work have to be cautious, as primatologist Frans de Waal explained in a 2019 interview. If you tickle a chimpanzee, he says, they laugh, exactly as Goodall found, but his colleagues still won't use the L-word. Instead, they say the chimps produce "vocalized panting."

Goodall didn't see the value in erasing the inner lives of her subjects in this way. Even after the criticism of her initial work, she continued to study the emotional, social, and sometimes human-like aspects of primates. After all, she reasoned, their emotions were real and could be observed and documented. Her empathy and openness were thus not at odds with her scientific work. They enhanced it.

Now we know that Goodall's approach changed the history of science. Her research didn't just pay off for primatologists; it influenced ecology and the budding science of environmentalism. And, as her mentor predicted, it has helped us understand our own heritage as human beings. There are very few scientists who can say they helped shape multiple new disciplines while revolutionizing others—but Jane Goodall can. And all her contributions would have been stamped out if someone had convinced her not to care so damn much.

Beyond just the *Sensitive Boost Effect*, which we described in Chapter 2, your sensitivity gives you access to five distinct gifts. Goodall illustrates one of the most powerful gifts of sensitivity: empathy. The other four are creativity, sensory intelligence, depth of processing, and depth of emotion. All these gifts are built, ultimately, on the environmental responsiveness you were born with.

As you read about these gifts, bear in mind that you may not identify equally with all five of them. This is normal—as a sensitive person, you can access all of them, but life experience will have led you to develop some more than others. Each gift, however, is a treasure in its own right, and each gives you an edge.

Empathy

The word *empathy* is a modern invention. It comes to us from the field of aesthetics, the study of what makes art beautiful. Just over a century ago, German philosophers debated how a piece of art can make you feel something, since it's only a collection of shapes and colors. Their best theory was that you "feel into" the art—*Einfühlung,* or empathy—bringing your own emotional perspective to what you see. Thus, when you gaze at a painting, you might imagine the emotions you would have if you yourself had made it—or if you were in it—and you feel something similar to what the artist might have felt. Emotions, empathy tells us, can be transferred by the physical senses, just like any other information. It didn't take long for this concept to leap to the budding science of psychology. If you can "feel into" a piece of artwork, then surely you can "feel into" a human being, too.

Sensitive people have empathy in spades, so much so that the difference can be seen in brain scans. In a study discussed in Chapter 1, participants looked at photos of people either smiling or looking sad. Some of the pictures were of strangers, but some were of the participant's own romantic partner. On a brain level, everyone showed some level of empathic response, especially for sad loved ones, but the most sensitive participants had more brain activity across the board in regions associated with awareness, empathy, and relating to others—even for the pictures of strangers. Sensitive people's brains also lit up in areas related to action planning. This indicates that—just as sensitive people frequently self-report—they could not watch a stranger in pain without feeling a strong desire to help. Sensitive people, it seems, are the varsity athletes of empathy.

This is the same trait that Jane Goodall credits for her success. And while Goodall's story might seem remarkable, when it comes to the power of high-empathy individuals, it's exactly what we should expect. In recent decades, a growing number of researchers have turned their attention to this once-underappreciated human trait, and their work has led to a slew of breakthroughs. Empathy, for example, is both genetic (some people have more of it than others do) and teachable (everyone can learn to have more). But perhaps the greatest discovery is that empathy is the root of two of the most important human activities: It powers our morality, and it drives progress.

The Opposite of Empathy

Psychology professor Abigail Marsh saw the power of empathy firsthand. She started studying empathy after she was in a car accident and a stranger ran across four lanes of freeway traffic, in the dark, to save her life. More than twenty years later, working with a team at Georgetown University, Marsh proved that the brains of highly altruistic people—as she would describe the person who saved her—are different from those of "regular" people and that the difference is largely empathy.

But Marsh didn't start her research by looking at these high-empathy individuals. She started by looking for people with no empathy at all.

One extreme example of a low-empathy individual, she knew, would be a textbook psychopath. This wasn't speculation: Diagnosed psychopaths have been shown to have a smaller, less active amygdala, the part of the brain that recognizes signs of fear or pain in other people and in turn allows empathy to happen. While psychopaths do have the capacity to empathize if they focus on it, neural imaging data suggests that their empathy system defaults to "off." This is the opposite of the rest of us. Whereas most people would have to make a focused effort not to be affected by someone's suffering, psychopaths must make an effort to be affected at all.

The absence of empathy drives much of what's so chilling about psychopaths. They tend to have cold personalities and lack the desire to help others. Although not all psychopaths commit crimes, they fall easily into behavior that is antisocial, callous, or even outright violent. Court cases back this up: Psychopaths are only about 1 percent of the general population but make up 25 percent of men in federal prisons.

Psychopathic people represent the low end of the empathy scale.

What does the high end look like? Do elevated levels of empathy also come with some kind of severe disorder? Not at all. In fact, it's the opposite: The individuals with the highest levels of empathy not only are healthy but also tend to be capable of extraordinary acts of compassion. People like the person who saved Marsh's life are driven not just by ideals, it turns out, but by a stronger-than-average ability to sense others' pain and a heightened sense of caring. Empathy, in many ways, is the difference between good and evil.

This quality is also the key trait that humanity may need to survive. As Stanford professors Paul R. Ehrlich and Robert E. Ornstein warn in their book *Humanity on a Tightrope,* civilization is unlikely to continue unless more people learn to put themselves in other people's shoes. They point to many of today's direst problems—such as racism, global warming, and war—that are fueled by a dangerous us-versus-them mentality that separates people rather than unites them. Similarly, Claire Cain Miller, writing for the *New York Times,* describes us as living through an "empathy deficit." "More and more," she says, "we live in bubbles. Most of us are surrounded by people who look like us, vote like us, earn like us, spend money like us, have educations like us and worship like us." This empathy deficit, she suggests, is "at the root of many of our biggest problems." That's where sensitive people come in with their gift of empathy—thanks to a remarkably active part of their brain.

Misunderstood Mirror Neurons

None of these findings would have surprised the eighteenth-century philosopher Adam Smith, who also wondered what makes humans act morally. Smith suggested that the answer might lie in, of all things, our ability to imitate one another. Just as we can copy things we see people do, he proposed, we can copy their feelings—mentally simulating what someone else is experiencing. We use this ability to judge one another, for better or for worse, but we can also do it in reverse: We can imagine how others would judge *us*. This ability, Smith said, is how we decide what's right and what's wrong. Actions that would win approval from an imaginary spectator must be moral; actions that would earn disapproval must be immoral. The human conscience was, in his telling, built on our ability to emulate the feelings of other people. Smith's contemporary David Hume agreed, but said it much more succinctly: "The minds of men are mirrors to one another."

Smith's theory was contentious in its time, but we now know it's largely right. Enter one of the trendiest—and most frequently misunderstood—concepts in neuroscience: mirror neurons. Mirror neurons are motor cells in the brain, the kind that help you move your body. But they also specialize in copying the way *other* people move and, by extension, the emotions that other people express. Think of it this way: If someone is staring off to your left, you might look that way too. If they're frowning, you might start to feel troubled. These specialized brain cells have variously been credited as an explanation for language, the birth of civilization, and even psychic powers. (Stephen King puts this explanation to good use with his character Molly in Hulu's *Castle Rock*. Molly's empathic abilities include disturbing visions that she controls, barely, with illegal painkillers.)

But there's no need to go that far. What is clear from the research is that the people who self-report the most empathy also have more-active mirror neurons, and this includes sensitive people. Much as Smith predicted, our ability to simulate feelings is closely tied to our ability to simulate physical gestures. You can see this connection in experiments where participants are prevented from mimicking facial expressions by holding a pencil in their mouths. They instantly become worse at guessing others' emotional states.

As for whether the mirror neuron system is at the heart of morality, the answer also seems to be yes. Marsh's work has demonstrated that selfless altruists who go out of their way to aid others, even at a high cost to themselves, tend to be high-empathy individuals. They are the "angel" to psychopaths' "devil." A litany of research backs this up, correlating high empathy levels in general, or mirror neuron activity specifically, with prosocial behavior of all kinds. Even the budding field of heroism science, the study of what makes people undertake selfless acts of heroism, has weighed in. Empathy, researchers in this field have found, is a key ingredient in what makes people risk their lives or their careers to help others.

The Foundation of Human Progress

As powerful as empathy is, it does more than drive human morality. In many ways, it's also key to human achievement. That's because innovation is mostly a group activity—it requires the exchange of ideas, and empathy is the lubricant for that exchange. To see this effect in action, you need look no further than the ancient Library of Alexandria. Most of us know of it for its wealth of books that were famously burned. What's rarely mentioned, however, is that it wasn't just a library, it was a think tank that gathered together brilliant minds representing countless cultures. The results were spectacular. By the second century B.C.E., researchers at the Library of Alexandria had invented pneumatics, built an automated waiter to pour wine, correctly calculated the circumference of the (round, they said, not flat) earth, created the world's most accurate clock at the time, constructed a device to calculate cube roots, and invented an algorithm to find prime numbers—basically mining for Bitcoin before it was cool. It was the act of bringing together multiple viewpoints that drove these great steps forward, and this act required empathy.

Eventually the Romans took over Alexandria—and relocated its thinkers. Every wealthy patrician wanted an Alexandrian genius to tutor his kids, so the scholars were spread out among them. The intellectuals continued their research, but, deprived of close contact with other perspectives, the wondrous inventions mostly ceased.

Empathy, it seems, helps drive success. This link between empathy, progress, and success is part of why Cambridge researcher Simon Baron-Cohen (cousin to the famous actor) believes that empathy is the "universal solvent." It improves outcomes in any situation, he says, because "any problem immersed in empathy becomes soluble." Thus, sensitive people are poised to make a massive impact on the world—if they learn how to tap their empathy effectively.

Creativity

The image of the sensitive artist is a cliché for a reason: It's grounded in truth. A mind that notices more detail, makes more connections, and feels emotion vividly is almost perfectly wired for creativity. That doesn't mean all sensitive people are creatives, but many creatives are indeed sensitive people, as anyone who works with them can attest.

Nina Volf, a researcher from the Russian Academy of Medical Sciences, decided to put that observation to the test. Volf assembled several types of tests to gauge both verbal and visual creativity, with an emphasis on seeing how original a person's ideas were, not just how many they could come up with. Participants were given, for example, sets of incomplete drawings and asked to make unique pictures out of them. Importantly, she used both "hard," quantitative criteria (how often had other people in the database come up with similar answers?) and "soft," subjective impressions (how did a panel of three judges rate the originality of the work?). She then gave this rigorous test to sixty people, running a DNA sample afterward. The outcome: People with the short *SERT* gene linked to sensitivity were more creative on all measures.

The more interesting question is *why*, and the answer has a lot to do with how creativity happens at a cognitive level. To be sure, creativity is hard to define and there are several theories of how it works. All of them acknowledge that intelligence plays a role, and they all prize originality as much as talent or skill—that is, a perfectly executed copy of someone else's painting would not be considered creative.

One prominent theory among scientists, however, began with the author and journalist Arthur Koestler in the 1960s. Koestler believed that true creativity arises when you blend two or more different frames of reference. You can see this principle at work in any metaphor or in stirring revelations like "We are made of star-stuff"—simultaneously a scientific truth and a call to a higher destiny. Koestler knew the power of such perspective-bending firsthand because it was how he lived his life. Born in Budapest, he was educated in Austria and naturalized as a citizen of Great Britain; meanwhile, he spent his early years as a passionate communist and his later life writing anti-Soviet propaganda. He couldn't help but notice the effect of all this border crossing—literal and otherwise—on his ability to generate original ideas. Koestler's experience might explain why so many other lauded creatives have a similarly multicultural life story, while countless more devote time to traveling and living abroad. The more perspectives you inhabit over your life, the more of them you can draw on and combine, creating something new.

Koestler's theory also explains the connection between sensitive people and creativity. Wired to make connections between vastly different concepts, the sensitive mind can blend frames of reference without ever leaving home. Sensitive people are perhaps the ultimate polymaths, thinking not in terms of science *or* poetry *or* lived experience *or* hopes and dreams, but in terms of the themes that run across them all. Many sensitive people speak this way, too, readily offering metaphors and linking different topics to make a point. Such talk can make purists uncomfortable, but it's a habit not only of great artists but also of brilliant scientists like Carl Sagan, originator of the "star-stuff" line above.

If you are a sensitive person, you may or may not work as a creative yourself and you may or may not have "creative" pastimes. But you have the raw components to do so. (One sensitive person, Elizabeth, told us, "I never thought I was more creative than other people until too many friends told me they had no idea how I imagined so much stuff. It never occurred to me that they couldn't do what I could do.") This creativity doesn't operate alone. It is built on the next three gifts of sensitivity—sensory intelligence, depth of processing, and depth of emotion—which together add up to a creative mind.

In Their Own Words: What Is Your Greatest Strength as a Sensitive Person?

"As a high school teacher, I could be standing in the middle of my students, not even facing all of them, and I could feel the emotional state they were in. There's always a lot going on with teenagers! I knew what to say and what to avoid saying so everyone could feel safe in my classroom." –Corinne

"I am a physician, and I have caught details that my patients' previous physicians have missed, leading to improved diagnosis and management of their health. I genuinely care about my patients, and my patients have commented that they can feel that and appreciate it." –Joyce

"My biggest strengths are empathy and compassion. I've noticed that I really hold space well for others in pain without destroying my own energetic capacity. I use these skills as a counselor, coach, and writer." –Lori

"I have an intuitive sense for groups of people: who has power, where the dynamics of a group exist, when people are shifting away from an idea, and what individuals want versus what the group wants. At my job, I was always several steps ahead of big decisions or movements of the company because of this 'superpower,' and it helped me climb the ladder." –Tori

"Being sensitive, I am always very aware of stressors and irritants in my environment, and am also highly attuned to the emotions of those around me, so I can tell when something is bothering someone. I therefore always strive to make my environment warm, comfortable, and welcoming–and I have been told my personality is the same. People feel at ease around me; they often open up to me when they might not open up to someone else. Even strangers in the grocery store end up telling me their life stories, their heartbreaks, their worries." –Stephanie

"My gift is that I'm at times moved to tears by the beauty and kindness in the world." –Sherry

"I am an artist. I don't just watch a sunrise, I *feel* a sunrise!" –Lisa

Sensory Intelligence

Sensory intelligence means being more aware of your environment and doing more with that knowledge. You may pay more attention to sensory details themselves (like the texture of a painting or a missing bracket in a line of code) or their implications (it rained yesterday, so it's going to be muddy when I go on my walk). Anyone can notice such things, but sensitive people tend to do so more readily, in a wide variety of situations—you could call it being *tuned in*. (As one sensitive person told us, he views himself as a "live wire" that picks up every signal.) Such insights can range from the mundane to the truly impactful. More than one sensitive person has saved an employer from a major debacle by paying attention to a nagging detail.

In some cases, this ability can seem almost mystical. Think, for example, of the swordsman Zatoichi, of Japanese B-movie fame. Zatoichi is blind, but he can always tell when he's being cheated at gambling because he can hear the difference in how the dice fall (and with his superior senses, he always wins the sword fight that breaks out next). That's fiction, of course; in reality, blind people don't have super hearing. They just use their brains differently, paying attention to the same tiny sounds that sighted people can hear but filter out. To a degree, sensitive people may do something similar with all five senses.

Sometimes, this level of sensitivity is a burden—no one wants to notice every whiff of cologne in the office—but it can also give astonishing results, as an Irish woman named Sanita Lazdauska found out firsthand. One morning, she woke up because she sensed a change in her husband's breathing—he always snored, but that day the noises sounded off. So she checked on him and saw that he had turned blue; he was in cardiac arrest. Lazdauska performed thirty minutes of CPR until the paramedics arrived. Few people are sensitive enough to wake up from a change in breathing. If she hadn't been attuned to his sleeping noises—or hadn't thought much of the odd one that morning—he would have died in his sleep. Her heightened sensory intelligence saved her husband's life.

This unique form of intelligence is the flip side of overstimulation. Sensitive people can certainly become overloaded in busy environments, because they're taking in so much more of their surroundings. But much of the time, rather than causing overload, their heightened awareness is an advantage, particularly if they take steps to avoid overstimulation in the first place—which we'll discuss in Chapter 4.

Sensory intelligence is an asset in a surprising number of fields. In the military, for example, it falls under the term *situational awareness*— the ability to know and understand what's happening around you—and it's the key to keeping yourself and your unit alive in combat. In fact, situational awareness is prized in any profession that involves safety: It's a major part of why airplanes don't crash, why nuclear plants don't melt down, and why crimes get solved. Sadly, the opposite is also true. A lack of situational awareness has been proven to be a primary cause of accidents involving human error, such as a hospital injecting anticoagulant into the wrong patient. (That really happened, and the case is now used in medical literature to train hospital workers to improve situational awareness. Thankfully, the patient was okay.)

Meanwhile, in sports, sensory intelligence is known as *field vision*. This is the ability to absorb what's happening on the entire playing field and read the game the way chess masters read the pieces on the board. Field vision makes the difference not only between good players and great ones but also between mediocre coaches and legends. Inexperienced coaches, researchers have found, tend to focus mainly on technical skills like passing in football or layups in basketball. Experienced coaches, on the other hand, prize field vision in their players because that is the skill that lets players pass to the right person or be in the right place to take a shot. Under a good coach, in other words, less-sensitive athletes get drilled on a skill that sensitive players are born with.

You've seen field vision at work if you've ever watched former hockey player Wayne Gretzky on the ice. Known as "the Great One," Gretzky has been retired since 1999 yet remains the player with the most goals, the most points, and the most assists in the history of his sport. He checked none of the boxes of a normal pro player, however. Gretzky was slow, small, skinny, and anything but aggressive, and he folded like origami if he was hit. Once he was out on the ice, though, Gretzky could see where everyone would be five seconds in the future. He explains, "I get a feeling about where a teammate is going to be. A lot of times, I can just turn and pass without looking." He had field vision—or as we would say, sensory intelligence. It made him so valuable that a teammate acted as his unofficial bodyguard on the ice, keeping opponents off Gretzky so that the famed center could put the puck where it needed to be.

NFL quarterback Tom Brady was much the same. He was a slow runner but was described by other players as having "lizard eyes" because he played as if he could see off to his sides and behind him. Sensitive enough that he cries when he talks about the day he was drafted, Brady led teams to seven Super Bowl victories and is widely considered the greatest quarterback in history.

Gretzky and Brady became top athletes in two of the fastest, most brutal sports in the world, because even those settings favor sensitive players. The truth is, sensory intelligence pays off in nearly all areas of life, from careers that "feel" sensitive like nursing and art to rugged ones like sports and policing. Sensory intelligence is often underappreciated by those who don't have it, but if you're sensitive yourself, you have a built-in radar that other people lack.

Depth of Processing

Sensitive people don't just take in more information; they do more with it. We saw in Chapter 1 how the sensitive brain processes all information in greater detail, but we didn't look at how this deep processing sets sensitive people apart. Imagine two tax accountants: The first one drops in your numbers, makes sure they add up, and sends them off to the government. Done. The second one goes further. They check supporting documents to make sure nothing is missed. They walk you through extra ways to save money. And they screen everything for red flags that might trigger an audit. Who would you rather have do your taxes?

If you prefer the second accountant, you understand the value of deeper cognitive processing. Of course, anyone can be thorough if they focus on it, but—like sensory intelligence—deep processing is the default setting of the sensitive brain. This capability tends to come out in several ways:

- More careful, often-better decision-making
- Thorough and broad-reaching thinking
- Creative connecting of the dots between different topics and ideas
- A preference for deep, meaningful ideas and activities
- Deeper dives into an idea instead of surface-level analysis
- Surprising, original ideas and perspectives
- Frequently, the ability to correctly predict how something will unfold or what effect a decision will have

Depth of processing doesn't just apply to long, complex tasks like taxes (thankfully!). In both humans and monkeys, individuals with the genes for sensitivity outperform others on a variety of mental tasks. In one study, for example, monkeys were specially trained to work on touchscreen devices, sipping water as they tapped away and receiving fruit snacks as rewards when they did well, not unlike a toddler with a learning app. The monkeys quickly gamed out how to get the most snacks possible—by succeeding on a series of tasks like assessing probability, noticing when patterns changed, and being observant enough to scoop up even very small wins. It quickly became clear that sensitivity was an asset on these mental tasks. The monkeys who were more sensitive not only performed better and reaped more rewards but also showed brain differences similar to those of sensitive humans.

Thus, deep processing can lead to better decision-making, especially when it comes to risk and probability. This gift is invaluable at work, in relationships, and in major life choices. Less-sensitive people may be impatient when you need to reflect before making a decision, but they should probably learn to wait; that short pause is your mind going deep. In many ways, sensitive people think like military strate-gists, considering all the angles to maximize the chance of a win. That propensity can lead to stunning results and is part of why sensitive people make great leaders (more on that in Chapter 9).

Of course, such instincts aren't sorcery, and a sensitive person can get something wrong just like anyone else. But sensitive people put far more mental resources into getting it right.

Depth of Emotion

Depth of emotion is perhaps the most misunderstood gift. Sensitive people really do have, on average, stronger emotional reactions than others do. And you may not think of them as a gift at all: If you are someone with stronger emotions, then anger, hurt, and sadness can be intense experiences for you. At times they can even overwhelm you. But your deep and powerful emotions also mean you are fluent in a language that some other people struggle to speak. That is a master key to the human spirit.

The source of this gift may lie in a tiny hub of the brain called the *ventromedial prefrontal cortex* (vmPFC). Located several inches behind your forehead and roughly the size and shape of your tongue, the vmPFC is a crossroads that brings together information about emo-tions, values, and sensory data. The reason we think of flowers as ro-mantic, and not just as colorful vegetables, is because of the vmPFC.

The ventromedial prefrontal cortex is a hardworking area in any brain, but for sensitive people, it's busier than a Jackson Pollock canvas. This heightened activity has the effect of coloring the world with added depth, causing sensitive people to see life in a more vivid emotional palette. That vividness can be hard sometimes. (Raise your hand if you want a more intense experience of sadness—anyone?) However, it also offers a number of benefits, especially in terms of intelligence and men-tal well-being. As far back as the 1960s, psychiatrist Kazimierz Dąbrowski theorized a connection between emotional intensity and the potential for high achievement. In his work, he showed that gifted people tend to be "overexcitable" or sensitive in various ways, including physically and emotionally. Gifted children, he suggested, are often accused of over-reacting but are just more acutely aware of their own feelings. Many gifted children, he found, carry on whole inner dialogues about their feelings—something not everyone does—and are so driven by compassion and human connection that emotions are simply a bigger concern for them. Dąbrowski even believed that emotional intensity was key to achieving higher stages of personal growth—what we would today call self-actualization.

Educators who work with gifted students get to observe this emotional intensity firsthand, and many of these educators agree that people with a deep intellectual life tend to have a deep emotional life, too. One possible explanation for the link has to do with memory: An event experienced with greater emotional intensity is more likely to be recalled later, so the people with the most emotional vividness—sensitive people—may be the most likely to absorb and integrate new information.

Today, though, we tend to focus on a different kind of smarts: emotional intelligence. To be clear, emotional intelligence is a skill, not something people are born with. Just as being tall does not automatically make a person good at basketball, being sensitive doesn't automatically give you high emotional intelligence. But like height in the playoffs, it sure does help. That's because emotional intelligence includes several components that really are strengths of sensitive people. For example, sensitive people tend to have a high degree of self-awareness; they notice and pay attention to their emotions, taking time to think about what they're feeling both in the moment and afterward. And they easily read and understand the emotions of others, making high emotional intelligence achievable with a little effort. That effort can pay off: Emotional intelligence has been proven to contribute to improved mental health, better job performance, and leadership ability. Your emotionality can launch you to new heights if you harness it.

Strong emotions come with other benefits, too. For one, they deepen relationships. They can also give you a powerful way of influencing people. If you're sensitive, your deep emotionality is why you're an exceptional listener, why people naturally trust you, and why you're probably the go-to confidant when anyone in your friend group needs advice. With practice, depth of emotion even lets you bring people together, rallying them around an ideal—the stuff that social movements are made of. (Martin Luther King Jr., for example, is thought to have been a sensitive person.)

On a personal level, depth of emotion also allows you to enjoy life in a rich way. Sensitive people have been shown to have stronger reactions to all kinds of experiences, both positive and negative, in studies gauging their emotional response. Fortunately, it's usually the positive experiences that get the biggest reaction. This may explain why sensitive people often have high ideals, form powerful bonds with others, and derive great joy from the little things in life, especially things of beauty, like a leaf-laden street on a sunny fall day or a song from a guitarist busking on the corner.

Although being wired for strong emotions comes with challenges, it also makes you exceptional. One not-highly-sensitive music producer, for example, who didn't want to be named, views sensitive musicians almost with awe. He described how he thinks of emotions as "the invisible world." He can see their effects in his work—something moves in the invisible world and, inexplicably, a deal falls through—but he cannot see the cause and effect, cannot predict what kind of emotional ripple a given action might create. (The sensitive musicians he works with, he said, can peek into that world, almost like a seer.) Because of his inability to read emotions, the producer, like a large swath of humanity, feels at the mercy of emotions. Sensitive people are the exception: They see the invisible.

Think back to Bruce Springsteen, who we discussed in Chapter 2, and you can see all the gifts of sensitivity at work. You'll find empathy, creativity, and depth of emotion in his music, in his sympathetic tales of losers and loners. Just listen to "Thunder Road," about a man who's "no hero" picking up a woman who "ain't that young anymore" for one last fling, and you'll feel it yourself. Springsteen even hears music differently than do most listeners, and he processes it deeply. When he was a boy, the records that held his interest were the ones where the singers sounded both happy and sad at the same time. "This music was filled with deep longing," he says, "a casually transcendent spirit, mature resignation and . . . hope . . . hope for that girl, that moment, that place, that night when everything changes, life reveals itself to you, and you, in turn, are revealed." For him, songs contain not just a rhythm and a melody but also shades of intention; they paint an entire world. Many musicians can relate, because many musicians are sensitive people. They listen differently—more deeply—than anyone else in the room.

Springsteen applies this depth and sensory intelligence to the way he reads and understands his fans. With his early band the Castiles, he describes revamping the set list when he saw that the crowd was all down-on-their-luck, leather-wearing greasers. "The secret ingredients were doo-wop, soul and Motown," he recalls. "This was the music that made the leather heart skip a beat." Springsteen could seemingly glimpse their whole lives—their struggles, their dreams—and tailored his music to suit them.

It's this thoughtful, perceptive approach that typifies his entire career. Turning his depth of processing on himself, Springsteen says he knew early on what he had to offer: that he wasn't the best singer or even the best guitar player but that he believed he could build a career on the strength of his songwriting. Then, trying not to lose himself as some of his musical heroes did when they reached a certain level of fame, Springsteen stayed close to his roots, living with his family on a horse farm in New Jersey. "I liked who I was when I was here. . . . I wanted to remain grounded," he says in an interview. It's this keen self-awareness that helped him not only succeed as a musician but also choose a life that felt right for him.

The working man's hero, it seems, is a sensitive hero, too.

chapter 4

Too Much, Too Loud, Too Fast

I have often lamented that we cannot close our ears
with as much ease as we can our eyes.
—Sir Richard Steele, Essay No. 148

No gift comes without some kind of cost. If you're a sensitive person, that cost is the flip side of the same deep-processing brain that gives you superpowers in the first place. As you've seen, such a brain gobbles up mental energy; it works furiously nearly all the time, and as a result, it requires frequent rest. More than that, it needs space. It asks for a little extra time, a little extra patience, a little extra quiet and calm. If given these conditions, the gifts of sensitivity are at their best and the sensitive mind whirs toward genius—by processing every scrap of information to its fullest.

Deprived of those conditions, however—rushed, pressured, and overworked—the same mind cannot hope to process everything it is fed. The physical and emotional inputs simply overload it like an over-stuffed laundry machine. Therefore, overstimulation is one of the costs of being highly responsive to your environment and one of the biggest challenges that all sensitive people face.

What should you do when you find yourself to be a sensitive crea-ture in a not-so-sensitive world? How do you deal with spaces that are too packed, schedules that are too rushed, and places that are too loud? When you have many gifts, but society sees your needs as a sensitive person as inconvenient? When you want to use those gifts to help the world, but you need calm, quiet, and rest to do so?

When There's No Escape

Alicia Davies had just been through a breakup while she was finishing a master's program, "one riddled with dissertation deadlines, long hours, and constant pressure," she writes on Sensitive Refuge. As if that weren't enough, she had one month left to figure out where she would live and what her life would look like when the year-long program fi-nally came to an end. It would be an overwhelming time for anyone, of course, but Alicia isn't just anyone—she is a sensitive person. What she needed was massive amounts of downtime to make sense of everything she had just been through. Now more than ever, she needed time in her sanctuary: her "lovely little bedroom" that was reminiscent of her child-hood, with its green velvet armchair and many plants, books, and can-dles on wooden shelves. This private space was crucial to her self-care because it evoked feelings of safety and calm.

Unfortunately, her landlord had a different idea: He had chosen this summer, of all summers, to do construction work on the house. This meant "drilling, sawing, and banging, every weekday, from early in the morning to late in the afternoon," right outside her bedroom. The construction crew spoke loudly, blasted their music, and seemed to pop up everywhere. Anytime she had to go somewhere in the house, she had to apologetically squeeze past them—and their messes. Soon they started to joke that *Alicia* was in *their* way. In this state, any privacy or downtime became impossible.

Understandably, Alicia's stress skyrocketed. Little tasks became huge in her mind. At one point, she realized, she couldn't even string simple sentences together: "Any sort of conversation felt painful—like when you've been listening to earbuds too long and you simply need to stop. It was as if my senses had tensed up and recoiled out of self-defense, and they had forgotten how to relax; I was fizzing over with input." Then the noise and chaos would start all over again the next day.

What she needed was an escape. She headed to a local café, but she found no refuge there. After she ordered her coffee, some energetic funk music started playing. A baby began to wail. That was the last straw: "I wanted to wail too, louder than that baby, and drown out all the sounds of the world."

Still in a full-on state of sensory overload, she left the coffee shop in a flurry of frustration and walked down the street. She muttered under her breath at anyone who made noise around her. She even swore at the too-loud hand dryer in a public restroom. Her anger wasn't rational, she understood, but neither is sensory overload.

Thankfully, she stumbled on an art exhibit. She wandered inside, where she was suddenly cloaked in silence. She walked around, spending time with each piece of art, feeling for the first time that day that her senses were slowly uncoiling, softening, reviving. There was a place for her in the world after all—in fact, a rather large place rich in beauty and stillness. Another woman—alone like Alicia—wandered into the exhibition with a peaceful energy about her. Alicia immediately felt close to her, as if this stranger somehow understood her need for solitude. When the two happened to glance at each other, Alicia found herself actually smiling.

Of course, Alicia's visit to the art gallery wasn't the complete end of her overstimulation. It was only the beginning of the end, a lessening of the symptoms, as if her senses were still brittle, ready to snap again at the slightest touch. Over the next few days, she figured out a few techniques to fully recover from the overstimulation, even with the construction crew still banging away in the house. She listened to music, which covered some of the noise and helped slow down her racing thoughts. And she spent time outside, hearing birdsong and breathing in the fresh air. Finally, Alicia found peace.

In Their Own Words: What Does Overstimulation Feel Like for You?

"When I feel overstimulated, I feel trapped and anxious, and I have an overwhelming need to find solitude. If I'm unable to escape or retreat, I then become what appears to be dazed or checked out, although my thoughts are still fully functioning. People around me will say things like, 'Are you feeling okay? You're too quiet,' and 'Are you having any fun?' If the overstimulation comes on fast or unexpectedly, I will also briefly experience an out-of-body feeling where my body feels completely unfamiliar to me. The only thing that helps when I'm overstimulated is to retreat to a warm, quiet, comfortable place." –Jessi

"I find it builds up over time. All physical comfort begins to disappear. Everything becomes an annoyance. Conversations become irritants. I used to run around trying to fix every irritant. That wouldn't work, and I would blow up with anger and frustration. Now I know I'm tired and need time to recharge my energy or have a good cry." –Mathew

"For me, overstimulation feels like I am getting poked by a ton of people all at once. It's kind of like a soft pressure that builds up all over my body and I can't get comfortable."
—Aly

Common Causes of Overstimulation

What Alicia experienced is not unusual for sensitive people, and maybe you've experienced something like it, too. If so, you're not alone, and there's nothing wrong with you. All sensitive people will face overstimulation at some point in their lives, and more likely, they will face it regularly as they work, care for their children, and socialize. Here are some of the most common causes of overstimulation for sensitive people. The following is not a comprehensive list; other things you may find overstimulating might not be included here. Which of these emotions or situations have sometimes felt overstimulating for you?

- Excessive, strong, or disruptive sensory stimuli (crowds, loud music, both repetitive sounds and irregular sounds, temperature, fragrances, bright lights)
- Worries, anxiety, or recurring thoughts
- Emotions perceived from others, especially negative judgment, stress, or anger
- Your own emotions
- Socializing and having lots of plans
- Tight deadlines, busy schedules, or being rushed from one activity to the next
- Information overload or upsetting information (e.g., watching the news or "doomscrolling")

- Changes (sometimes even positive ones, like getting your dream job or finally having a baby)
- Novelty, surprises, and uncertainty
- A chaotic schedule or getting thrown off a familiar routine
- Clutter in your environment (e.g., a messy room or desk)
- Doing tasks—even familiar ones—while someone observes you (e.g., a performance review at work, competing in a sport, typing on a keyboard as someone looks over your shoulder, giving a speech, or even attending your own wedding)
- Too many things demanding your attention at once

Why Overstimulation Happens

The things on the preceding list might overstimulate anyone, sensitive or not, especially if more than one is happening at once—but sensitive people will reach that state faster and feel it deeper. Why does this happen? Imagine an invisible bucket that we all carry around with us. Some people have a big bucket, while others—sensitive people—have a smaller bucket. No one gets to choose the size of their bucket; we're all born with a different nervous system and a different capacity to deal with stimulation. Yet no matter the size of the bucket, every sound, every emotion, and every scent fills it a little more, says Larissa Geleris, an occupational therapist who works with children and adults who have sensory processing difficulties.

If your bucket is running dry, you feel bored, restless, or even depressed. But if your bucket is overflowing, you feel stressed, fatigued, and overwhelmed—maybe even panicked, angry, and out of control. Everyone, then, has a certain threshold for stimuli, and everyone seeks to have their bucket filled to just the right level so they are neither under- nor overstimulated. A child with attention deficit hyperactivity disorder (ADHD), for example, may always feel as if this bucket is running dry. So they rap fingers on their desk or jump out of their seat in school in an effort to stimulate themselves. For you, a sensitive person, it's the opposite: Your bucket fills quickly just from everyday activities, like a day at work or taking care of your kids at home. "Once the bucket is full," explains Geleris, "it spills over and we see dysregulation or over-stimulation. Essentially, it's your sensory system saying, 'Nope, no more. I have processed enough, I have filtered enough, I'm overworked, and I just don't have the capacity to deal with it anymore.'"

For Geleris, the bucket analogy is more than just theory; she is a sensitive person herself ("My therapist says I'm one," she laughs, as we speak over Zoom). So, she frequently finds her bucket too full. Most recently, it happened when she was changing her three-month-old daughter's soiled diaper. Her daughter was crying, toys were strewn all over the floor, and, as every parent has experienced ad nauseam, the mess of the diaper went everywhere. As a result, Geleris began to feel overwhelmed, and her emotions spiraled out of control: "I could feel that I was holding on as much as I could," she says. To make matters worse, she had suffered a concussion not long before this. The injury had caused her to physically and mentally struggle with navigating such cluttered spaces—leaving her effectively trapped at the changing table. "I turned around, saw all the mess and the toys, and just started crying," she recalls. The panicky feeling didn't end until her husband came to her rescue, moving the toys and helping her escape the sensory bombardment.

In Their Own Words: What Makes You Feel Overstimulated?

"For me, overstimulation is an easy state of mind to slip into. Sometimes something as simple as running five minutes late is enough to trigger it. I have to be very mindful not to unload my emotions on the ones I care most about." —Joseph

"It often happens when I feel like all the people and

things around me (like chores, mobile phone alerts, traffic noise, neighbors being noisy, etc.) demand my attention, and I can't escape from it." —Jana

"I can handle loud concerts and airports, usually because they are planned activities that I have mentally prepared for. It is simpler, more innocuous stuff that can trigger me. My young son makes a particular sound that he knows I can't handle, but being a child, he pushes those boundaries. My whole body becomes tense, and it feels like my every nerve ending is on edge. If I can't escape, which often I can't, it triggers anger and rage, as I try to regulate from the irritant." —Tanja

"I feel my most overstimulated when there are too many emotions happening around me, whether it's in a crowd or just one person. It makes me want to cry because I feel closed in. Taking a hot bath with a nice-smelling bath bomb or going into a dark, quiet room by myself or with my cat helps me calm down." —Jessica

Your Body's Eight Sensory Systems

What happens in the body, exactly, when our bucket spills over? Let's take a closer look at our body's sensory systems. Although we think of ourselves as having five senses, the body has eight sensory systems:

1. Visual: sight
2. Auditory: sound
3. Olfactory: smell
4. Tactile: touch
5. Gustatory: taste
6. Vestibular: the sense of balance and head movement; located in the inner ear

7. Proprioceptive: the sense of one's own body's movement; controls and detects force and pressure; located in the muscles and joints

8. Interoceptive: a monitoring system for activities within the body, like breathing, hunger, and thirst; located all over the body, in the organs, bones, muscles, and skin

All day long, your sensory systems work both together and separately to keep you safe, regulated, and on task. This includes big things, like completing a project at work, but it includes little things, too, things you probably aren't even aware of. To take just one example, this morning, when you got dressed, your brain had to decide whether what was touching your arm was safe or dangerous. A shirt? *Safe. Your brain sends a signal to your body to ignore it.* But what if it was a mosquito? *Dangerous. Your brain sends a signal to your body to swat it.* This process of taking in a stimulus, interpreting it, and then responding to it happens constantly. Your brain filters out background noise so that you can hear people talk. As you cut vegetables to prepare dinner, your brain adjusts the amount of pressure your hands use on the knife to keep you safe. Even now, as you read this sentence, your brain is working to focus your eyes and decode the meaning behind the marks on this page. "Throughout our day, we never have a moment when we are not using this skill of sensory processing," Geleris explains.

All told, that's eight streams of nonstop information jacking into your brain every second of every day. Add in any emotions you're feeling or higher-level tasks you're doing, and the input adds up fast. As we've seen, sensitive people have a nervous system that is more responsive to certain stimuli, especially to the sensory inputs of sound and touch, notes Geleris. Just as your arms get tired after doing push-ups, your senses get tired, too. Yet unlike your arms, which can take a break, your body's sensory systems are always on.

Drive, Threat, Soothe

When you're overstimulated, it can feel as though your body is under attack. You might experience racing thoughts, muscle tension, intense panic or anger, and an overwhelming desire to escape the situation. Clinical psychologist Paul Gilbert calls this state Threat mode. Gilbert has spent his career learning the mechanisms that underpin human motives and emotion. Ranking among the most cited researchers in the world, Gilbert produced work so pivotal to science that the queen awarded him the Order of the British Empire, one of the most prestigious awards a British citizen can earn. He believes we use three basic systems—Drive, Threat, and Soothe—to regulate all our emotions. Learning to pay attention to which emotion system you may be using in any given situation can help you keep it in check.

The first one, called *Threat*, is our most powerful system, because it has the greatest ability to seize control of the brain. Its goal is to keep us alive, and its marching orders are, "Better safe than sorry." Even animals use it, such as when they fight off a predator, growl, or puff themselves up to look bigger than they really are. Associated with the fight or flight response, or what psychologist and author Daniel Goleman calls an "amygdala hijack," the Threat system is always on, scanning our environment for hazards, whether it's a bus speeding toward us or a significant other not returning our texts. Responding to both real and perceived threats, it turns up a lot of false positives. For example, your spouse's sarcastic comment or your toddler's tantrum probably isn't really a danger to your life, but Threat can make it feel like it is. When you feel fear, anger, or anxiety, you've entered Threat mode. Self-criticism can also be a part of this mode; in this case, the body believes that you yourself are the danger.

If the first system keeps us alive, then the next one helps us "get more." Called *Drive*, this system makes us feel good when we obtain resources and achieve goals. You're in Drive mode when you complete items on your to-do list, ask for a raise at work, buy a new house or car, go out with friends, or swipe through dating apps. Animals also use Drive when they build nests, attract mates, and store food for the winter. When balanced by the other two systems, Drive "gives you these buzzes of joyfulness and pleasure," Gilbert tells us. But if it gets out of whack, as it often does in our too-much culture, Drive can spiral into an insatiable quest of "never enough." With this spiral, notes Gilbert, "people become absolutely obsessed with achieving, having, doing, and owning, and can start to feel like failures if they don't." Think out-of-control gambling, food and drug addictions, and greed. A good example of this mindset is the movie *The Wolf of Wall Street*, which tells the true story of stockbroker Jordan Belfort's crimes. We can see Drive in overkill when Belfort remarks, "The year I turned twenty-six, as the head of my own brokerage firm, I made forty-nine million dollars, which really pissed me off because it was three shy of a million a week."

Because of the powerful nature of Threat and Drive, we're at our happiest when we keep these two systems in check, using them only on a part-time basis. Unfortunately, and without even realizing it, most of us spend the majority of our time in these systems (and we feel justified, because it is, after all, what the Toughness Myth demands). Both Threat and Drive can contribute to the feelings of overstimulation that we as sensitive people face.

But there's an antidote to overstimulation: the third system, called *Soothe*, which switches on naturally when there is no threat to defend against and no goal to chase. Others have called it the "rest and digest" system, because once in Soothe mode, we feel calm, content, and comforted, like a baby rocked to sleep by a parent or a kitten cuddled against its mother to feel safe and warm. Soothe, which is used by all mammals, allows us to relax, slow down, and enjoy what we're doing in the present moment. You might use Soothe when you savor your morning coffee, get a massage, or mindfully appreciate the fresh blossoms in your garden. This system allows us to open ourselves to other people and extend compassion to them, rather than seeing them as a potential danger. When you feel safe, happy, secure, cared for, and calm, you've entered Soothe mode.

However, even though Soothe is the most pleasurable of the three systems, it's the easiest for us to ignore. For many of us, Soothe is underutilized or even completely blocked because of trauma or a difficult childhood. Learning to activate it regularly is a game-changer for sensitive people, and we'll give you techniques for doing that later in this chapter.

The Difference Between Occasional and Chronic Overstimulation

Thankfully, occasionally slipping into Threat mode is not dangerous in and of itself. Nor does it harm your health. As Alicia found out, as soon as she was able to take refuge in a quiet, calm place (the art museum), her stress and anger began to dissipate. She writes, "Thankfully for me (and for everyone around me), I discovered that overstimulation is only temporary. With the right techniques, it goes away and barely even leaves a trace."

However, chronic overstimulation is a different story. It occurs when our bodies are constantly plunged into Threat mode because of certain unavoidable, ongoing situations. Maybe a colleague is making your workplace toxic, or maybe you are the main caregiver to your young children. Or you might live or work somewhere that is overstimulating by its very nature. If you've ever said that you're getting burned out or just can't handle things anymore, you're probably experiencing chronic overstimulation. Fatigue is another sign of chronic overstimulation; if you feel tired all the time—or even after you've rested—it may be because your nervous system is in overdrive. As the saying goes, "It's the kind of tired that sleep can't fix." Other signs are that you find yourself crying more easily (sometimes for no real reason at all) and may even have physical symptoms—like muscle pain, head-aches, or digestive issues—with no clear physical cause. While you can bounce back from occasional bouts of overstimulation, chronic over-stimulation is a more serious problem and may eventually hurt your job performance, your relationships, your mental and physical health, and your happiness.

If you're experiencing chronic overstimulation, you need to step back and evaluate the situation carefully. What, exactly, triggers the overstimulation? Is it certain people, tasks, noises, something else? What can you do to avoid or minimize these triggers? Could you spend less time with the person, only communicating with them through email instead of face-to-face? Could you wear headphones to cover the noise, take more frequent breaks, cut back your working hours, dele-gate some of your responsibilities, or ask someone for help? Sometimes the only way out of chronic overstimulation is to remove yourself from the situation, relationship, or job. Leaving isn't an easy step, but if that's what it takes, give yourself permission to do so.

A Toolkit to Lessen Overstimulation

The key to dealing with overstimulation, both chronic and occasional, is to create a lifestyle that works *for* your sensitivity, not *against* it. First, you need reliable ways to activate the Soothe system and end the over-stimulation in the moment. Then, you need realistic methods to build a long-term lifestyle that nourishes your sensitive nature.

Taking these steps doesn't mean you'll completely stop getting over-stimulated or never face a challenge related to sensory overload. Even Lama Lodro Zangmo, a sensitive Buddhist nun who spent eleven years in nearly nonstop seclusion,* sometimes found herself overstimulated by the prayer and meditation practices of the monastery. As she puts it,

---

* Zangmo also happens to be Andre's sister.

it left her with "a feeling of lightning inside." If she talked to other people, the feelings intensified, and by the end of the day, she would become overwhelmed. Over time, she learned how to be comfortable with this energy as she came to understand it as a natural part of her, and she let go of trying to control it or make it disappear. Rather, she explains, "If I kept silent, it was like letting the wind die down, and then I would feel comfortable with what was going on inside."

Tom Falkenstein, author of *The Highly Sensitive Man,* puts it another way: "The tendency to become overstimulated can't be completely avoided because it's impossible to steer clear of all potentially challenging situations—be it a visit to a busy supermarket, your brother's birthday party, giving a presentation at work, organizing or booking your next vacation, or an upcoming parents' evening about how well your kids are doing at school." Plus, he points out, if we arranged our lives to completely avoid any opportunity for overstimulation, we'd probably end up leading, well . . . a pretty boring life. Rather, sensitive people should accept their tendency toward occasional overstimulation and draw on tools to lessen it.

As we've seen, there's no single way that overstimulation shows up, so there is no single technique that tackles it every time. That's why we recommend the toolkit approach: having a variety of strategies at your disposal so you can choose those that will help you the most in the moment. Most important, all the tools in your kit involve soothing yourself in one way or another. Remember, the point is to switch from Threat or Drive to Soothe, not to follow a script. So customize each tool as you see fit. The only thing you shouldn't change is the habit of using these tools early and often.

Develop an Early Warning System for Overstimulation

Before you get sick, you might get a tickle in your throat or just feel off—early warning signs of a cold or the flu. In the same way, before you reach a state of full-on overstimulation, your body gives you early warning signs. The more you can become aware of these signs, the easier it will be to sidestep overstimulation before it gets too "big." Throughout the day, check in with yourself. Ask yourself these questions:

- How am I feeling right now?
- What thoughts or images come to mind?
- Where in my body am I experiencing these emotions?
- How does my body feel, physically?

If you feel restless, wound up, distracted, irritated, or a desire to cover your ears or eyes to shield them from sensory input—or if you have muscle tension, a tight feeling in your chest, a headache, or stomach pain—you may be on the verge of overstimulation.

If Possible, Take a Break

When overstimulation strikes, the best thing you can do is to move away from the thing that is overstimulating you, whether it's a sound or a conversation. Take a break. Close a door. Go on a short walk. Step into a restroom—whatever it takes. If you do need to walk away, make sure to communicate what's going on to those around you. Try, "I'm getting overstimulated. I need a short break to calm my body down." Or for a more work-appropriate heads-up: "I need to take a few minutes to sort out my thoughts, and then I'll know how to do my best work. I'll be back in five."

The toughest part of taking breaks may not be knowing when you need one but *giving yourself permission to take one*. However, breaks are crucial to interrupting overstimulation. Remember, if you really don't want to explain, the bathroom usually goes unquestioned. (As one sensitive man put it, "Another name for 'bathroom' is 'refuge.'")

While taking your break, bring your awareness to your body. Recognize that you're not really under attack, even though it feels that way. "In the moment, when you're overstimulated, you feel so helpless," says Geleris. "I think that's the most important thing to recognize. You may feel helpless, but you are not. Your nervous system is saying, 'Hey, we're in danger,' but you're not in danger. Remind yourself of that."

Give Yourself Calming Sensory Input

More often than not, we cannot escape the situation that is overstimulating us. That's when we need some other tools to lower our arousal level. When our Threat system turns on, we must interrupt the body's physical response (because Threat mode is, essentially, a physical reaction from your body). The way to disrupt that response is also physical. For example, you can put your back against a wall and push firmly against it. Lie on your back on the floor. Do mini push-ups on the kitchen countertop or your desk. Wrap your arms around your body and give yourself a tight hug (or if it is appropriate to do so, ask someone else for a hug). Proprioceptive input, the sensation you receive when you move your body against resistance, is the most calming type of sensory input, says Geleris. The best part of proprioceptive input is that you can trigger it anywhere and anytime, on your own, and nobody's the wiser. (Proprioceptive input is also the reason people enjoy weighted blankets.)

Move Your Head Less

The vestibular system is the sensory system that, among other functions, tracks where your head is in space. When you turn your head, the brain lights up with electrical activity, and all your other senses become heightened—which can contribute to overstimulation. So, position yourself in a way that reduces head movement. For example, if you're cooking dinner (often an overstimulating task for parents of babies and toddlers), gather everything you need from the cabinet first so you don't have to flip back and forth as much. If you're at a dinner party, sit at the head of the table so that you can see everyone at once. Preferably, place your back to a wall so you don't have to filter sensory input from behind; this makes your "Threat brain" feel safer because "predators" can't sneak up on you. (It's also why we like cozy spaces and prefer the seat that's against a wall in a restaurant or a conference room.)

Comfort Yourself as You Would Comfort a Child

As every parent has learned, kids get overstimulated easily because their young brains are learning and processing so much, all the time. So, extend to yourself the same compassion that you would to an overstimulated child. "You wouldn't have calmed down or stopped crying when you were a baby or a child if your parents had shouted at you, criticized you, or left you in a room on your own," writes Falkenstein. "So it's vital that in difficult moments you are able to use emotional regulation to look after yourself and comfort yourself instead of criticizing your tendency to become quickly overstimulated and to feel things intensely ('Oh, here we go again!'). This only increases the tension you feel and your emotional arousal and doesn't help you calm down more quickly." You might try imagining yourself as a young child and speak comforting words directly to this little person. "I know this isn't easy for you," "I can feel your pain," "You're not alone, I'm here with you," "Tell me what's wrong."

Activate Your Cognitive Brain

We have, effectively, two brains—a cognitive brain and an emotional one. Sensitive people tend to spend more time in their emotional brain, says psychotherapist Julie Bjelland, who specializes in the trait of high sensitivity. "When your emotional brain is activated, your thinking brain basically goes to sleep," she explains. (If you've ever felt as if you couldn't think clearly when you've been mad or stressed, your emotional brain has overridden your cognitive brain.) Just as Threat and Soothe can't be activated at the same time, neither can our cognitive brain and our emotional brain. Waking up your cognitive brain will lower the intensity of the emotions you feel when you are overstimulated. Bjelland suggests getting a piece of paper and writing down the emotion(s) you're feeling and what she calls some "cognitive facts." In this case, cognitive facts are observations that counter the message of your emotions. For example, your emotions might be telling you, "I botched the presentation and made a fool of myself." Here are some cognitive facts that might counter that message:

- I performed to my personal standards.
- My coworkers told me I did a good job.
- My boss wouldn't have asked me to lead the presentation in the first place if she hadn't believed that I could perform well.

Write down at least three cognitive facts for every emotion, advises Bjelland. Because the cognitive brain is in charge of language, the mere process of putting your feelings into words is one way to activate this part of your brain.

Create Your Sensitive Sanctuary

Set up your physical environment in a way that nurtures your sensitivity. It isn't always possible to, say, feel calm in an open office or a classroom, but you should have at least one space that brings immediate peace. That's where your *sensitive sanctuary* comes in. This sanctuary is a room or another space that's all your own. It's where you decompress and escape the noise of the world. If your own room isn't possible, start with a cozy chair, your own desk, or any quiet corner. Decorate it with soothing colors or whatever makes you happy. Physical comfort is key, so include pillows, plush surfaces, soft lighting, and comfortable furniture. Stockpile the things that bring you the most joy, such as books, journals, candles, religious items, calming music, and your favorite snacks. The specifics don't matter so much as the idea that this is *your* space, set up in a way that lets you process and come down.

Most important, make sure to tell your family or roommates about your sanctuary. Stress that your "me time" in your sanctuary is important for your physical and mental health. Many sensitive people create a sanctuary space instinctively, but unless they have clear boundaries about their space and how they use it, others may intrude, interrupt, or even take it over. Remember, the idea that anyone might need a special private space just to do nothing—or relax—is an unfamiliar concept to some people. For example, if it's important to you that no one rearrange the items in your sanctuary or interrupt you while you enjoy your tea there, make sure to communicate these preferences clearly.

Set Healthy Boundaries

Speaking of boundaries, chronic overstimulation often occurs because our boundaries have holes, that is, places where we haven't set or communicated a clear limit. (Raise your hand if you're a sensitive person who hates setting boundaries because you don't want to hurt anyone or let them down!) Boundaries can feel as though they go against the sensitive person's natural empathy. However, the limits you set don't have to be walls or dividers; they are simply a personal list of things that are okay or not okay with you. For sensitive people, healthy boundaries might sound like these statements:

- "I can't come to that event this weekend."
- "I can only stay for an hour."
- "That doesn't work for me."
- "I won't be doing that."
- "I'd like to, but I'm not available without advance notice. What's a different time that would work?"
- "I'm sorry you're having such a difficult time. I would love to help, but I would be overcommitting myself if I did ___. Is there something else I can do?"
- "I understand it's an important topic, but I'm not able to talk about it right now."
- "When I share my thoughts with you and get criticized, I close up. I can only talk with you if you respond respectfully."
- "I'm struggling and need to talk to someone. Are you in a place where you can listen right now?"
- "I need some 'me time.' Would you take the kids for a few hours?"
- "I'm feeling tired. I need to rest."

Hear the Message Your Emotions Are Telling You

When you're overwhelmed by intense feelings, remember that emotions in and of themselves are not the problem, explains Steven C. Hayes, co-author of *Get Out of Your Mind and Into Your Life*. Like an alert on your phone or a postcard from a friend, emotions are merely the messengers.

Because they are messengers, we don't have to act on every emotion, but at the very least, the messages deserve to be heard. Sometimes our emotions tell us when an important boundary has been crossed, when it's time to take action, or when our needs in a relationship aren't being met. They often show us lessons and opportunities for change. Although it may be tempting to tell yourself that you are overreacting—after all, you may have heard this your whole life—don't ignore your emotions or feelings of overstimulation. They aren't meant to be clung to, but they aren't meant to be avoided, either. "They are meant to come and go, flowing through you in their own time," explains Hayes. "They contain important lessons when things are off, and beautiful rewards when things fall into place." When strong feelings arise, he says, take a moment to reflect on these questions: "What does this emotion ask me to do?" and "What does it suggest I am yearning for?"

Make Time to Laugh and Play

Sing along with the car radio, skip down the hallway, play fetch with your dog, build a snowman, go on a bike ride with no destination in mind, or grab one of your kid's toys and play along. Look for the humor in the situation. Psychologists call this focus on play and the willingness to engage in it the *play ethic*. It's about embracing your inner child and making time for fun. As therapist Carolyn Cole writes on Sensitive Refuge, this playful side often "gets covered up over the years by the fear of not fitting in, being overly focused on responsibilities, and feeling like you simply don't have time for this part of yourself anymore." She recommends cultivating a play ethic to all her clients, but especially to her sensitive ones, to help curb overstimulation before it starts. Humor, in particular, requires the use of the prefrontal cortex, the part of the brain that's at odds with emotional overstimulation. In other words, you can't laugh at something funny and feel overwhelmed at the same time.

Give It Time

When you're overstimulated, your emotions feel overwhelming and your body may be flooded with anxiety or stress, so it can be hard to remember to use any of the tools described here. Geleris herself admits that when she was overstimulated while changing her daughter's diaper, all her techniques flew out the window—even though she's a sensory processing expert who teaches these tools to others. So perhaps the most important piece of advice to deal with overstimulation is to simply give yourself time. "If you can, ride the wave a little bit, and as you come back down, that's when you can implement your tools," she says. "It will end. It feels like it won't, but it will."

Accept that sometimes, overstimulation simply can't be avoided. Remember, overstimulation is your brain doing what it does best: going deep. In these moments, do what you can to draw on your tools, and be kind to yourself if the results aren't perfect. As the saying goes, this too shall pass.

chapter 5

The Pain of Empathy

Sometimes I think, I need a spare heart to feel all the
things I feel.

—Sanober Khan, "Spare Heart," in
A Thousand Flamingos

Rachel Horne was in trouble. She had worked against all odds to get
into a prestigious university program devoted to the art of administer-
ing global charities. Unfortunately, the job market for people who want
to make a difference in the world is competitive at the best of times. A
year after graduating, she found herself buried in student loans and in
desperate need of any job. There was an opening for a manager of a pal-
liative care home for older adults with dementia. Here, she thought,
maybe she could help people, even though the work wasn't what she

had originally planned to do. Maybe it would even be something she was good at, because she is a sensitive person.

Elder care is important work, but for Horne, it became a heartbreaking career. Her days were filled with a nonstop rush of caretaking, logistics, and actual life-and-death decisions, all of it to be done with a smile. Her "office" was wedged into the activity closet, heaps of dart boards teetering over her computer and the panicked beep of flatlines sounding through the paper-thin walls. There were beautiful moments, to be sure, times when she managed to get through to someone lost in dementia and offer a sunbeam of joy. In one instance, she played music for a patient even though her coworkers said she was wasting her time because he was too far gone. Then, one day, he turned to her and sang a line from the song. It was the only time she ever heard him speak, but on that day, she knew she was making a difference.

But these moments were hard to come by, partly because slowing down enough to provide them put everyone behind schedule. There were also moments of loss. It wasn't uncommon for a staff member to form a real bond with a person one day, only to find them dead the next. Horne didn't understand how her coworkers could go on as if nothing had happened; their attitudes seemed so callous, so cold. "It was impossible for me to put professional distance between me and the patients' suffering," she told us. "I couldn't be like, 'Okay, it's five o'clock. Time to close the door and go out with my friends.' I would be like, 'Somebody just died. What?'"

Other times, people on their deathbeds opened up to her and shared their feelings, regrets, and even family secrets they didn't want to take to the grave. As a sensitive person, Horne could listen nonjudgmentally and bring them some comfort. But this emotional labor took a toll on her. "I could hold it together in front of the people that needed me to," she says, "but as soon as I got in my car and closed the door, I started crying."

In theory, Horne was making a difference, but she wasn't getting enough sleep, and she went home many nights in tears, only to start crying again the next morning. After just five months on the job, she was physically and emotionally at her limit, and she needed a change.

That was when she met a French man named Florian. His kind eyes and carefree demeanor reminded her of herself back when she still had space in her life. Florian had plenty of space: He was hitchhiking around the world. He happened to be camping on her friend's land for a few nights, and then he'd be back on the road. With no meetings to go to, and no tragic deaths he was supposed to "manage" like lines on a balance sheet, his life seemed utterly serene.

That night, Horne and Florian talked long into the evening, as she lobbed question after question his way. He answered each one patiently. No, he wasn't wealthy. No, he didn't feel unsafe. No, he had never been shouted at while pitching his tent. Yes, he was happy—was she? Slowly, Horne admitted that she envied him. Most people would say they could never do anything like what Florian did, but she started to see his journey as a viable, maybe even preferable, alternative to her job.

The next day, Horne found herself striking a deal. She would wrap things up at her job, and Florian would hitchhike to her flat with a tent and backpack at the ready. With his help, she would do what every parent hopes their child will never do: take off into the wilderness with a stranger. She knew she could lose everything, run out of money, maybe even end up in real peril. But she also felt lighter. For the first time in years, the constant bombardment of other people's needs and emotions seemed far away.

The Dark Side of Empathy

While empathy is one of the greatest gifts of all sensitive people, it can also feel like a curse. That's because empathy can be painful. It requires us to truly take in what another person is feeling, even to experience that feeling *with* them, but in our own body. Like all emotions, that experience can sometimes be overpowering, and like all emotions, it's messy. As a result, empathy comes with some side effects.

One of those side effects is the weight of internalizing the world's most troubling moments, whether you watch them on the news or experience them yourself. Another side effect is so-called giver burnout—also known as compassion fatigue—which happens when the constant effort of caring for others becomes too much. Giver burnout is what Horne experienced. Teachers, nurses, therapists, stay-at-home parents, and others in caregiving roles are especially at risk of giver burnout. Case in point: In 2021, in the midst of the pandemic, burnout was reported as the number one reason that so many health-care workers left their jobs. Even by 2022, one in five doctors and two in five nurses said they intended to leave their practice within two years, according to the American Medical Association. Another one-third wanted to reduce the number of hours they work.

Ask any sensitive person, though, and they'll tell you that one of the most regular side effects of high empathy is absorbing unwanted emotions. For some sensitive individuals, emotions are like a tangible presence in the environment, and the result is the sudden sense of being invaded by feelings that seem to come from nowhere. One minute, you're enjoying your coffee; the next, you're nervous and afraid, looking around the café wondering why. As one sensitive person told us, she seems to feel her mother's emotions, like anxiety, even when she and her mother are not physically close to one another, like when they are shopping in different parts of a store.

To a less-sensitive person, this dark side of empathy has a simple solution: Dial it down. Sensitive people, however, have been hearing this advice their whole lives. They cannot shut off their empathy any more than they can shut off their physical senses or their deep thinking.

In Their Own Words: How Do Other People's Emotions Affect You?

"When I walk into a room, the first thing I do is visually notice every person. All my senses tune in to their emotions. Positive emotions keep me upbeat, while negative emotions drain me. Sometimes I think I can even feel pets' feelings." —Jackie

"Dealing with other people's emotions is very challenging for me. Men are not supposed to notice that kind of thing. In fact, I have learned subtle ways to ignore other people's eyes, tone of voice, body language, manner of speaking, and other things, in order to 'turn down' the volume on their intrusive emotional states. People who are angry or have malicious intent can disrupt my nervous system for days if I have to interact with them, and sometimes they can even provoke a trauma response. After a lot of work, I can now usually distinguish which emotions belong to me and which ones don't." —Trent

"I can feel and even visualize other people's emotions. It's often difficult to know where their emotions end and mine begin. When in a room of strangers, it is the worst, as I have no justification for the feelings, and I often think they are my own. If I'm overstimulated, then the emotions of others will push me into a negative headspace. If I'm not overstimulated, then I can often use them as clues to help people. But even then, I have to be very careful not to let too much in." —Mathew

"I absorb everything! I'm working on managing it, but I'm like a human thermostat—I can tell the 'temperature' of a person or even a whole room." —Kay

Emotional Contagion

As sensitive people know all too well, emotions are infectious—they spread as easily from one person to the next as does the common cold. In fact, psychologists don't call the spread of an emotion empathy at all. They refer to it as *emotional contagion,* and we all catch emotions to some extent, whether we're sensitive or not. And it isn't just negative emotions, like stress and anger, that spread: The whole point of a party is to absorb happy feelings from friends through smiling, laughing, and dancing. Catching others' feelings is, in fact, a key part of what makes us human—and, like sensitivity, it helps our species survive. When a group of humans catches inspiration, they work together toward a common goal. When they catch fear, they mobilize against the threat and react quickly in the face of danger.

The spread of emotions is made possible, in part, by what researchers call the *chameleon effect.* Like a chameleon blending into its surroundings, we unconsciously mimic the mannerisms, facial expressions, and other behaviors of the people around us, the better to match our social environment. For example, if your coworker smiles at you as the two of you pass in the hallway, you probably smile back—automatically. This social response is a good thing: When you mirror the behavior of another person, that person feels good about you. The chameleon effect also explains why a group of friends develops similar ways of talking and joking, or how we can build rapport with strangers within seconds by "returning" their emotions. Research shows that high-empathy individuals—as sensitive people are—show the chameleon effect to a greater degree than others show it. This finding also explains why sensitive people often report that strangers feel comfortable telling them their life story (as Horne's patients did). Without even realizing it, sensitive people tend to mirror others' emotions automatically, and this mirroring builds trust.

This biological process of catching and returning emotions happens in three observable stages. The first stage is the chameleon effect, when you mimic another person's cues, either a smile or a frown. Then comes the second stage, a feedback loop. With your body taking on the *appearance* of an emotion, your mind starts to *feel* that emotion, either happiness or concern. During the final stage, the other person may begin to talk about what they're feeling or what they experienced. From their own words, ideally, you learn what caused a person to feel joy or stress—and by extension, why you feel the same way. This stage can be helpful, especially when you're confronted with painful emotions, because it allows you to put the emotion in context and get a "why" for the "what" you're feeling. But this stage can also heighten the feedback loop. As the two of you become synchronized, your initial frown becomes a true sense of distress. Worse, if the two of you don't communicate—perhaps because you've gotten the emotion from someone who doesn't want to talk about it—anxiety and uncertainty get added to the mix. Imagine, for example, that your coworker is called into a meeting with the boss and comes out looking on the verge of tears, then gathers their things and leaves. It would be stressful enough to absorb your coworker's fear and sadness (even if you knew why they were being laid off), but when you absorb those feelings with no explanation, you're left wondering if you're on the chopping block, too.

If you don't consider yourself a sensitive person, you may now be getting an idea of why those who are this way talk so much about their feelings. They go through this cycle all the time—their empathy can leave them carrying the stress of everyone around them. Sharing someone's emotions can be beautiful, but when it's constant, it can also be a source of pain.

The Most Potent Super-Spreaders

It's one thing to absorb a stranger's emotions but another thing entirely to absorb the emotions of those closest to you. In fact, research shows that emotions are far more infectious when they come from a loved one. One study found that spouses deeply influence one another's stress levels. The shared stress consequently plays an important role in marriage satisfaction (or the lack of it). As one sensitive wife told us, when her husband swears or gets agitated—even when the problem has nothing to do with her—her body immediately has a physical and emotional response, such as panic or even tears. Her husband, however, struggles to understand why his venting of emotions is "such a big deal." (Interestingly, one researcher found, women are more susceptible to emotional contagion than men, especially to catching stress and negativity. This may be because women are more socialized to attend to the emotional needs of the people around them.) Another study found that depression in a spouse frequently leads to depression in their partner; the same is true of parents and children and even people who live together as roommates.

It doesn't help that negative emotions spread more easily than positive moods. In one study, observers were asked to watch an unfortunate test subject give an unplanned speech and complete mental arithmetic problems in front of an audience. The subject's stress was so infectious that observers had measurable increases in cortisol, the stress hormone, even if they only watched through a one-way mirror—indeed, even if they merely watched on video from another location. No wonder many sensitive people report being unable to stomach certain TV shows or movies, such as ones that are intense, suspenseful, or violent.

These findings underscore the importance of choosing your inner circle wisely. You would do well to sidestep chronic complainers, perpetually negative and toxic people, and those who express strong feelings but are not very responsive to other people's emotional states. These people are the world's emotional super-spreaders; they pass on the most negative emotions, much like how nursing homes and indoor restaurants quickly spread Covid-19 during the pandemic.

Empathy, as the saying goes, is "your pain in my heart"—and it can sometimes be overwhelming. But if you step back and think about it, the people who are suffering don't actually need us to feel what they're feeling for us to help them. Of course, everyone wants to feel that their loved ones support them and understand the hardship they are going through—and sensitive people excel at holding that emotional space for others. But when we become overwhelmed, this response is counterproductive, like hearing a baby crying and responding by crying back. If the emotions are painful enough, we may even turn away from those who are suffering. If you've ever changed the TV channel when a commercial about abused animals comes on, then maybe you can relate.

But how can empathy be so problematic? How is it that empathy—the foundation of human morality and a driving force in human achievement, as we saw in Chapter 3—does not necessarily lead to people helping people?

The answer is that empathy is a fork in the road. It can lead to distress and pain. But with practice, it can also lead to something much more beautiful—something that will help both you and the party that is suffering.

That thing is compassion.

Going Beyond Empathy

The "happiest man in the world" earns no money. He has no house or car. In the winter, he isolates himself in a tiny hermitage in Nepal with none of the typical comforts or even heating to fight back the cold. That man is Matthieu Ricard, a French molecular biologist turned Buddhist monk.

Ricard is a little embarrassed by this title. It was coined by a British newspaper over a decade ago; he says it's all just media hype. Yet there's something to this label. When Ricard participated in a twelve-year study on meditation that included multiple brain scans, the scans showed something highly unusual: In areas associated with positive emotions, his brain had a level of activity never before seen in the scientific community. In other words, he was wildly content.

As the story goes, Ricard was in an fMRI scanner at the Max Planck Institute in Germany, being shown images of people in pain. He was told to tune in to his experience and just sit with the pain of witnessing another person suffering. (Essentially, he was asked to tap his empathy.) After doing this for a while, he is said to have begged the research team, "Can I please switch to compassion practice? This is getting too painful to bear." Astonishingly, once he added compassion to his empathy, he found that he could continue witnessing others' pain indefinitely—without the emotional overload.

The Brain-Changing Power of Compassion

That's the magic of compassion—a trait closely related to empathy, but subtly different. Whereas empathy involves mirroring the emotional state of someone else, experiencing it *with* them, compassion involves a response of concern, caring, or warmth. Compassion also implies action: Empathy can be as simple as feeling for someone and moving on, but compassion involves a desire to help them or act on their behalf. Thus, it moves us from a place of stress and overwhelm to a place of warmth and love. Compassion makes us active rather than passive; we become the helping hand, not just the sponge soaking up pain.

When we switch to compassion, we change our very brain chemistry. Indeed, leading compassion researcher Tania Singer found that different parts of the brain are activated when we share someone's pain (empathy) versus when we want to respond warmly to someone's suffering (compassion). Our heart rate slows, we release the "bonding hormone" oxytocin, and the parts of the brain linked to caregiving and pleasure light up. Once compassion enters the picture, we do not necessarily experience other people's pain with them, explains Singer, but we feel concern for them and a strong desire to help. Rather than turning us away from others, our compassion connects us even more deeply to them and strengthens our social ties.

To be clear, empathy is, in itself, a wonderful thing. It's a superpower all sensitive people share. But empathy alone can become overwhelming. That's where compassion comes in. It's what allows us to use our empathy to make a difference.

UNDERSTANDING EMPATHY VS. COMPASSION

Empathy	Compassion
Experiencing the same emotion as that experienced by another	Not necessarily feeling the same emotion
Inward focus (our own feelings or understanding)	Outward focus (desire to connect with and act in support of another)
May lead to pain, suffering, or distress; may cause us to pull back to reduce the pain we are feeling about another's suffering	Hormones and brain activity physically prepare us to help, connect, and give care
Facial expressions and actions often signal distress, pain, or concern (cringing, protective gestures like covering the heart in sympathy, looking shocked or worried)	Facial expressions and actions signal a commitment to the other person (leaning toward them, physically approaching them, making eye contact, light touches, expression of sincere interest)
Increased heart rate and tension	Decreased heart rate and calm
Brain activity associated with negative emotions	Brain activity associated with positive emotions
Can lead either to connection and caregiving or to pain and avoidance	Always linked with a motivation to approach or assist
Basic biological response; can be automatic with no training needed	Requires effort; not as easy to trigger compassion without practice or intention

Even more beautiful, moving from empathy to compassion makes a difference in our too-much world. We see the impact of this transition in countless everyday people who respond to tragedy with compassion, such as Susan Retik, whose husband was killed in the September 11 attacks. Her life was shattered, but she saw firsthand how much the outpouring of public support for 9/11 widows helped her cope. Then she saw a group of women who were not getting that support: Afghan women who were war widows in the country where her husband's killers had trained. Without their husbands, these women often fell into poverty or even lost their children. So, at a time when many other Americans gave in to Islamophobia and other forms of hatred, Retik opened her heart, sensing that she and the Afghan women were not enemies but had something in common. She began raising funds and reached out across the two warring nations to help. And before she knew it, she had cofounded an international aid organization helping Afghan women build the skills they need to earn an independent income. Retik went on to receive the Presidential Citizens Medal, the highest U.S. nonmilitary award, but she says it all started with a humble goal: to give even one woman in Afghanistan the same level of support she had received in her darkest hour.

Retik is not an outlier, at least not by the standards of high-empathy individuals. She also serves as a case study showing that empathy, a built-in strength of sensitive people, isn't just a feel-good quality but is one of the most important superpowers a human can wield. Or at least it can be, when sensitive people learn how to move beyond emotional contagion to compassionate empathy.

The question is, How do we do that?

How to Move from Empathy to Compassion

The answer comes from neuroscience as much as it does from meditation—and it's as simple as where you put your attention. Attention is like a spotlight, illuminating certain things and leaving others dark. Whatever it falls on becomes brighter in your mind, and these things, in turn, become your inner experience—your thoughts and emotions. For example, call to mind the last performance review you had with your boss. Your manager may have told you five good things about your work—and only one bad thing!—but if you shine your spotlight on the one bad thing, you will leave the meeting with your head hanging low. On the other hand, if you focus on your boss's mention of the many things you're doing well, you will feel calmer and more balanced.

So, to cultivate compassion, we must refocus our spotlight—placing it on the other person, not on our own feelings and reactions. "Empathy, without care and compassion, is a self-focused experience," explains neuroscientist Richard Davidson. "We ourselves become distressed and try to cope with our own response. Compassion is just the opposite. . . . We don't get caught up in our own feelings and reactions. Our attention, infused with care and the motivation to help, is with the other person. Compassion is always—by definition—other-centered." Compassion says, "What I'm feeling is beside the point. In this moment, it's about you."

Switching to compassion can be hard in the moment, but with practice, it becomes easier. You don't even have to generate warm, fuzzy feelings for the other person; you need only shift your attitude or "orientation," as Davidson says—and offer help, if you're able to. Compassion can be a small gesture, such as sending a text to check on a friend or carrying a heavy grocery bag for your neighbor. Other times, compassion means standing up to bullies, righting injustices, and addressing our world's biggest problems.

A Compassion Meditation

One proven way to shift your attention is through compassion medita-tion. There are many variations on this type of meditation, often under the name loving-kindness practice and drawing on Buddhist roots, while others that are fully secular; the results are the same either way. You can easily find audio guides for compassion meditation online or in meditation apps. Our favorite is "Wishing Your Loved Ones Well: Seated Practice," a meditation created by Davidson's nonprofit organi-zation, Healthy Minds Innovation. It's available in the Healthy Minds Program app, which is free, or as a free track on SoundCloud.

This kind of meditation involves first focusing your compassion on yourself and then extending it to those who are suffering and, eventu-ally, to the wider world. You may reflect on or repeat phrases like "May you experience less hardship" or "May you be happy, may you be safe, may you be healthy and strong." These simple affirmations do not, on their own, improve lives, but they do prime your mind to react differ-ently when compassion is needed. The point of the meditation is to carry that calm, compassionate mindset with you throughout your day—an outlook that better equips you to respond to people who are suffering. If you do the meditation regularly, this attitude starts to be-come automatic.

Ricard, the so-called happiest man, uses practices similar to this one and views compassion much the same way that Davidson does. If thinking about other people's pain just increases our distress, Ricard asserts, "then I think we should see it in another way." The answer is to "not center too much on ourselves." Rather, when we tap compassion, he says, we increase our courage. And courage, ultimately, is what sen-sitive people need to make a difference in our too-much world—because it allows us to be strong in the face of suffering.

When sensitive people practice compassion, it doesn't just give them a rudder in the storm. It makes them an ark unto others. Almost nothing is more calming than the presence of a person with unflinching compassion. They care, but they don't panic; they speak up, but they do not command. Compassion is a language all of us understand, and sensitive people are among those who can speak it fluently. When they do, they radiate trust and trustworthiness, care, and authenticity—just what our world needs most right now.

Other Ways to Lessen the Pain of Empathy

Here are some other things you can do to strengthen your compassion and lessen the pain of empathy.

Prioritize self-compassion. Some researchers have suggested that empathic distress plays an important protective role in our lives: It kicks in to keep us from giving and giving until we're spent. With that understanding, you can meet your own needs without feeling selfish. Indeed, self-care and self-compassion are research-validated ways to make sure you have the mental resources available to give compassion to others. Recognize when you're starting to feel overwhelmed by other people's emotions and give yourself permission to take a break from them. Turn off the news or put down your phone. Set boundaries with people who constantly exhaust you with their stress and negativity. Your boundaries don't mean you are indifferent to their suffering or you don't feel empathy for them. Rather, you are showing compassion to yourself and setting healthy limits on how much you will give. Or to put it another way: Caretaker, caretake thyself.

Find smaller, actionable steps. Research has shown that people are less likely to move to compassion and more likely to feel empathic distress when they believe that they can't make a difference in a situation— for example, when you hear about war, violence, or other suffering in the news. As a result, identifying small steps you can take makes a big difference both for yourself and for those in need. When helping feels daunting or even overwhelming, look for ways to break down the need into smaller, more achievable pieces. For example, if you're heartbroken about the number of abandoned animals who are euthanized, you may not be able to find a no-kill shelter or even volunteer at one, let alone take in every creature in need. But you may be able to donate money to one of these shelters or temporarily foster one dog or cat until it is homed. Or you could share the animal's profile on social media to encourage friends and acquaintances to adopt.

Focus on catching positive emotions. Whenever possible, cultivate empathic joy. To nurture this kind of joy, you double down on your empathy, except in the opposite direction: You focus on trying to absorb other people's happiness. Research shows that when we celebrate other people's good fortune, we activate our own brain's reward system; this activation improves our well-being and is linked to greater life satisfaction and more meaningful relationships. It is also associated with a stronger desire to help others and a greater willingness to do so (compassion). You can catch other people's happiness in a number of ways, such as sharing in their victories and milestones, recognizing and calling out their character strengths like kindness or humor, or even watching a child or animal play. Another way is to focus your attention on the positive effects of the helping efforts you make. When you're feeling overwhelmed with sadness, for example, call to mind the lives that you *have* changed, rather than dwelling on the people still in need.

Practice mindfulness. Brooke Nielsen, a therapist and the founder of the Therapeutic Center for Highly Sensitive People, offers a simple mindfulness practice to help you pinpoint emotional contagion. She says to take a moment to ask yourself, "Is this feeling mine, or does it belong to someone else?" The answer may be obvious, or it may take a moment of sitting with your emotions. If you realize you've been feeling a certain emotion after interacting with someone, then the emotion may have come from that person. Beware of sneaky emotions that seem as if they belong to you. For example, you feel heavy-hearted after getting coffee with a friend. Deep down, the emotion came from someone else—your friend was devastated about her breakup and you absorbed that feeling. If the emotion isn't yours, it's time to label it that way. Imagine two buckets in front of you, one labeled Mine and another labeled Not Mine. Take the emotions and mentally put them in the Not Mine bucket, and then imagine handing it back to its owner and letting them take it away—it's now officially theirs to deal with. Since emotions can be sticky, you may want to take the visualization a step further. At the end of the day, Nielsen likes to visualize using a vacuum cleaner to suck out all the stress and emotions she has unnecessarily collected throughout the day. This practice helps get rid of contagious emotions that she hadn't even realized she'd absorbed, and it creates a clear mental boundary showing that she is done dealing with them.

Get curious. It's easy to notice other people's feelings and think we understand them. After all, sensitive people excel at reading body language and other cues. However, our observations aren't always correct—nor do they show us the full picture—because no one can truly know for certain what's on another person's mind. Someone who appears to be radiating anger may not actually be angry but may just be tired from a lack of sleep or disappointed about an unrelated issue. So get curious and ask questions about what they're going through. Even when our assumptions are correct, people appreciate being heard, and gaining a deeper understanding of their situation can help you keep your own feelings separate, rather than being at the mercy of emotional contagion. If the person is expressing very strong emotions, focus on observing the feelings but not absorbing them. One way to do this is to imagine a glass wall between you and the other person. The wall allows you to see the person's feelings, which can't go through the glass; instead, they bounce back to the person.

Life at the Edge of the World

Perhaps the first sign that Rachel Horne was in over her head was the advice she got from locals: "I hope you packed something warm." She and Florian were backpacking in the Scottish headlands, and all she had was a thin sleeping bag and a couple of wool sweaters. These would prove to be little match for the cold North Sea wind. Officially, it was summer, but Horne spent many nights shivering in the dark, sometimes even descending into the early stages of thermal shock. Only Florian and his silver emergency blanket kept her from needing urgent medical attention.

Their diet wasn't much better. They spent weeks on uninhabited islands and had to bring food that was light, calorie-dense, and easy to cook. Mostly, that meant plain boiled pasta. Desperate for seasoning, Horne learned to gather seaweed as local Scots had done for centuries. Some days, she foraged under a clear sky; on others, she was caught in sheets of horizontal rain. It was, she says, the hardest time of her life.

It was also the best. Horne spent her days walking along vast beaches, hiking, or sitting on the edge of a sea cliff with nothing but the sky before her. Eagles soared overhead while dolphins dove in and out of the ocean. Sometimes she composed poetry; other times she simply enjoyed being where she was. Best of all, her sensitive mind got to run free without disruption. She shared her experience with us in an interview:

> For the first time in my life, I had the time and space to heal. No social media telling me to lose weight with detox tea, no advertisements telling me that the hole inside me could be filled with a new bikini and nice high heels. No beep-beep-beep of the washing machine, or the phone, or the supermarket checkout. I had a break from the rushing around of modern-day life and a break from soaking up a

hundred different people's emotions as I passed through the day. I totally checked out of the mainstream, and it was the most precious gift I could have ever given to myself.

After three months wandering the islands, she and Florian upgraded. They fixed up an old van and turned it into a tiny mobile living space. They'd park it in the mountains or the remote beaches of France, and the only time they returned to civilization was to buy groceries or to see friends. In these travels, Horne met scores of incredible people, people who wanted to make a difference in the world as she did: off-gridders, foragers, organic farmers, and more. And these people, she says, eventually inspired her to "stop running." She and Florian married, then settled down in a cottage in France, where Horne now tends a regenerative garden. She even got a new job, one that is less taxing on her sensitive nature but that still allows her to make a big difference: She is a full-time research writer for an international educational charity.

Horne would be the first to tell you that her unconventional life wouldn't suit every sensitive person. But for her, it was what she needed to hit pause on the overwhelming emotions she felt. That pause gave her the chance to build a life that works for her sensitive nature, not against it—one that allows her to tap her deep well of empathy in a different way.

"Highly sensitive people process everything so deeply," she writes, "and we aren't going to be content just to bury our authentic emotions and live like we are told we should. Whether your dream is to live on the open road or in a mansion, it doesn't matter. What matters is having the guts to ask yourself what you really want from life, and then stepping toward your dreams with trust and courage."

chapter 6

Full-Hearted Love

There are such relationships which must be a very
great, almost unbearable happiness, but they can
occur only between very rich natures . . . they can
unite only two wide, deep, individual worlds.

—Rainer Maria Rilke

When Brian met Sarah, it wasn't exactly love at first sight. "I was that annoying kid who was friends with her brother," he says, laughing. Although they knew each other in high school, they didn't really connect until decades later, when they started messaging over Facebook. At the time, Sarah was a single mom of two young children. Her family didn't, in Brian's words, "look kindly" on her divorce.

But Brian was different from the other people Sarah knew. He was kind. He was gentle. He was willing to listen to her without judgment and support her in the struggles she faced. Soon they were talking for hours every day and seeing each other every weekend. Speaking to us from his home in Michigan, Brian chose his words carefully and stopped often to reflect. He told us, "I may not be the most romantic guy in terms of making big gestures, but I can listen to her and be there for her emotional needs." Sarah fell in love with him not in spite of, but because of, his sensitivity, he says.

It wasn't long before both of them were ready to take the next step. After just eight months of dating, they married at a local reception hall as their friends and family looked on. Brian, Sarah, and her kids all moved into a house together; it was "instant family," as Sarah puts it. Brian became a stepfather, sharing a love of baseball with his new stepsons. Unlike some other men, he had patience with the boys, even when they misbehaved or made a mistake.

But soon, things began to fall apart. Family life—and all the stress that raising children brings—was very different from Brian's single, quiet life. Brian and Sarah found themselves arguing more and more, and these arguments exacerbated the differences in their personalities. "She's the kind of person who wants to resolve things right now," Brian told us. "I'm the kind of person who needs to step back and reflect first." Sarah agreed that they are "completely different" in how they handle disagreements, and it can be hard for Brian because she's "so direct."

For reasons he didn't understand or couldn't fully explain to Sarah, these arguments really rattled Brian. He just knew that after they fought, he had the strong urge to withdraw from the family for long periods. He would watch TV on the couch or walk outside alone. Sometimes it would even be three or four days before he would feel like talking to Sarah again. And it wasn't just after they fought that Brian wanted to be alone. He found himself withdrawing after a busy day at work or on a Saturday night when the family finally had some downtime—time when Sarah thought they should be going on dates or making plans with friends.

To Sarah, these retreats made no sense. It seemed as if Brian was being dramatic and self-absorbed; his avoidance of the issue that had caused the fight made her even more upset. Worse yet, he didn't seem to enjoy spending time with her anymore.

Their marriage crumbling, Brian felt like a failure not only as a husband but also as a man, and he developed severe depression. "Being sensitive is something men are not supposed to do," he told us. "It's something society frowns on as a man." At one point, Sarah asked for a divorce, and Brian agreed. Later that same afternoon, both of them changed their minds when they realized they didn't want to spend their lives apart from each other. Nevertheless, something had to change— not just for their sake but also for the sake of their kids. Brian, it seemed, was about to lose the love of his life.

The Sensitive Person's Relationship Dilemma

As we've seen, sensitive people tend to be conscientious and have high levels of empathy—so you might think that strong, healthy relationships come naturally to them, whether it's friendship or love. Yet all too often, sensitive people say otherwise: Relationships are one of their greatest challenges in life. Here are some of the things that sensitive people report as being challenging in their marriage and friendships. How many have you experienced?

- Needing more downtime than your partner or friends need to recover from stimulation
- Getting easily overwhelmed by arguments, raised voices, or other expressions of disappointment or anger (like a slammed door) and needing more time than others need to recover from conflict with loved ones
- Putting your spouse's, children's, or friend's needs ahead of your

own, to the point of exhaustion, burnout, or disconnection
from yourself
- Reading others so well that they cannot hide their emotions
from you, and in turn, taking those emotions personally
- Getting taken over by bigger, louder, and more aggressive
personalities and, consequently, feeling resentment, hurt, or
taken advantage of
- Being targeted by narcissists or other toxic or controlling people
- Deeply feeling the impact of other people's words, especially
criticism and blame
- Getting easily worn down by drama, gossip, or small talk
- Feeling misunderstood by others, because you experience the
world differently as a result of your sensitivity
- Craving a deeper mental, emotional, and sexual connection
than many people are able to give
- Finding "your people"—those who understand you and who
not only respect but also cherish your sensitivity

Again, if you've experienced any number of these things, there's
nothing wrong with you, and you're not alone—you're simply a sensitive person in a not-so-sensitive world. Sensitivity expert Elaine Aron
even goes as far as to say that relationships are generally less happy for
sensitive people overall than they are for their less-sensitive counterparts. This was her conclusion after running a series of studies comparing sensitive people and less-sensitive people in marriages. Specifically,
sensitive people reported feeling more "bored" and "stuck in a rut" in
their marriage; these feelings are key predictors of an unhappy relationship later on. To dig into why, Aron asked them questions like, "When
you are bored in a close relationship, is it usually because you wish the
conversation were deeper or more personally meaningful?" and "Do
you like to spend time reflecting or thinking about the meaning of your
experience?" Not surprisingly, sensitive people said yes to both.

In Their Own Words: In Relationships, What Is Challenging for You?

"I am constantly prioritizing my spouse's needs at the expense of my own. This sometimes causes me to miss some of the classic signals of burnout. There are times when I have begun to feel overlooked, neglected, and taken for granted, pouring out of my highly sensitive love bucket without feeling as though I was receiving a reciprocal effort." –Raneisha

"My greatest challenge is finding people I can really bond with who understand and hear me–my 'people.' It seems at times I am always finding the wrong people to attach to, people who push my boundaries and set off some of my personal weaknesses: moodiness, conflict avoidance, and standing up for myself. In love, I am a hopeless romantic, a dreamer of perfect love, an idealist with high expectations that are often tempered by reality." –William

"I am very aware of subtle changes in my husband's face, for example, when he is not impressed by something. Although he thinks he's hiding it, I see it, react to it, and feel hurt by it. Then I question why he feels that way and dig to find out why." –Emma

"I feel like the worst is not being understood by my husband and not being able to have those deep conversations at any time of the day. He's capable of having pretty deep conversations, but then if I go even deeper, he just doesn't get it or doesn't want to. He thinks very logically, and he's very literal, so it's sometimes very difficult to be heard and understood." –Laura

Why else might relationships be less happy for sensitive people? There are several possible reasons, although not all of these will apply equally to every sensitive person or relationship. One reason is that sensitive people simply experience the world differently and have different needs. Often, sensitive people pair up with less-sensitive people, and generally, this matchup is a good thing: A less-sensitive friend can lead the way on a new adventure, and a less-sensitive spouse can step up when the partner feels overwhelmed. Yet when opposites attract, as was the case with Brian and Sarah, there are sure to be misunderstandings.

Just as sensitive people's bodies have an inherently stronger reaction to, say, the stiffness of a new pair of jeans, their hearts have a stronger reaction to a critical comment. And sensitive people—even extroverted ones—also need more downtime than others do. Less-sensitive partners or friends may take this need as an insult or see it as wrong. One sensitive woman told us that her tendency to get overwhelmed in social situations creates tension in her marriage. She quickly gets fatigued at big parties or in loud restaurants. Then she becomes irritable and distant and wants to go home—while her husband wants to stay and enjoy the scene. In this case, neither person is wrong for their reaction; they are simply inhabiting the world differently. But if these misunderstandings go unaddressed, sensitive people can be left feeling lonely and isolated.

Stress is also a factor. As we've seen, the sensitive brain processes information deeply, so sensitive people tend to feel stress and anxiety quicker than do their less-sensitive friends or spouse. Brian, for example, found it difficult to adjust to the loud, chaotic family life that inevitably accompanies young children. Other sensitive people report finding it stressful to share a living space with roommates or family. As we saw in Chapter 4, they reach a state of overstimulation faster and need a quiet sanctuary to retreat to, although finding a retreat can be an impossible feat when you're surrounded by people who don't get it.

The Need for Something More

Ultimately, however, there is one factor that stands above the others. It's something sensitive people tell us over and over again: They require more depth in their relationships to feel satisfied. Without this depth, something will always be lacking for them. That's certainly true for Jen, a sensitive woman who finds it hard to meet people who desire the same level of authenticity and vulnerability that she does. "Talking about personal struggles and deep, gritty issues feels too scary and uncomfortable for many people," she told us. And small talk doesn't cut it. As a result, she has grown more selective about who she engages with and, unfortunately, has therefore never really had a best friend.

Jen isn't an outlier. In fact, the search for meaningful relationships is getting measurably harder. According to the most recent American Perspectives Survey, Americans have fewer close friendships than they once did, talk to their friends less often, and rely less on their friends for support. This *relationship deficit* is even more pronounced for men. Americans are also marrying later than ever and moving around more, two trends strongly associated with isolation and loneliness. Blame who you want—cities, social media, the nuclear family, car culture, or just our busy too-much world—most people aren't getting their needs for human connection fully met.

Here we can take a lesson from sensitive people. As society experiences its relationship deficit, sensitive people seek to draw us closer. They want more out of their relationships—more depth, more connection, more intimacy—than the average person. That instinct, it turns out, is a good one: Strong relationships have numerous benefits, such as helping you live longer and recover from illness quicker, and making you happier and more productive on the job. Harvard Medical School goes as far as to say that your social connections are as critical to your health as getting a good night's sleep, eating a healthy diet, and not smoking. Another study concluded that relationships are the most valuable things in our lives: When we feel loved and accepted by others, we value physical possessions less. We focus less on possessions, probably because meaningful relationships provide a sense of comfort, security, and protection.

Yet, as we've seen, many people—sensitive ones in particular—find their relationships lacking. So what is a sensitive person supposed to do? Can you have the kind of relationships you crave? The answer is no . . . and yes.

It's no secret that the purpose of marriage or any other long-term partnership has changed over time. Matches were once based not on love but on economic security—perhaps in the form of a dowry, some farmland, or simply to unite two families that practiced the same trade. Historians suggest this pattern held not just among the well-off but also for commoners and even among bands of hunter-gatherers. Marriage was a way to pool resources, share labor, and build bonds between families. In some parts of the world, this is still the norm today. In South Sudan, for example, a dowry is paid in cattle as part of any marriage. The price of the dowry is discounted if the couple has a spark, but the wedding can go forward either way; love is more of a bonus feature than a necessity. Our obsession with deep, soul mate-style love is comparatively recent and uniquely Western.

But according to social psychologist Eli Finkel, in today's world, even love is not enough. Finkel set out to map changing expectations about marriage, and he says that many couples now expect their relationship to contribute to a sense of personal fulfillment and growth. We still want chemistry, certainly, but we also want someone who will help us become our best selves and reach our full potential. Understandably, this expectation puts great pressure on a marriage, and most marriages fall short in this regard. In fact, according to Finkel, the average marriage today is weaker than the average marriage of the past, in terms of satisfaction and divorce rate. But he found something else in his data: The best marriages today are much stronger than the best marriages of the past—indeed, these good unions are the strongest the world has ever seen. Clearly, then, a highly satisfying relationship is achievable. It's just, well, a lot of work.

Finkel would be the first to say that this kind of relationship isn't for everyone (and that's okay). It also involves ongoing effort of the most uncomfortable kind: challenging oneself emotionally. He compares it to a scene from the movie *Sideways,* in which Paul Giamatti's character, a wine connoisseur, muses about how much harder it is to grow pinot grapes:

> *It's thin-skinned, temperamental, ripens early. It's—you know, it's not a survivor like cabernet, which can just grow anywhere and thrive even when it's neglected. No. Pinot needs constant care and attention. You know, and in fact, it can only grow in these really specific little tucked-away corners of the world. And only the most patient and nurturing of growers can do it, really. Only somebody who really takes the time to understand pinot's potential can then coax it into its fullest expression. Then, I mean, oh, its flavors, they're just the most haunting and brilliant and thrilling and subtle and ancient on the planet.*

In other words, sure, a good pinot—or a romance built on deep fulfillment—is a thing of rare beauty, but it's rare for a reason. It's hard to cultivate. And that's where Finkel offers hope. As with pinot grapes, he says, it takes time, effort, and a certain kind of person to foster a deep, meaningful relationship. What kind of person? Finkel says they must have traits like emotional investment, empathy, and self-reflection—basically a checklist of the strengths of sensitive people. Sensitive people, in other words, don't just enjoy drinking pinot. They are uniquely suited to grow it.

In Their Own Words: What Are Some of the Strengths You Bring to Your Relationships?

"I believe being sensitive allows me to be a better friend and wife. I'm able to empathize with my people on a cellular level! I don't have the ability to give a superficial 'congratulations'—I experience true happiness from others' joy. Conversely, I am able to walk with my people, with hands on their back, as they experience difficult or trying situations. To be able to be a safe haven for my husband and friends is a special experience for me." —Raneisha

"My sensitivity makes me less selfish, so when I make decisions, I try to do what is in everyone's best interests and not just mine." —Jen

"My strength as a sensitive person is that I know when someone is feeling painful emotions. They may say they are okay, but I can feel when something is wrong. Trusting my instincts helps every part of my life and my relationships." —Vicki

"Many of my friends have told me that I am one of the kindest people they know. My best friend loves that she and I can have deep conversations about anything with no judgment." —Phyllis

How to Make Your Relationships More Meaningful

How, exactly, can sensitive people tap into their strengths to create the "pinot" relationships they crave? The best partnerships, according to Finkel, are those in which two people bring high expectations to the relationship and then invest enough in that relationship to make sure that it meets those expectations. To this end, two people might double down on the strengths of a marriage—the ways in which the two of them are compatible—and take the pressure off (or lower their expectations) in areas where there is less compatibility. Take, for example, the sensitive woman who felt overstimulated by parties and restaurants. Finkel might say that the woman and her spouse could take the pressure off by simply accepting that they are different in this way. Rather than her begrudgingly attending these events—and getting exhausted—her husband could agree to go alone or with a friend, with the woman only attending on the most important occasions. The couple could then double down on something else they both enjoy, such as traveling or watching certain movies together.

Unlike this couple, you may be in a relationship with someone who is just as sensitive as you are—or more sensitive. Making a life with another sensitive person can be wonderful; both of you are probably conscientious and caring and prefer to go deep in your conversations and interests. You and your partner probably have a strong desire for closeness and meaning, and both of you may prefer a slower, simpler pace of life. However, both partners being sensitive is not a guarantee that a relationship will progress smoothly or be exceptionally meaningful. In some ways, this pairing might be extra tricky. For example, perhaps you both avoid conflict or are easily overstimulated by daily life. Or perhaps you are sensitive in different ways—one of you may be really bothered by clutter in your environment, while the other takes messes in stride and is sensitive to noise. In this case, you and your spouse need to honor how each of you is sensitive and look for compromises that won't overload you or push you past your limits.

Here are some more ways to make your relationships stronger as a sensitive person. We also discuss some habits that will limit any relationship's capacity for meaning. These strategies will be helpful whether the other person is sensitive like you or not.

Make Conflict Safe

As Brian discovered, arguing with your partner can be incredibly over-stimulating when you're a sensitive person. Researchers have found that couples' conflicts have the same physiological effect as combat stress, complete with a galloping heartbeat, agitation, inaccurate perceptions of incoming information, and, of course, Threat mode. Megan Griffith, writing for Sensitive Refuge, explains it this way: "When my husband and I disagree, I can't even focus on the actual topic we're fighting about. Instead, I get swept away in my husband's feelings—and my own—and it becomes so overwhelming that I either shut down or just start crying." Many sensitive people feel this "combat stress" of conflict even more intensely, so no wonder many report that they tend to avoid it. Or, like Brian, they need long periods of downtime after conflict to soothe their overworked nervous system.

However, avoiding conflict is a surefire way to limit the depth of any relationship, says April Snow, a marriage therapist who specializes in working with sensitive people. Of course, every relationship will call for times when you "go along to get along," but this approach shouldn't be the status quo. When someone crosses an important boundary, you should speak up. And when someone else initiates conflict, it's not necessarily your job to appease that person or hide your reaction to keep the peace. Although these tactics may work in the short term to calm the intensity of the disagreement and reduce the overstimulation you may feel, they will eventually lead to more anger, resentment, or other forms of emotional buildup.

When we avoid conflict, "the other person never gets to know the real, full you," Snow says. The people closest to you never learn what's on your mind, what kinds of things bother you, or how you really feel. Although it seems counterintuitive, conflict can actually strengthen a relationship because, she explains, "You learn how to resolve problems and can practice supporting each other through difficult moments."

One way to instantly make conflict feel safer for sensitive people is to banish shouting, door-slamming, eye-rolling, insults, shame, intimidation, and other strong expressions of anger or disappointment from your relationships. If you or the other person experiences strong emotions during a conflict, take a break from each other until those emotions feel less intense. One sensitive, loving couple came up with a code—"storm warning"—that either of them could invoke at any time. If either partner said the code phrase, both of them immediately had to stop the discussion, note the time, and take a thirty-minute break. During the break, they would do something to ground themselves, such as journaling, going for a walk, or taking up a creative project. Then, after thirty minutes, they would continue the conversation or set up another time to talk within twenty-four hours. This practice reassured them that issues wouldn't be dismissed or ignored, and it allowed both partners time to reflect on their thoughts before responding. When they came back together to discuss the problem, they could do so in a more productive—and less emotionally charged—way.

Snow also recommends that sensitive people take a mindful approach to conflict. In the heat of a disagreement, she says, it's easy to spin into your imagination or let anxiety take over. To counteract this tendency, bring your mind back to the here and now by engaging your senses. Do some mindful breathing, feel your feet pressing into the ground, find an object to concentrate on, or deploy any other strategy from your overstimulation toolkit. Try to stay connected with your own experience instead of getting swept up in the emotions of the other person. To this end, you might break eye contact from time to time and quietly notice what's happening inside you—your own feelings and bodily sensations. Remind yourself that it makes sense to feel uncomfortable during conflict and that, at the same time, your feelings and needs are just as valid as those of the other person.

What if you truly are dealing with a high-conflict person, someone who frequently yells, twists the truth, or unfairly blames you? Bill Eddy of the High Conflict Institute defines *high-conflict people* as those with a pattern of behavior that increases conflict rather than reducing or resolving it. These people blame others for the problems they create themselves, engage in all-or-nothing thinking, aren't in control of their emotions, and have extreme reactions to situations. You can't control what a high-conflict person does, but you can work on learning to control how you respond (and you can decide how much of their behavior to allow in your life). If your friend or loved one is a high-conflict person, we recommend learning specific strategies to respond to them. These strategies are available through Eddy's books or the High Conflict Institute's free podcast.

Ask for What You Want

In light of her thirty years of working with couples as a clinical psychologist, Lisa Firestone reveals that most people have an easy time pointing out what they don't want in a relationship—their partner's flaws—but they have a harder time asking for what they do want. Sensitive people are no exception, and in fact, they may find it even harder to speak up. Their reticence usually springs from a place of good intentions: Sensitive people tend to be conscientious and don't want to burden or inconvenience others. However, this tendency can leave their needs unmet, which can erode the meaning in any relationship. On the other hand, asking for what you want builds emotional intimacy. As Firestone explains, "When you speak about your wants honestly, directly, and from an adult point of view, your partner is more likely to be open, responsive, and personal in return."

Sensitive people may also fall into the trap of expecting others to read their mind and anticipate their needs. It's easy to see why: Sensitive people themselves excel at reading other people and anticipating others' needs. However, if you're a sensitive person, you may need to get comfortable being direct, perhaps more direct than you wish to be—even more so if you are in a relationship with a less-sensitive person. Don't expect others to be able to read you as well as you can read them. Remember, you are different, and most people you meet will simply not possess your superpowers.

If you're a sensitive person, you might even experience low self-esteem, feeling broken or flawed because of your sensitivity. You may question whether you even deserve to ask for what you want. Please know that your needs and desires are just as important as those of others. You would never tell a friend that she doesn't deserve to rest when she's tired or that she doesn't deserve to ask someone when she needs help. We teach children the Golden Rule: Treat other people the way you would want to be treated. Sensitive people often need the Golden Rule in reverse: Treat yourself the way you treat others.

When you ask for what you want, avoid using victimizing language. Your words should be an authentic expression of what you desire, explains Firestone, not a demand for what you need or an expectation of what you're entitled to. Likewise, avoid "you" statements that cast blame. Here are three examples of how to ask for what you want in a relationship, from Firestone:

- Instead of "You don't seem excited to see me anymore," try "I want to feel wanted by you."
- Instead of "You're always distracted," try "I want your attention."
- Instead of "You never help," try "I feel so much more relaxed when I have help with this or that."

Be Willing to Get Vulnerable

Vulnerability has been getting a lot of attention from researchers lately, most notably from social scientist Brené Brown, the bestselling author of *Daring Greatly*. Brown found that healthy vulnerability in relationships increases a sense of trust and connection with others. It can also lead to the deeper, more personally meaningful conversations that sensitive people crave. Healthy vulnerability is about opening up and showing your "rough edges and human imperfections," as author and marriage therapist Robert Glover famously wrote. Sensitive people naturally show their vulnerability, but at some point in their lives, they may have been made to feel as if they shouldn't. Society tends to view vulnerability as a weakness, because of the Toughness Myth.

Artists also know that to share their art, they must be vulnerable. There is no other way: You are laying bare something that came from your heart and soul, and once it's out there, it will be judged, interpreted, and criticized. And yet artwork is how we share meaning. Seth Godin, in his picture book for adults, *V Is for Vulnerable: Life Outside the Comfort Zone*, explains it this way:

> *Vulnerable is the only way we can feel when we truly share the art we've made. When we share it, when we connect, we have shifted all the power and made ourselves naked in front of the person we've given the gift of our art to. We have no excuses, no manual to point to, no standard operating procedure to protect us. And that is part of our gift.*

Vulnerability does not mean oversharing aspects of your life or being painfully blunt or harsh. Nor is it a means to an end; vulnerability shouldn't be used to guilt, control, or manipulate others. Here are some healthy ways to add more vulnerability to your relationships:

- Admit when something is hard, frustrating, or scary for you.
- Tell someone when you admire, respect, are attracted to, or love them.
- Be willing to share stories from your past, whether they were positive or negative experiences.

- Tell others when they have hurt you.
- Express your true feelings—even negative ones—rather than covering them up for the sake of politeness (sadness, frustration, disappointment, embarrassment, etc.).
- Share your opinion, even when you think others will disagree.
- Ask for help when you need it.
- Ask for what you want.

Beware Narcissists and Other Toxic or Controlling People

If you find yourself in a relationship with a narcissist (or another type of abusive or controlling person), you may not be able to put a name to what you are experiencing, but you have a nagging feeling that something isn't quite right. Narcissists believe they are superior to other people, although this attitude may show in subtle ways. They may, for example, ignore expert advice or be overly critical of the restaurant service. Narcissists lack empathy—even for their friends and family—and they believe they are entitled to attention, success, and special treatment. "Ask anyone who is a highly sensitive person and they will tell you that at some point in their lives, they have been in a relationship with a narcissist," explains Deborah Ward, author of *Sense and Sensitivity*. "Most did not know it at the time, but increasingly, they began to feel taken advantage of, used, and wondered how to get out." Even though you may feel a strong connection to this person—especially at first—a relationship with a narcissist will inherently lack real intimacy and meaning.

At first, this person may be charming, funny, and profoundly interested in you, but as time goes on, you feel exhausted, controlled, manipulated, or confused. Then, the harder you try to fix the relationship, the worse it gets. Sensitive people don't consciously choose these kinds of partnerships or friendships, but they are especially at risk for them, because of their empathy. Sensitive people are acutely aware of other people's emotions. They often consciously (or unconsciously) work to make others feel comfortable—and narcissists love being on the receiving end of such attention and care. When narcissists share stories of trauma or wounds from their childhood, sensitive people want to help—including helping them process their buried emotions, of which the narcissist has many. In the narcissist's eyes, it's a match made in heaven.

Healthy boundaries are an important part of any relationship, but they are even more important when you're dealing with a narcissist or another controlling person. First, you must get very clear on what you want to happen or what boundary you are trying to enforce, explains Sharon Martin, a psychotherapist who specializes in helping people create healthy relationships. Narcissists, especially, will work to throw you off balance and keep you confused, using gaslighting, lies, or other manipulative tactics. Write down your boundary so you don't lose sight of what needs to happen. Then, communicate your boundary clearly, calmly, and consistently. Stick to the facts, and don't blame, overexplain, or defend yourself—even when the narcissist gets upset and throws emotional grenades, which are attempts to bait you into conflict.

Unfortunately, all too often, controlling people won't respect your boundaries—that's a big part of what makes them controlling in the first place. That's when it's time to consider your other options, Martin says. Is the boundary negotiable? Some boundaries are more important than others, so consider what behavior you're willing to accept and what behavior is a complete no-go. Compromise and flexibility are good things if the other person is also willing to make changes. But if someone repeatedly disregards your most important boundaries, you have to consider how long you are willing to accept such mistreatment. "I've seen people accept disrespect and abuse for years and years, hoping a toxic person will change only to look back in hindsight to see that this person had no intention of changing or respecting boundaries," notes Martin. At this point, you have to choose to either accept their behavior as-is or disengage from the relationship.

Forcing other people to change never works. That's where a practice called *loving detachment* can help. When you detach, you make a conscious decision to stop trying to change the other person or control the outcome of the situation. Detaching doesn't mean you don't care about them; it means you're choosing to be realistic about the relationship and show compassion to yourself. Martin says you can practice loving detachment in these ways:

- Letting them make their own choices and deal with the consequences of their actions
- Responding in a different way, such as shrugging off a rude comment or making a joke of it (instead of taking it personally), and thereby changing the dynamics of the interaction
- Choosing not to participate in the same old arguments, or taking a break from an unproductive conversation
- Saying no to invitations to spend time with them
- Leaving an uncomfortable or dangerous situation

And if you think there's even a slight chance that you're dealing with a narcissist, you should find several trustworthy people, such as friends, a therapist, or members of a support group, to talk with. "Narcissistic and 'toxic' people are skilled at getting us to doubt ourselves and our intuition," Martin says. "As a result, many people spend a lot of time second-guessing whether the person is truly toxic or whether they are overreacting or maybe even causing the person to behave poorly." Although sensitive people read others well—and have strong intuition— they may have been conditioned over time not to trust their "gut" impressions, because the Toughness Myth says that emotions are weak. Narcissists, especially, like to mess with your head and attempt to scramble your otherwise reliable intuition. That's why it's crucial to develop a support network that can help you see things for what they truly are.

You always have a choice when it comes to narcissists and other controlling people (even though they may make you believe you don't). Sometimes, the only way to protect yourself is to stop spending time with them. When you choose to limit contact with them (or break things off completely), it isn't meant to punish them—it's a form of self-compassion. If someone is hurting you, whether physically or emotionally, you owe it to yourself to put some space between yourself and this person.

A Happy Ending

Brian doesn't remember the exact moment, but things were beginning to change. His marriage to Sarah was getting stronger. He was attending therapy, and he had stumbled on some life-changing information: He learned that he is a highly sensitive person.

In Brian's words, because he falls on the "extreme end" of the sensitivity scale, he needs much more downtime than Sarah needs and he takes her words personally when they disagree. He realized that his main issue was about perfection, a common struggle of sensitive people. When Sarah seems to be insinuating that he's doing something wrong, her observation hurts, because he wants to be a perfect spouse. Now, he and Sarah are learning to handle conflict differently—and to meet in the middle when it comes to other issues. "I don't need to change who I am, but I do need to meet her partway," Brian says.

His sensitivity may have created some challenges in his marriage, but ultimately, it was also what saved the relationship, he believes. Being a sensitive person allowed him to reflect deeply on his relationship and consider how he and his wife's dynamic could change. Under such pressure, a less-sensitive person may have given up before finding healing or may have lacked the self-awareness to bring about real growth. But Brian reflected on his strengths and weaknesses and learned to play to his strengths—such as his ability to be there for Sarah emotionally, read her cues, and show her that he really cares. Now, after eight years of marriage, Brian says their love is even more solid than it was when they first met.

He also has advice for anyone who has a sensitive person in their life: "It's not a character defect; it's not us trying to be difficult. I think that's what my wife thought for a while. Being sensitive is a real personality trait. I hope that those who are not highly sensitive take the time to really learn and understand that being with a sensitive person can be challenging but ultimately very rewarding."

Brian's advice applies not only to the adults in our lives but to our children as well. Much like sensitive adults, sensitive children come with their own challenges and rewards, which we explore in the next chapter.

chapter 7

Raising a Sensitive Generation

> When you were a kid . . . you saw life through very
> clear windows. Small windows, of course. But very
> bright windows. And, then, what happened? You
> know what happened. The grown-ups began to equip
> you with shutters.
>
> —Dr. Seuss

It began in the first few hours, and even minutes, of your baby's life. When the doctor shined a light in Sophie's eyes, she cried. When you sneezed loudly, she cried again, almost as if she were in physical pain. Later, after being passed from relative to relative—each one holding and admiring this tiny, perfect creature—she seemed too wound up to sleep. Of course, every newborn cries and has trouble sleeping at times, but Sophie seemed different from your other children when they were her age. There is nothing physically wrong with her, the doctor assured you; it's just her personality. Other adults used different descriptors: "fussy," "high-needs," or even "difficult."

As she grew up, Sophie was a typical child in many ways, but in other ways, she stood out. She was creative and clever, and you wondered if she might be gifted. As a toddler, she repeated big words after only hearing them once or twice, and she surprised you with her insights, her mind seemingly able to grasp concepts beyond her years. From the way she played, you sensed she had a rich imagination. She was also a keen observer. One day, she spotted a plane in the distance—hardly a speck against the morning sky—and she always pointed out when her teacher wore new earrings.

However, overstimulation was never far off, and Sophie's insights vanished when she became overwhelmed. She felt overwhelmed after busy days or even fun activities like a birthday party or a trip to a crowded indoor play park. During these times, Sophie was prone to fearsome tantrums and meltdowns. Nearly all young children have such episodes, but Sophie's were more frequent and intense. Sometimes, little things set her off, like a pebble in her shoe or macaroni noodles that were not, in her opinion, the right shape. At other times, the triggers were nearly existential: She came home in tears after witnessing another child being bullied, even though she had nothing to do with the situation. When she got older, she refused to eat hamburger after learning where meat comes from.

Along with her meltdowns came big emotions. Sophie danced when she was happy. She buried her head in your chest and wailed when she was sad. Although her feelings sometimes overwhelmed her, she was surprisingly aware of her own mental state and the emotions of others. As a result, she seemed to know when you were hiding something from her or having a bad day—something her siblings, who were older than her, missed. Sophie's thoughtfulness helped her make friends easily, although she was timid in large groups of her peers and became nervous when she had to perform in front of them, such as when giving a speech or competing in a sport. Generally, though, she was conscientious and kind. Able to read between the lines and sense what her teachers wanted, Sophie easily pleased them and earned good grades. In fact, you worried that she was a little too nice and too honest. At times, her perfectionism drove her to those all-too-familiar tears.

Sophie had other quirks that you learned to accept. Even as a teenager, she was bothered so much by certain textures and flavors that she would not eat certain foods. Certain smells bothered her, too, like the sweaty odor of the gym locker room, which she refused to enter. Whenever life took a sudden turn, such as when a pet died or a friend moved away, Sophie was shattered with grief, unable to shake the heartache for a long time. Even positive life changes could make her anxious because there were new situations to navigate and new routines to learn. Sometimes she spent hours mentally preparing and rehearsing for these events.

Over the years, you've tried to help Sophie stretch her comfort zone while also making space for her big emotions. But raising her was far from easy. At times, you felt as if you didn't know what she needed or how to help her. Perhaps other parents have told you that this frustration is especially common among those with sensitive kids.

Is Your Child Sensitive?

Sophie is not a real child, but her portrait is based on examples of numerous sensitive children. Not every sensitive child will be like Sophie. Just as sensitivity presents itself differently in adults, it presents itself differently in children, too. Here are some common traits of sensitive children. Your child does not need to check every box to be considered sensitive, but the more boxes they check, the more sensitive they are.

MY CHILD

- ☐ Learns new things quickly
- ☐ Expresses strong emotions
- ☐ Reads people well
- ☐ Struggles to cope with change
- ☐ Dislikes big surprises or disruptions to their routine
- ☐ Has strong intuition about people or events
- ☐ Responds better to gentle correction rather than to harsh discipline
- ☐ Cries or withdraws when yelled at or scolded
- ☐ Has a hard time falling asleep after a fun or exciting day
- ☐ Jumps at unexpected noises or touch
- ☐ Complains when things feel off (scratchy bedsheets, itchy clothing labels, tight waistbands, etc.)
- ☐ Refuses to eat certain foods because of their smell or texture
- ☐ Has a clever sense of humor
- ☐ Asks many questions
- ☐ Makes insightful comments and seems wise for their age
- ☐ Wants to save everyone, from a stray dog to a bullied child in their class
- ☐ Must do things perfectly
- ☐ Stresses over grades and homework deadlines
- ☐ Wants to please the adults in their life
- ☐ Has been bullied by their peers (this is especially true of sensitive boys)
- ☐ Avoids certain places (like public gyms or perfume counters) because of their strong odor
- ☐ Dislikes noisy places
- ☐ Notices when other people are upset or hurt
- ☐ Thinks before speaking or acting—they "look before they leap"
- ☐ Worries a lot

☐ Avoids taking risks unless they have prepared carefully ahead of time

☐ Feels physical pain intensely

☐ Notices new things, such as a teacher's new outfit or when furniture has been moved

Still not sure if your child is sensitive? Take a look at how some parents describe their sensitive kids. Do you see similarities between their children and yours?

In Their Own Words: What Are Your Sensitive Child's Greatest Strengths and Challenges?

Jenny, the parent of a seven-year-old boy: "My son is very attuned to his own emotions as well as other people's emotions. He loves to understand how things work. He is an animal lover and a nature lover, and he takes to heart why we should take care of the planet. My son doesn't like to be alone (it seems like a punishment to him); his constant need to be with someone is hard for the whole family at times. He has a hard time with groups and isn't a risk taker or willing to try new things (like a new sport or riding a bike) until he has observed them repeatedly. Because of these tendencies, he sometimes feels left out of activities with friends."

Sarah M., the parent of a nine-year-old girl: "School is often overwhelming and stressful for my sensitive daughter. She can be very hard on herself and reacts strongly to the subtle cues of those around her. She is easily triggered by harsh words or tone of voice even when it is not directed at her (like when teachers address other students). Out in the world, she holds in all her big feelings, then releases them in the safety of her home. On bad days, she closes up and questions her very existence in the world. But she has a big heart with a huge well of love to give. She's picky about who she loves, but she loves fiercely. She's a deep thinker and comes up with some amazingly insightful comments."

Sarah B. H., the parent of a five-year-old girl: "My sensitive child notices every detail and has such an incredible love of learning. Her compassion for other living things high-lights her heart of gold. She's wise beyond her years and so considerate of others. However, just as Superman has his kryptonite, my daughter is aware that her body and soul need extra breaks. Learning to regulate her emotions (espe-cially when her sense of overwhelm presents itself as rage) has been challenging. While she has a toolbox full of calming tactics, overstimulation sometimes hits so hard and fast that it's impossible to stop. Usually the overstimulation is due to her being off her schedule, her inability to do certain things that she'd like to do, and, most often, time constraints."

Maureen, the parent of two sensitive boys, ages six and nine: "One of the biggest challenges that my sensitive boys struggle with is managing their big emotions, especially when it comes to anger. My husband and I have always made it a point to let them know that big feelings are okay. But as they grow, we are working hard to give them coping tools. Also, they don't always fit in with other boys, because their interests are not sports-related. We have worked very hard to help them make friendships with like-minded children by providing many opportunities for one-on-one play and get-togethers. As they have grown, they have been able to develop some strong friendships, but it took a lot of encour-agement and help from us to build those friendships."

Olivia, the parent of a sixteen-year-old boy: "When he was younger, he was incredibly thoughtful. When a neighbor's husband passed away, he wrote her a long letter, at eight years old. He once left money for the tooth fairy as a thank you for collecting his teeth. Adolescence, particularly high school, has muted some of that vulnerability, and he has anxiety. I also notice a lot of avoidance tactics. He has one year left in this school, and I'm hoping that with maturity he will be able to feel more comfortable in his own skin."

Vicky, the parent of an eighteen-year-old girl: "When she was younger, she would frequently feel distraught and overwhelmed that she couldn't fix the world and its problems. As she has matured, she is able to better manage and actually celebrate her sensitivity. Now we laugh at challenges instead of crying. I am immensely proud of her."

Common Misconceptions About Sensitive Children

As we've seen, sensitive adults don't always look sensitive, and the same is true for children. One common misconception is that all sensitive kids are timid. While some sensitive kids are indeed shy, the label doesn't apply to all of them. (And if we're being honest, we the authors are not fans of the *shy* label, anyway; a better way to describe many sensitive kids would be to say they look before they leap or need time to warm up.) Ahlia is a sensitive fifteen-year-old who is social and outgoing. According to her mom, she fell in love with acting at a young age, performing roles in large musicals. Recently, she had to perform a scene that required her to act sad in front of her class. In this regard, her sensitivity was an asset: Tapping her deep well of emotions, she cried on cue, impressing her teacher. Ahlia used to be embarrassed by how easily she cried, but not anymore.

Another misconception is that sensitive kids are passive, submissive, or even weak. Although many sensitive kids could be described as gentle and calm, others could be described as having strong personalities. Maria, for example, is a sensitive child who is determined and ambitious. As a baby, she would cry for over an hour at a time, and she could only be soothed in specific ways, such as with a pacifier, which she needed almost always. As a toddler, her daily tantrums were extreme. Her mom told us, "I could tell there was a sensitivity to just being in the world." Now, as a six-year-old, Maria is still highly responsive to her environment, but she is also what her parents describe as a type A personality: extremely intelligent and a natural leader. She's orderly and precise and will arrange her toys in a clearly defined way, such as by color, height, or size. At a young age, she taught herself to read using only the subtitles on the TV.

A final misconception is that boys can't be sensitive—or that boys who are sensitive aren't "masculine," in the heteronormative sense of the word. As we've seen, sensitivity is equally common in both males and females, and being sensitive is actually an advantage in many traditionally masculine activities like sports and military service. Still, from a young age, boys feel pressure to conceal their sensitivity because of the Toughness Myth. In fact, researcher Elaine Aron found that by the time boys become teenagers, they score lower on her self-test for sensitivity. The reason for this discrepancy is obvious, she writes: "It is so difficult to be highly sensitive in this culture if you are a man. So most sensitive men and boys are trying to hide their sensitivity. Often they do not even know what they are trying to get rid of. But the last thing they want to do is to answer a list of questions that seems to uncover something in them that they fear is not masculine." Rather than trying to toughen up sensitive boys or change them to be like the other kids, we need to offer them *more*—more love, more affection, more acceptance of who they are.

The Sensitive Child's Secret Advantage

One characteristic, however, unites all sensitive children—in fact, it defines sensitivity itself. For sensitive kids, *environment really matters.* As we've seen, sensitive people suffer more than others do in toxic or otherwise negative environments: They report higher levels of stress, pain, illness, anxiety, depression, panic disorders, and other problems. On the flip side, they get more benefit than others do from supportive and otherwise positive environments: the *Sensitive Boost Effect.* In the right environment, sensitive people show more creativity, empathy, awareness, and openness than less-sensitive people show; they enjoy good mental and physical health and are happier and have stronger relationships. Their gifts—the ability to listen, to love, to heal, and to create art and beauty—shine through. The Boost Effect is especially powerful in sensitive children, and numerous studies bear this out.

To take just one example, let's turn to a study done in Khayelitsha, one of the poorest areas of South Africa. The majority of its people live in shacks cobbled together from wood, cardboard, and tin; many must walk the equivalent of several blocks to access drinkable water. Nearly half the people living there are unemployed, and for many families, food shortages are common. In such an environment, it's difficult for any child to thrive, sensitive or not, but an international team of researchers wanted to know how a child's personality would affect their response to an intervention. To find out, the researchers collaborated with an area nonprofit that was helping pregnant women provide an emotionally healthy environment for their babies. Trained community health workers from the nonprofit worked with the mothers during the last trimester of their pregnancy and the first six months of their baby's life. During this time, the health workers came to the mothers' homes and taught them how to interpret their baby's cues and respond to what the baby needed—skills which can be tricky for any new parent. As the mothers became more responsive to their children, the health workers hoped they would establish what's called *secure attachment*. A child's secure attachment, or sense of safety, is particularly hard to achieve in an unstable environment like Khayelitsha but is also particularly valuable, because it helps them achieve more in school, avoid violent behavior, navigate hardship with less trauma, and form healthier relationships as adults. By focusing on secure attachment, the nonprofit was using its limited resources to give local children a lifelong boost.

At least, that was the hope. And indeed, the children whose mothers received the intervention were much more likely to develop secure attachment by eighteen months of age, and many of them—but not everyone—still showed benefits in a follow-up at age thirteen. This is where the researchers came in. During the follow-up, the researchers collected DNA samples from the children to see how many of them had the short *SERT* gene—the gene variant described in Chapter 2 which is likely to be associated with sensitivity. Once the gene was taken into account, a striking pattern emerged. The children with the short *SERT* gene were more than 2.5 times more likely to benefit from the program and were more likely to develop a lasting secure attachment. The children who had the low-sensitive version of the gene, on the other hand, got virtually no benefit from the nonprofit support. It was as if it had never happened.

Other studies have come to similar conclusions:

- Sensitivity researcher Michael Pluess found that boys who have a larger left amygdala (a brain region associated with processing emotions) were more sensitive to their early childhood environment and took more benefit or harm from it. Specifically, if raised in low-quality environments, these boys had more behavioral problems than did less-sensitive boys. But when the sensitive boys were raised in high-quality environments, they had the fewest behavioral problems of *all* the boys and were rated by their teachers as showing the most prosocial behavior.

- A study from the University of Maryland found that newborn babies who are "difficult" (they cry a lot and are hard to soothe) are more sensitive than others to the quality of care they receive from their parents. If parents are responsive to them—such as attending to their cues and soothing them when they cry—they have a higher chance than other babies have of growing into sociable, engaged toddlers. On the other hand, if parents are not responsive to these sensitive babies, they are more likely than others to be withdrawn as toddlers.

- Pediatrician W. Thomas Boyce, author of *The Orchid and the Dandelion,* found that sensitive children living in stressful environments have more injuries and illnesses than other kids have, but that in low-stress environments, they have fewer injuries and illnesses than do less-sensitive children.

If you are the parent, the grandparent, or another caregiver of a sensitive child, all these observations should give you hope: You have more power to shape who your child will become, more so than if your child were not sensitive. The love, patience, and learning opportunities you give your sensitive child will go further. Yes, parenting this child may be tough at times, and yes, your child will need you more than another child might. But you have been entrusted with a child who can do great things. You, more than any other person in their life, have the power to activate the *Sensitive Boost Effect* and launch them toward a life of unexpected heights. Give them acceptance and approval, and they will not just be "typical" kids. Compared with their peers, they are capable of earning better grades, developing better emotional and so-cial skills, having a stronger moral compass, and contributing to the world in significant ways. Be consistent with your approach, and over time, you will see your child harness the gifts of sensitivity. They will grow comfortable with their own thoughts and emotions, avoid overload, and turn their talents into success. Here are some ways you can help them do that.

Embrace Sensitive Kids for Who They Are

Without meaning to, adults often have a way of making children feel as if something is wrong with them. When it comes to sensitivity, they may see their child's big emotions or tendency to get overwhelmed as bad. Even caregivers who are sensitive themselves may be biased against sensitivity—unconsciously—because of the negative messages they received about it when they were young. (Think of Bruce Springsteen's dad, who wished that Bruce would toughen up, when it turned out that he, the father, was "soft.") Instead of seeing your child's sensitivity as a weakness, make a conscious choice to see it as a strength. When you model love and acceptance of your child's sensitivity, you make it easier for them to love and accept this part of themselves, too.

One way to better understand—and therefore embrace—your child's sensitivity is to get curious about their world. Make a point to observe them in different circumstances and at different times throughout the day. Set aside time to talk and play with them one-on-one, separate from their siblings. Ask open-ended questions. For example, "What was hard for you today?" will create more room for conversation than, "Did you have a bad day?" Keeping an open mind, try to understand what your sensitive child experiences in their body and through their five senses. Their answers might surprise you.

Sometimes, this acceptance and support will mean advocating for your child. This support can be as simple as sharing books or articles about sensitivity with extended family or fellow parents or explaining the trait in your own words. One particularly important place to advocate for your sensitive child is at school. Talk about sensitivity at the start of the school year, when you meet with your child's teachers, before any potential misperceptions can arise.

Your child will notice you speaking up for them, and maybe one day in the future, they will see how it paid off for them. You don't have to wait for that day, though. Tell them today that you are proud of them and share with them your pride in the specific things they've done lately; perhaps they've applied their imagination, their knack for people, their emotions, or other sensitive gifts. These soft and beautiful words matter to a sensitive heart. And that softness will come in handy in other situations, too, like when you need to correct their behavior.

Gentle Discipline Is Best

Embracing your child's sensitivity doesn't mean you don't discipline them or help them grow. We all want our kids to flourish in life, and that growth inevitably includes steering them in healthy directions. Discipline is a part of this learning, but with a sensitive child, the method matters even more. Because sensitive kids feel things more acutely than do other children, their feelings become more easily hurt, and it's difficult for them to not take correction personally.

Being sent to your room, a parent yelling in a moment of frustration, a stern talking-to from a teacher—these are situations that most of us can recall from being young. We might even consider them ordinary parts of growing up, laughing about them almost fondly as adults. But for many sensitive kids, situations involving punishment—even if it appears light—can feel debilitating. The memories of feeling wrong can cling to them for years, even following them into adulthood. Such memories may be accompanied by shame and a fear of punishment, fueled by worries about not being good enough.

In some cases, these forms of punishment only escalate the sensitive child's already-big emotions, making it even harder for them to calm down. Maureen Gaspari, author and founder of the blog *The*

Highly Sensitive Child, found that when she put her sensitive boys in time-out or sent them to their room, the result was more screaming—both from them and her. "They would have trouble calming themselves down on their own and would get so worked up," she says. "By the time I would come get them out of time-out, they needed so much help calming down that the original reason they were in time-out got overshadowed."

As a parent or a caregiver of a sensitive child, you may already realize that a "normal" level of discipline is too much for your kid, who will go out of their way to please and rarely means to cause upset. Compared with other kids, a sensitive child is more likely to blame themselves for difficult situations. In a review of studies on sensitivity in educational and parenting settings, Monika Baryła-Matejczuk, a researcher in educational psychology, found that sensitive kids have a heightened awareness of criticism from others and are likely to criticize themselves severely. They may avoid situations that lead to disapproval (such as getting a bad grade) or that involve a sense of wrongdoing (such as breaking a rule). These are noble instincts, but when they come with feelings of shame, this predisposition can lead to other, less desirable outcomes: Sensitive kids may become easily frustrated when trying something new or avoid new situations entirely.

Moreover, sensitive kids are more likely to experience lower self-esteem during childhood than other kids, says Baryła-Matejczuk. This diminished sense comes back to their heightened reception to criticism and their tendency to self-criticize—two factors that can affect self-esteem. The child might even start to anticipate negative responses to their actions, becoming overly perfectionistic and anxious as a way to avoid doing anything perceived as wrong.

And as you probably already know, your sensitive child has a solid inner moral compass. Before they receive punishment or feedback, if they know they've potentially done something wrong, the chances are high that they've already punished themselves internally. Author

Amanda Van Mulligen, who has a sensitive boy, says it well: "They tend to act as their own disciplinarians; their sense of shame is often so strong that they beat themselves up mentally for what they have done, and feel terrible without an adult saying a word to them." Sensitive kids are so receptive to a stern tone that they may feel shame just from hearing *another* kid being disciplined, such as when their teacher scolds other students in the classroom.

In response to raised voices or anything they see as punishment, a sensitive child might burst into tears, withdraw into themselves, or exhibit disproportionately intense signs of anxiety. That's why Baryła-Matejczuk advises parents and teachers to avoid putting the child in situations where they feel shame. Instead, gentle forms of correction work best for sensitive kids; they receive reassurance that they are loved and that their sensitive nature is not to blame for any mistakes. They can also process a gentle correction with a calm attitude instead of heightened emotions and stimuli. Further, gentle discipline conveys the message that mistakes are a part of life and an opportunity to learn from, rather than to avoid at all costs.

How to Do Gentle Discipline

Gentle discipline is about paying attention to what you say and how you say it. Raised voices can easily overwhelm a sensitive system. Instead of having the desired effect, a loud voice can cause the child to block out what you're saying as their bodies go into Threat mode. Instead, using a level voice and a calm tone is best. A sensitive child will also remember your words, and harsh ones—such as sarcasm, teasing, or name-calling—will cut deep. Besides your tone of voice, the sensitive child will notice your body language, the tension in your eyes, and other indicators of disapproval or disappointment. Although it may be hard when you're angry or frustrated with your child, try to speak gently while communicating clearly.

Touch is also a powerful tool for gentle discipline. Lightly touching a sensitive child's arm or shoulder can help get their attention without your having to raise your voice. Of course, some sensitive children have extra trouble with physical stimuli, so this is another area to adjust as needed for your child.

Here are some more gentle discipline tips:

- Correct a sensitive kid in a quiet location away from others. Otherwise, the embarrassment of other kids or adults knowing they're "in trouble" will just make the child feel worse. If you and your child are at someone's house or running errands, wait until you are home to discuss the issue with your child.
- Avoid statements that shame your child. Don't say, "How could you do that!" or "You're being too sensitive!" or "Stop crying!"
- Rather than putting them in time-out, you may want to create a calm-down spot—their own sensitive sanctuary. This is a place where they can go if they are having trouble regulating their emotions. Include stuffed animals, a weighted blanket, toys, or any other comfort items.
- After disciplining, give them hugs and reassurance, and point out their strengths. Sensitive kids think about their experiences deeply, and without these affirmations, they may come to the conclusion that you don't love them anymore after you have disciplined them.
- Be aware of your own stress level. If you yourself are frazzled or overstimulated, it will be harder to use gentle discipline. Care for your own emotions and allow yourself to take breaks, too.

Set Expectations Ahead of Time

By understanding common traits of sensitive kids, you can often lower the need for discipline at all. For example, because sensitive people tend to need time to think things through, you'll find that setting expectations ahead of time helps you avoid power struggles later. This can be as simple as saying, "Today we are going to visit Aunt Joanne in the nursing home. We'll need to use inside voices and calm bodies because some people there don't feel well." Knowing the expectations ahead of time gives the child a choice: They know what will happen if they meet those expectations, and they know there will be consequences if they don't.

Transitions can be tough for sensitive kids, who tend to get deeply immersed in whatever activity they are doing, especially ones they enjoy. When it comes time to end the activity—such as leaving the playground—give them a ten-, five-, and one-minute heads-up before it's time to go. This forewarning can help any child, but especially sensitive kids, who do best when they have time to process their thoughts and mentally prepare for something new.

Finally, monitoring your child for signs of overstimulation will also help reduce the need for discipline. Signs your child is becoming overstimulated include seeming tired, cranky, or upset; cooperating less with requests; crying; acting clingy or clumsy; or throwing a tantrum. Give your sensitive kid plenty of downtime, even if this means saying no to other invitations or activities.

Remember, you won't always do gentle discipline perfectly, and that's okay. Sometimes you will lose your cool or say something that you regret. Although sensitive kids are more affected by your words and actions than another kid would be, it doesn't mean they require perfect parenting to thrive. Gaspari has dedicated her career to advocating for sensitive kids, and even she says she makes mistakes with her sensitive boys and doesn't always perfectly implement the advice she gives to other parents. "I am not perfect," she says. "Let me reassure you that it's okay if you struggle with disciplining your sensitive child as well." When you make a mistake, use it as a learning opportunity to show your child that even adults misstep sometimes.

Other parents or family members might not understand your gentle approach to discipline at first. You might get feedback about being too delicate or "letting them off easy." Remember, sensitive kids aren't bad or wrong—they're simply overwhelmed. The gentle process might seem too soft to parents with children who are not receptive to lower-key forms of discipline, but trust that you know your child best. Research shows that gentle correction is ideal for helping sensitive kids grow into thriving sensitive adults. The world might not get their sensitive nature, but parents and teachers who do get it will be the child's greatest advocates and will set them up for success down the road.

When to Push Their Comfort Zone

Gentle discipline doesn't mean you never challenge your child or that they shouldn't challenge themselves. In fact, if done with care and compassion, helping a sensitive child expand their comfort zone is one of the best gifts you can give them. The key is to start by teaching them to set healthy boundaries. Having limits like these allows sensitive kids to push themselves in a way that feels safe. In particular, help them notice their limits and when they need to rest. For example, you may bring your child to a birthday party but leave immediately when they give you the prearranged signal that they are beginning to feel overstimulated.

For many children, fear is a typical response to new situations, but this fear can be magnified for sensitive kids, as they tend to be extra cautious and risk averse. Teaching them to manage their fear is an important part of pushing their comfort zone. Nor should you let your own fear get in the way. At some point during an event or an activity, your child will probably get hungry, grow tired, or even throw a tantrum, but don't let your worry about this possibility stop you from trying new things with them. If they are old enough, teach them how to solve certain problems on their own (like packing their own snack) to help them build resilience.

You'll also want to take small steps. If you want your child to learn to play basketball, for example, first watch a movie about basketball or go to a basketball game together. Then, by setting goals they can easily achieve, you will help them build their confidence in their abilities. For example, don't expect your child to master dribbling all in one day. Instead, start small, such as having them practice using only their fingertips, not their palm, to push the basketball. Also, remain flexible and be willing to change your plans if you notice that something isn't working. Try to keep the new activity enjoyable, and don't push your own personal agenda. If you push too hard, your child may end up deciding that they don't want to do it again. Most important, celebrating each success is another way to build your child's confidence in the skills they are learning. Give them a hug, praise them, tell others about their accomplishment, let them pick the meal for dinner, or anything else that shows you are proud of them.

Here are some more tips to help you gently push your child's comfort zone:

- If appropriate, go with your child to new settings, like sitting in the bleachers during basketball practice or waiting in the car in the parking lot. Don't hover, but remain nearby.
- Talk with your child about what to expect in new situations. Don't assume your child knows what basketball practice is like (or a wedding, a museum, an after-school club, etc.). You may even want to conduct "dress rehearsals" of important conversations and events, for example, by walking the school grounds or talking with their teachers before the first day of school.
- Talk to them in a nonjudgmental way about their fears. "What

makes going to the doctor scary?" Don't dismiss their feelings, even if their fear doesn't seem warranted to you.

- Validate your child's feelings: "That *does* sound scary!" or "I feel afraid, too, when I have to get my blood drawn." But don't go overboard with reassurances, because doing so might reinforce in their mind just how dangerous or scary the thing is. Quickly move to making a plan together that will help your child feel braver in the situation.
- Give your child some control over frightening situations by asking them to name something that would help: "What's one thing we can do that will make you feel better at your doctor appointment?"
- Set time limits on overstimulating activities (like birthday parties) and give your child permission to "be done" when they feel overwhelmed or tired. Make it easy to exit: "If you're not enjoying yourself, we can just leave."
- Point out their successes. "You were nervous to get into the pool, but now look at how much fun you're having!"

The gentle approach to pushing their comfort zone will also make space for their big emotions and help sensitive kids learn to cope with uncomfortable feelings—a crucial part of emotional regulation.

Be Your Child's Emotion Coach

Emotional regulation is the skill of being in control of your emotional state, how you think about it, and how you do (or don't) act on it. Although we can't always control whether we feel, for example, angry, we can control how we react: whether we yell or remain calm, whether we think about the issue in extremes or put it in perspective, and—especially important—what comes out of our mouth in the grip of it.

A core skill for all children, emotional regulation is even more vital

for sensitive kids. Perhaps that's no surprise since, as we know, sensitive people feel emotions intensely and spend more time thinking about them. One study even found that sensitive people do less emotional regulation than other people do. Because sensitive people often have strong emotions, the study found, they may come to believe that their negative emotions will not pass or will last a long time and that there's nothing they can do to make themselves feel better. These beliefs are typically signs that an individual lacks emotional coping strategies. Their feelings seem to take over and are too big to confront. When sensitive people did use emotional regulation strategies, the study found that doing so helped prevent anxiety and depression—two concerns that many adults have for sensitive children.

As the parent, this is where you come in. You are already teaching your child emotional regulation skills every day by modeling how you yourself handle emotions, whether it's your own stress or your child's meltdowns. The more intentional you can be about this, the better the example you set. Generally speaking, parents who are responsive and who accept their child's emotions end up with kids who have a calmer central nervous system, more self-confidence, better performance in school, and more balanced reactions to intense emotions. These outcomes are particularly likely the more that parents talk about emotions with their children. Frequent discussions about feelings help kids learn to identify their own emotions as they come up, rather than feeling as if the emotions spring up from nowhere.

According to psychologist John Gottman, parents model emotional regulation using one of two styles: emotional coaching or dismissiveness. Each style is a different way that parents can respond to their child's emotions, and both types can come from parents who mean well. However, all children—but especially sensitive children—need emotional coaches who teach them to deal with their feelings in a healthy way.

Emotional coaches understand that a range of feelings is normal for

kids (and for adults, for that matter). These parents see emotions as an opportunity to learn, self-soothe, and connect. They get an intuitive sense of when it's best to explore their child's feelings with them or to give them space to work through their feelings alone. Emotional coaching can also look like teaching your child not to hold on to a single emotional reaction. For example, you could suggest that your child sleep on it and see how their mental state has changed in the morning.

If modeling emotional regulation sounds difficult, it's okay: breathe. (Or perhaps: regulate thyself.) You do not have to be perfect at emotional regulation yourself to model it well for your children. In fact, a big part of teaching good emotional regulation is having the talks with your kids that many of our own parents never had with us. This means listening when your child is upset and helping them explore those feelings, problem-solve, and potentially take constructive action. These approaches can be taken even by those of us who never had our own feelings validated or who perhaps struggle to regulate our own emotions to this day.

The Dangers of Dismissing Emotions

The other side of the coin is parents who fall into the emotionally dismissive or emotionally neglectful camp. Perhaps they consciously or unconsciously buy into the Toughness Myth: They see emotions as distractions from handling the matter at hand or a sign of weakness, and they believe they are helping their child by teaching them to stop crying or ignore their feelings. They may say things like "It's not a big deal" or "You'll be fine" when their child expresses a fear like nervousness about the first day of school. For sensitive children, this approach can play into the shame that comes from being taught that their emotions are too much or that they are too sensitive. It also plants a dangerous lesson in a child's head: They should not ask for help in alleviating bad

feelings and doing so will make things worse. In reality, we need other people to help us process big emotions; we need to talk with them and be listened to.

Unsurprisingly, emotional neglect in childhood is where a lack of emotional regulation often begins. Compared with sensitive children who have emotional coaches in their lives, those who grow up with emotionally dismissive parents don't learn how to regulate or respond to their emotions. Stress and heightened emotions remain overwhelming, and the child might turn to destructive behaviors or thought patterns—such as bottling things up until a breakdown happens. They don't learn to label their emotions or accept that all emotions have a place, so they might hold on to shame or embarrassment for feeling so intensely. Emotional neglect can have long-lasting effects. In adulthood, it can stick around as unnecessary guilt, self-anger, low self-confidence, or a sense of being deeply, personally flawed.

Notably, gender roles play a big part in these outcomes. Parents tend to model emotions differently for boys and girls, rather than embracing a full range of emotions from both. Girls tend to learn that certain emotions won't be accepted, so they often cope by substituting "acceptable" emotions for unacceptable ones. For example, they might show puppy dog eyes instead of making a firm request, or they might show sadness rather than anger. Boys, on the other hand, tend to learn that they shouldn't display any emotions at all and thus don't learn how to regulate them. This may help explain so-called male anger: Anger is perhaps the hardest emotion to suppress.

Boys and girls also tend to see different sides of their parents. According to the data, parents talk more about emotions with their daughters than they do with their sons. Parents also use more emotion-related words with girls than with boys and are particularly comfortable sharing their sadness with their daughters. Sons are more likely to suffer from punitive parenting and get little emotional talk other than their parents' displays of anger. All children are damaged by this dismissive approach, but boys, researchers have found, are especially vulnerable to emotional neglect.

You can help support your sensitive child's emotional development by focusing on emotional regulation techniques. Researchers have identified three essential regulation techniques: noticing emotions, controlling the intensity of emotions, and managing emotions. These skills can help anyone respond to intense emotions, and parents as coaches can help their kids practice these techniques.

Noticing and Identifying Emotions

The ability to notice, name, and understand the intensity of emotions helps kids get more in touch with how they're feeling. This technique is crucial for emotional regulation. For example, toddlers who can use language to describe how they feel can self-regulate during a challenging time by talking themselves through it or turning to someone who can help them process those feelings.

One way to help kids do this is by introducing *feelings check-ins* to teach them to regularly recognize what emotions they're experiencing. A feelings check-in can be as simple as asking, "How are you feeling in this moment?" Encourage your child to use specific, descriptive words; instead of, "I feel bad," perhaps they feel tired, achy, disappointed, hurt, or overwhelmed. (There are plenty of free lists of emotion words available online to help your child expand their emotion vocabulary.) From there, you can transition to teaching your child about managing the intensity of their named emotions.

Controlling the Intensity of Emotions

A child who doesn't learn emotional regulation will struggle to stop intense emotions before they boil over. Unchecked, these emotions may show up as kicking, yelling, tantrums, withdrawal, or other destructive behaviors. But learning to sense the intensity of a feeling will help a sensitive child stay in tune with their emotions and manage them in a healthy way. One simple way to help your child do this is to tell them when you've noticed a change in them: "You seem a little quiet" or "You didn't want to play with your friends today." Then invite them to tell you about the cause. If you think you know the cause, bring it up gently: "Maybe you're feeling sad because your friend is moving away." In this way, you help your child learn to notice their feelings before they become overwhelming.

You may also want to introduce a *feelings thermometer* to ask your child where their emotions lie on the thermometer—anywhere from cool, or feeling calm, to the hot zone, which would represent strong emotions. The image helps children visualize their emotions while also providing a simple way to describe them. (Again, there are free printable thermometers online, or you can make your own.) Like the feelings check-in, the thermometer allows the child to monitor how they feel so they can maintain control more easily.

Managing Emotions

After a person recognizes emotions and lowers their intensity, the final step is to develop tools for managing those emotions. Sensitive kids experience intense emotional reactions to many areas of life, so managing emotions is an invaluable skill to learn as early as possible. There are many strategies you can use to teach your child to maintain control and de-escalate their emotions, including deep breathing and imagining themselves taking a step back from whatever is upsetting them. They could also imagine that an invisible umbrella over their head is protecting them from the upsetting situation or words. (The strategies offered for overstimulation for adults in Chapter 4 can also be adapted for children.)

These tools make a difference from a young age. During preschool and elementary school, children gain a better understanding of emotional expressions and the culturally defined rules attached to them. For example, a child learns that appearing more upset than they actually are might get them more sympathy. On the other hand, they might learn to put on a smile when they're not feeling happy or to hide emotions from their face. Young children learn quickly that their expression of emotion doesn't always have to match what they feel. This tendency increases into adolescence, with boys being more likely to suppress sadness and girls more likely to hide anger. By the teen years, kids have become even more aware of the opinions of others regarding emotions. As a parent, you can help your sensitive kid develop healthy emotion management and expression during these years through continued coaching and emotional regulation techniques.

Have Hope

Your child's environment may have a bigger impact on them than it would on a less-sensitive child, but that gives you all the more power to help them build a good life. As your child grows into the adult they will become, you'll see your effort and patience come to fruition, and more important, you'll be able to see sensitivity at its finest. The loving, supportive home you are working to give them today will help them achieve future success and happiness.

chapter 8

More Than Just a Paycheck

The truly creative mind in any field is no more than
this: a human creature born abnormally, inhumanly
sensitive.

—Pearl S. Buck

If you look closely, you might spot the sensitive employees. Maybe they are the ones escaping to their desk after some brief morning hellos. Or the ones holding back tears as they try to catch their bearings in the middle of a stressful workday. If you were to ask them why they're upset, the answer may surprise you: Maybe a conference call was so emotionally draining that focusing on other tasks feels impossible for them. Or the boss's comment about their messy desk—although meant to be playful—cut like a knife; to them, their clutter is a reflection of being overwhelmed. Or they could be frazzled by the constant phone calls and message notifications, yet feel guilty because everyone else seems to be handling the chaos better. Or perhaps the culprit is an uncomfortable chair, a coworker tapping repeatedly on a desk, or the too-bright fluorescent lights.

Sensitive people also know that going home won't solve all their problems. The emotions they experience at work trail behind them like a shadow and linger as a back-of-the-mind thought that needs to be processed before they can let it go. The problems are exacerbated if a sensitive person can't take breaks throughout the day to rest and reflect on an experience, whether they work in an office, a classroom, or a retail space.

Yet for all the stress that sensitive people feel at work, there is another side to them. They might be the ones who get through to that struggling student who no one else could reach. The ones who put in the extra time to wow a client, to make a routine lesson plan fun, or to dig deep into the data. The people who "just know" when something isn't right and see tiny gaps before the holes become big problems. These people save their company time and money or, in a medical setting, a patient's life. At the same time, they are masters at anticipating the needs of the people around them—needs that are often invisible to those higher up the ranks. For example, sensitive people might read between the lines and recognize when their teammates are burning out or when an important client is unsatisfied. Coworkers are often drawn to a sensitive colleague because they feel safe to speak about their frustrations, insecurities, and fears without judgment.

As managers and leaders, sensitive people are capable of bringing harmony to the workplace and creating the conditions that allow others to thrive. As innovators, investors, and entrepreneurs, they spot trends and valuable gaps in the market. To put it simply, a sensitive employee may be one of the best workers you'll ever have. Rather than being leery of workers who are "too sensitive," employers ought to court them.

If this portrait of sensitive workers seems contradictory, it's because they often experience contradictions at work: Although they tend to be high performers, they also experience high levels of stress and burnout on the job. One survey even found that sensitive people were the best performers of all, despite feeling more stress. The survey was run by Bhavini Shrivastava, an organizational psychology graduate student who was studying sensitive people in the workplace and included workers at a large IT company in Mumbai, India. Combining reports from managers and self-reports from workers, she found that employees who tested as sensitive people were rated by their managers as better performers than their less-sensitive colleagues. However, the sensitive workers also reported more stress and scored lower in their well-being overall. These results make sense, given what we know about the *Sensitive Boost Effect*.

Many great sensitive IT professionals, the survey suggests, have likely left their companies because of this stress but perhaps could have been retained if their role or working environment had been tweaked. As we saw in the previous chapter with sensitive children, environment really matters for sensitive workers. Depending on the conditions, these workers can either become your top talent or burn out from stress.

In Their Own Words: What Are Some of Your Strengths—and Stressors—at Work?

"I have been told by some of my students that they would not have been able to complete the semester had it not been for having me as a professor. They said that they appreciated that I had a degree of empathy and understanding that they did not receive from other professors in times of need. The downside is that I care possibly too much about the bad situations that arise in their lives. I get very emotional and worry when one of them tells me they are struggling in their personal life." –Shelby, college professor

"I've worked in sales for twelve years and have been very successful at it. But I've also spent most of those years frazzled and burned out. My strengths are my relationship-building skills. I can quickly build rapport, as I imagine how the customer feels. I'm also very conscientious, so I never miss deadlines. However, I get very burned out constantly communicating with people all day. The phone ringing, emails flying in, people walking in . . . there's always a lot going on!" –Emma, recruitment and sales

"I find that I am able to create a safe space that allows clients to open up about their struggles. The benefit of this is that it helps us get to the root of their problems more quickly so they can make changes that give them lasting results. I also find that my sensitivity helps me find the right approach that works best for each individual. My biggest struggles are having the clinic schedule my clients back-to-back without any downtime for me to recharge between clients. I find that when I have to go at a fast pace without breaks, I am much more likely to become a sponge to everyone's emotions, and I become mentally and emotionally depleted." –Daphnie, clinical health coach

"I feel that the biggest strength attributed to my sensitivity would be my ability to process and analyze data at a deep level. I also have high attention to detail. My biggest weaknesses would be that I do get overwhelmed easily, especially when I have a lot of deadlines to hit, and I am unable to filter out external stimuli when I'm working in the office (as opposed to working in silence at home), and that makes it extremely difficult to focus and do my job." –Traci, commercial liability insurance underwriter

The Right Physical Environment for Sensitive Workers

So how do companies create the right environment that sensitive workers need to thrive? How do they avoid losing the employees who have the potential to become their top performers? In the workplace, two things must be addressed: the physical environment and the emotional environment.

As we've seen, sensitive people tend to do best in physical environments that are calm. Specifically, in the workplace, they need an amount of stimulation that doesn't overwhelm their ability to work comfortably and effectively. Background noise, the activity of their coworkers, bright lights, and stiff chairs are all examples of things that some sensitive people can't easily ignore. Things that might seem minor to others, such as a coworker's strong perfume, can make it feel impossible for a sensitive person to focus. Remember, sensitive people aren't purposely being difficult by requesting changes to their environment—their brain is wired differently than many of the people around them.

Creating the right environment can be challenging since the typical workplace isn't set up with a sensitive person's nervous system in mind, but there are ways to make it more accommodating. Basic practices that would help any worker feel less stressed will go even further for sensitive workers. Of course, the setting will vary with the field and your position. For example, if you work from home, you could face just as many potential distractions as you could in a collaborative in-person work environment like an office or a call center.

If you're a sensitive worker, you will benefit from the following practices:

- Reducing or eliminating visual clutter in your workspace (or around your house if you work from home)
- Making full use of your office door (if you have one) to shut out ambient noise
- Investing in a good pair of noise-canceling headphones
- Using an air purifier to reduce stuffiness and allergens in the air
- Decorating or furnishing your workspace (if allowed) in a beautiful, calming, or inspiring way
- Taking regular breaks to stretch, get a glass of water, have a snack, or walk around

If you work at home, you have even more freedom to create the physical environment that works best for you. You might play white noise or calming instrumental music or even install paneling in your office to shut out noise. It can also help to declare quiet hours—a time when everyone agrees to keep down the noise, not interrupt one another, and so forth—with your roommates or family.

Sensitive people also need coworkers, or at least managers, who understand their needs in the physical environment. If you're the employer of sensitive people, the rule is simple: Give them as much control as possible over their workspace. Perhaps this means allowing them to work in a quiet corner of the office, come in early or stay late to work when fewer people are there, or work from home a few days a week.

Open communication is another important policy. Sensitive people are often concerned about others' feelings, so they may not speak up about their needs, because they don't want to burden or inconvenience others. The sensitive worker might even feel trapped in their current environment if they aren't comfortable asking for accommodations. So, ask all your employees at regular intervals if there's anything they need to do their job better—and suspend judgment on any requests that seem odd to you. Routinely touching base like this will make it easier for sensitive employees to be honest about what causes them stress and prevents them from working effectively.

The Right Emotional Environment for Sensitive Workers

People and relationships tend to be the number one challenge that sensitive people face at work. Unlike physical distractions, which can often be blocked, there's no way to silence the emotions and attitudes of the people around you. If the work culture is toxic, the emotions in the room are what become most draining. Juggling different personalities, energy levels, and demands is a challenge for anyone, but for sensitive people, it can have an outsized impact on their mental health. The emotional environment may be the difference between a tiring workday that still leaves them feeling fulfilled and regular breakdowns because the energy and demands of their job are too much to maintain. Add loud, stressful workplaces with rushed deadlines and a lot of pressure into the mix, and a sensitive worker will quickly feel burned out.

And when you're sensitive, you more easily take on the emotions of the people around you. In a workplace, you're often near people over a roughly eight-hour (or longer) period. These people are often stressed, worried about deadlines, and feeling a range of emotions, both positive and negative. When you absorb those emotions, you may have trouble concentrating on your own work. If you take those emotions home, the mental and psychological burden can strain your family relationships and harm your quality of life. Similarly, because sensitive people tend to be conscientious and want to please others, you may become weary of the constant push and pull between your own needs and your colleagues' desires.

So, just as sensitive workers need the right physical work environment, they also need the right emotional setting. To this end, you'll want to set healthy boundaries and speak up for what you need. Although no one—especially a sensitive person—likes to be *that* person in the office, direct communication is the best way to help others understand your needs. Here are some sample phrases you might use for setting boundaries at work:

- "I need some time to think about your question. I'll get back to you later."
- "I'm feeling overwhelmed right now, and it's hard for me to focus on your feedback. I'd like to take a short break."
- "I wish I could help, but I'm not available this weekend to work an extra shift."
- "It sounds like an interesting project, but I wouldn't be able to give it the time it deserves."
- "I can see the importance of the project, but I'm also working on X, Y, and Z. Which of those would you like me to pause?"
- "I know this is a little awkward, and I doubt it was your intent, but when you said/did X, I felt uncomfortable."

Remember, you have just as much value as your less-sensitive coworkers have. There is nothing about being a sensitive person that needs to be fixed. In fact, if you believe that something is wrong with you, others will see it that way too and treat you accordingly, says Linda Binns, a career coach for sensitive people. Rather, it's about embracing the many gifts you have as a sensitive person. "When you see yourself this way," explains Binns, "you will gain confidence, become better at knowing and asking for what you need, and be good at setting boundaries. Others will naturally begin to respond more positively to you, which will grow your confidence even more." This confidence, in turn, will help you advocate for the environment you need to do your best work.

The Desire for Meaningful Work

Along with needing the right work environment, sensitive people also have a high need for meaning on the job. Rather than just collecting a paycheck, they also want to know that their efforts make a difference for other people and contribute to the greater good. Of course, no one, sensitive or not, wants to think that their work is pointless, but many sensitive people feel the need for meaningful work so strongly that they organize their entire lives around finding it. As writer and sensitive person Anne Marie Crosthwaite puts it, "They are often driven by an internal search for meaning, and if something doesn't feel meaningful, they can't just 'do it anyway.'"

A meaningful vocation is a key part of a happy, sensitive life. So, what exactly is meaningful work? The answer will vary from person to person, but generally, work is meaningful when you see a real connection between the tasks you do and a higher purpose beyond yourself. That higher purpose might be saving a life, fighting climate change, or just making someone's day run a little bit smoother.

Having a sense of purpose is satisfying, but it's also valuable: It contributes to our personal well-being and our companies' bottom lines. According to research by management consulting firm McKinsey, employees who feel a strong sense of purpose at work are healthier and more resilient. Not surprisingly, they are also more satisfied with their jobs. Work satisfaction is linked with increased productivity—by one estimate, meaningful work generates an additional $9,078 per worker per year. Companies also retain their satisfied employees longer, saving an average of $6.43 million in turnover-related costs for every ten thousand workers per year. Here we can take another lesson from sensitive people, who intrinsically know the value of meaningful work.

Yet for all the benefits of meaningful work, many sensitive people say their job doesn't feel valuable or important. So let's look at some ways that you as a sensitive person can make it more meaningful.

The Best Jobs for Sensitive People

Our readers at Sensitive Refuge often ask us to name the best jobs for sensitive people. Here they are, in order:

- Any
- Job
- You
- Want
- To
- Do

That's it. There is no magic list of jobs that will automatically make work meaningful for you as a sensitive person. Sensitive people can thrive in any position, from CEO to construction worker.

With that said, there are certain professions that sensitive people tend to be drawn to more than others, and often those are jobs that tap their empathy, creativity, and attention to detail. Many sensitive people excel in caring professions such as therapist, teacher, doctor, nurse, clergy, childcare or eldercare provider, massage therapist, or life coach. Aleshia is a sensitive person who works as a recreational therapist inside a behavioral health unit at a hospital. Being sensitive allows her to better respond to the emotional needs of her patients: "I have often walked into a room prepared to do a particular therapeutic intervention and completely changed the intervention at the last minute based on how the group feels," she told us. However, caring jobs are not right for every sensitive person, because high levels of stress and secondhand emotions are usually part of the package. Aleshia went on to say that caregiver burnout poses a serious challenge to her: "Being hypervigilant to others is exhausting. Every day I work, it shuts me down for the evening. I am a single mom to two teenagers, and unfortunately, they don't get the best of me when I come home."

Sensitive people also excel in creative professions, such as writing, music, and the arts. In fact, some of the world's most successful artists are sensitive people. Take, for example, the actor Nicole Kidman, who has won multiple Emmy and Golden Globe Awards. She says that she is a highly sensitive person and that "most actors are highly sensitive people"—although they have to "develop a thick skin" to deal with the constant critique of their lives and work. Other famous creative people who say they are sensitive include Dolly Parton, Lorde, Elton John, Yo-Yo Ma, Alanis Morissette, and of course, Bruce Springsteen. Creative people tend to possess some seemingly contradictory traits: They are sensitive but also open to new ideas and experiences, notes the famed psychologist Mihaly Csikszentmihalyi. This dual character explains how they can be both emotionally vulnerable and easily overwhelmed but at the same time charismatic and striking. "Creative people's openness and sensitivity often exposes them to suffering and pain, yet also to a great deal of enjoyment," Csikszentmihalyi explains.

Jobs that require attention to detail—whether it's paying attention to people, your surroundings, or numbers on a spreadsheet—can also be a good fit for sensitive people. Work of this nature can be found in fields like event planning, accounting, finances, research, science, architecture, gardening and landscaping, trade work, law, and software development. One sensitive woman who describes herself as social, emotional, and artistic told us that she purposely chose a role that was the opposite of all that: financial systems analyst. Dealing with numbers all day is calming and gives her a break from her emotional side.

The ideal work for a sensitive person may not be a job at all. Barrie Jaeger, author of *Making Work for the Highly Sensitive Person,* recommends self-employment for sensitive people, because many of her sensitive clients report feeling more satisfied with self-employment than with a traditional job. Self-employment might look like design, photography, videography, furniture restoration, social media management, launching a business, consulting, or the freelance version of your current job. On the upside of self-employment, it gives sensitive people control over their work environment and schedule, making them less prone to overstimulation. Of course, there are downsides, such as the lack of a regular paycheck and, for certain roles, the need to market and network, which can be draining. So, like any other type of work, self-employment will not be right for every sensitive person.

Again, sensitive people can do any job they want to do, including ones not mentioned here. However, when you are choosing the right career path, there are definitely some things you should avoid. These will exact a heavy toll on your nervous system and will cause over-stimulation and burnout. Moreover, they will go against your need for meaning as a sensitive person. We recommend avoiding any job with a great amount of the following attributes:

- Conflict or confrontation
- Competition, high stakes, or extreme risk
- Noise or a hectic physical environment
- Interaction with people with few breaks
- Repetitive tasks that lack a clear connection to a larger mission
- Toxicity in the company culture or unhealthy management styles
- Demand to set your principles aside to make money

Unfortunately, you will probably encounter some (or all) of these elements at one point or another in almost any job. The key is to avoid jobs where these things happen regularly, not just on a bad day (or a stretch of bad days). Listen to yourself. Your emotions and intuition will point to whether the overstimulation is chronic or just occasional. It's one thing to feel tired and mentally worn down at the end of a busy workday, especially if you're a sensitive person. It's another thing en-tirely to experience chronic overstimulation on the job. Also pay atten-tion to the physical sensations in your body. Do you regularly experience muscle aches and tension, an upset stomach, a tight feeling in your chest, trouble sleeping, pain, or fatigue? If these symptoms don't have a clear physical cause (such as an illness or an infection), then they may be another way your body is trying to communicate with you.

Deep Work and Slow Productivity

For one reason or another, we can't always choose the perfect job. Maybe job opportunities are limited where you live, or perhaps you don't yet have the degree or training for the work you want. Maybe you're locked into a contract for a certain period. Or, considering other factors in your life, maybe it's just not practical to change jobs right now. Building a meaningful career takes time—in some cases, a lifetime—and many of us temporarily accept jobs that are less than ideal because we have bills to pay. Even the two of us have taken on various jobs to pay the bills: Jenn cleaned buildings, and Andre was a line cook. For whatever reason, if you choose to remain in your current job, there are ways to make it more meaningful and less overstimulating.

One tactic that sensitive people can try is to build in more *space*—specifically, mental space. Mental space enables you to concentrate on a task without interruptions or distractions. Everyone works better this way, but as a sensitive person, you need mental space to do the deep processing that produces your best work while you feel calm and comfortable as you do it. Mental space looks different in different jobs. For a systems analyst, it may mean quietly focusing in a private setting with no interruptions from email or meetings. For an auto mechanic, it may mean playing music loud enough to drown out other activity in the garage and focus on the car in front of them.

Unfortunately, mental space can be particularly hard to come by in a modern office setting. The reason, according to researcher and bestselling author Cal Newport, is our own instincts. As human beings, we all have a drive to accomplish things and see tasks completed; a project accomplished is one of the most satisfying parts of work. Yet for many office workers, many tasks are never truly complete. Think of the inbox that can never be emptied, the Slack channel that pings while you sleep, and, yes, the dreaded calendar full of dubiously useful meetings. It feels good to check off these items—to see that you've replied to everything— but within seconds, you have to do it again. Your hunter-gatherer brain, Newport says, starts freaking out: "We haven't finished the hunt! The harvest must come in! People are counting on us!" Yet the hunt will never be finished, and the ancestral part of your brain has no idea that all this anxiety is meaningless. So, it keeps yelling inside your head, and you keep jumping from email to Slack to texts, and your mental space vanishes—even in a private office with a closed door.

Newport calls this style of work the *hyperactive hive mind*, because in theory, it's a way for knowledge workers to collaborate (that's what all those messages and meetings are for, right?). Instead, he told us, "It's a disaster. It fatigues us and we can't think clearly, and it makes us miserable." For sensitive people, the hive mind is even worse—and not just because of overstimulation. "It's extra bad for sensitive people," Newport says, "because, from an empathy standpoint, you're exposed to lots and lots of people who need things from you that you are not able to get back to at the moment. Even if you know, logically, these are not urgent emails, it hits something deeper down. Because you know there are people who need you." Every unanswered email feels like someone you're letting down.

Newport knows what he's talking about; he has built his entire career around going deep, teaching others to do the same, and eliminating as much "shallow" and overwhelming work as possible. (Rather than a contact form, for example, Newport's website has a list of options that funnel requests to various colleagues and no-reply inboxes, the better to maintain his focus on the work that matters. He made time for us, he said, because he's a sensitive person himself—and says it's the reason for his success as a writer.)

But Newport says the hyperactive hive mind isn't necessary to do good work—not even office work, and not even in a tech-driven economy. In fact, because this approach actively undermines productivity, the hyperactive hive mind is as bad for your employer as it is for your day-to-day mental health. Most organizations, he believes, don't want much of your time spent on these low-value tasks like continuously dealing with email or attending meeting after meeting. But people tend to fall into these tasks by default, because many employees have vague goals and not enough direction.

An alternative is what he calls *slow productivity*: the art of doing fewer things but doing them better. Whereas the hive mind devours mental space, slow productivity cultivates it. Slow productivity is the ideal model for sensitive people, because it depends on careful planning, thoughtful decision-making, and high standards of perfection, the things that sensitive people are best at. In particular, it lends itself to what Newport has christened *deep work*, or long periods of focused, uninterrupted time on high-value tasks. When you're cleaning out your inbox, you're doing shallow work; it pulls you back to the hive mind. When you block out an hour, silence your phone, and finish that slide deck, you're doing deep work.

How Sensitive People Can Do More Deep Work

Newport suggests you may have more autonomy over your work style than you think. Some amount of slow productivity can be "permission-less": You can start practicing it without talking to your boss. He advises making changes that won't affect anyone else directly—like scheduling into your day an hour-long deep work session, during which you won't check communication, or switching to checking email only twice per day. In fact, he advises not even telling colleagues about these changes; it's unlikely they'll even notice, and you can avoid any misperception that you're going to inconvenience them.

Similarly, Newport says, if you do approach your manager about changes to your work style, frame it as a decision you want their input on, and be explicit about the trade-off involved. A good script for the conversation might go something like this:

> *"I'd like to talk to you about how much deep work versus shallow work I should be doing. Deep work is completing my part of our project or finishing my work plan. Shallow work is things like replying to emails and attending meetings. Both are important, but for my job, what's the ideal ratio?"*

This is a dramatically different conversation than one saying you have too many emails or meeting requests (many of which come from your boss). Instead, you're focusing on the goals your boss values. You may find that you get significantly more buy-in than you might have expected. If you do, you now have marching orders to decline more meetings or go somewhere you can close a door and do deep work. This suggestion isn't just theory: When Newport recommended that his readers have this conversation with their managers, he received numerous reports telling him how surprised they were by the changes that occurred—even in what they thought was a very entrenched culture. In many cases, the managers took the idea and ran with it, working out ratios for their team and allowing them to be "out of touch" for half the day to focus. The managers sometimes even banned internal emails altogether. "These things would happen that you think would be impossible," Newport says. "They really just needed a number and a rationale." Offering these kinds of workplace modifications also taps into sensitive people's natural abilities as job crafters.

Natural-Born Job Crafters

When researcher Amy Wrzesniewski wanted to learn what makes work meaningful, she decided to meet people with one of the least glamourous jobs of all: janitors at a hospital. She expected that they would be unsatisfied by their work, which is grimy, routine, and often thankless. Indeed, she found plenty of janitors who griped, but she also found exceptions. A few janitors spoke about their jobs glowingly. They described themselves as ambassadors for the hospital or even healers who kept the place sterile so that patients could get better. They didn't just enjoy their work; they were fulfilled by it.

Intrigued by this subset of workers, Wrzesniewski followed them to learn what set them apart. She found that they did the same work that the other janitors did but went out of their way to add other tasks—often with meaningful touches. Some made a point to chat with patients and give extra time to those who had no visitors (one even exchanged letters with patients long after they were discharged). To avoid irritating anyone's health condition, they took time to research how their cleaning chemicals would affect patients. One janitor went as far as to rotate artwork in the coma ward on the chance that the change might help stimulate patients' brains. All these steps were outside their job duties and were, effectively, extra chores. But these efforts also underscored why their work mattered and how the janitors were truly serving people. These workers proved that meaning doesn't rest entirely on what job we're doing but comes from how we do it.

In light of this understanding and other research, Wrzesniewski developed what she calls *job crafting*: the art of turning your ho-hum job into a meaningful one. Job crafting, she says, is a way to think about your job that puts you in the driver's seat. Since then, countless studies have proven that job crafting works—in everything from blue-collar jobs to skilled professional roles, and even for stressed-out CEOs.

Job crafting is effective largely because, like deep work, it's permissionless. (Supervisor buy-in will give you even more options, of course, but that can come with time.) In fact, since job crafting tends to enhance performance, supervisors who do notice the changes often encourage them. Likewise, sensitive people excel at this practice. When researchers compared job crafting success with personality traits, they found a correlation with traits like empathy, emotional intelligence, agreeableness, and conscientiousness—all traits common among sensitive people. For this reason, many sensitive people are natural-born job crafters.

Ways to Craft Your Job

Part of job crafting means changing your perception of the tasks you do and looking for the way they connect to a higher purpose. If you think this step sounds like a mental trick—a way of making yourself enjoy your current job rather than changing jobs—you're only partly right. Of course, how you think about your job makes a big difference in how you feel about it, but job crafting has real results, too. Often, this cognitive change—which expands your vision of your work and what you're capable of doing—allows you to transform your role over time. The transformation means real change in terms of what you do day in, day out, and potentially more opportunities later on, such as promotions and career advancement.

This aspect of job crafting, called *cognitive crafting*, involves two mental shifts. First, you *expand your view of your own power*. This means accepting that you have the power to change the boundaries of your own job. (This step is, in a sense, giving yourself permission to craft your job.) And second, you *expand your view of your role*. Many of us see our jobs as a specific set of prescribed tasks—understandably, because that's what's in a job posting. With this view, however, your ability to do meaningful work is constrained by your position description. In reality, you have the power to make a difference in outcomes far beyond your official duties, and it's those big-picture outcomes you should use to define your job.

For example, a nurse's job may seem inherently meaningful, but when the focus is on the assigned small-picture tasks—technical skills, like inserting a catheter, or rote tasks, like following a checklist—the job becomes divorced from its higher purpose of healing people. A nurse taking a big-picture view of the same job might say, "I am part of a team that delivers total patient care." Or simply, "I get every patient the best outcome possible." If you describe your role with these big-picture statements, you suddenly have a duty to go beyond your job description. You might check for problems not indicated on a chart, ask patients questions, help them resolve needs not directly related to the care you're providing, or engage in patient advocacy on their behalf. In other words, you'll be what everyone wants in the person taking care of them. This pattern repeats in every profession. It's the line cook who sees their job as making nourishing cuisine; the vice president who sees their job as creating a product that will change lives.

None of this is to say that there aren't obstacles to job crafting. Every job will have obstacles. (And as one chef who loves his work told us, "Every job has its bullshit.") Rather, job crafting helps you work around those obstacles. Here are some more ways you can craft your job.

Adjust the Tasks You Do and How You Do Them

With this step, called *task crafting,* you can include some new tasks on your own initiative or, if you have the leeway, drop some tasks. It can also mean altering the way you do a task or shifting how much time and attention you give to different responsibilities on your plate. For example, a retail worker who puts extra effort into arranging a fashion display might be asked to do all the displays going forward and flex their creative muscles. Or a teacher who tweaks their end-of-day dismissal procedure might be asked to find more ways to improve the dismissal process throughout the entire school. Sometimes you will need supervisor approval to do these things, but you can often start doing a task informally rather than waiting for an official mandate.

Change Your Interactions

Research shows that having meaningful relationships at work is one of the most important factors of job satisfaction, even more important than the work environment or the actual tasks you do. In one study, employees who had emotional support and friends at work reported being happier in their jobs. You can probably remember a time when you stayed in a job that was hard or low-paying because you liked the people you worked with; this research explains why. Yet when it comes to job crafting, the point isn't to make friends with everyone. Rather, it's to think about who you're spending time with and why.

This process of being intentional in your work relationships is called *relational crafting*. The hospital janitor was doing relational crafting when he chatted with patients who had no visitors, because he chose to give more time to those who might be lonely. Likewise, you can make an effort to get to know your regular customers, clients, or patients, and then remember them. Treat it as your job to get them good outcomes, even if on paper it's not. Talk to colleagues about problems you all share and do it in a solution-oriented way. Think about the people you *don't* interact with much but who you really should. They might be people you respect for their knowledge or someone whose work involves one of your interests or strengths. Similarly, check in with newer teammates to see if they need help, and let them know you're available to assist. On the flip side, identify coworkers or clients who drain your energy, and put healthy boundaries around your interactions with them.

Job Craft Regardless of Status

You will have to tailor your approach according to your rank because people at different levels of an organization have different barriers preventing them from doing meaningful work. If you're in a nonmanagement position, you're probably held to a specific set of tasks, which means your main barrier is autonomy. So, you might focus on correcting inefficient processes, building strong relationships, and building trust through your performance so that managers are open to your suggestions and requests. If you're in a higher-ranking position, job crafting will look different, because you likely have much greater freedom over how you use your time. On the other hand, you're beholden to a set of goals or outcomes you need to meet (often with very high stakes, like launching a product on time). Thus, your main barriers are your own limited time and getting buy-in from other leaders. With this in mind, you might focus on delegating work that has become routine in order to free up time of your own, or running a small pilot version of an innovative project so you can take the results to the next leadership meeting or company retreat.

Master Rare and Valuable Skills

According to Cal Newport, jobs that offer more autonomy and mastery of skills will inherently feel more meaningful. Not all jobs offer these features, which are seldom found in entry-level positions. Yet Newport says the lack of autonomy in your position shouldn't worry you. Instead, it should give you a game plan: If you want more meaningful work—including the ability to call your own shots—you should start mastering skills that most other people in your industry do not have. Sure, this could mean getting a Harvard law degree, but that's not the only way. For example, we spoke to a web developer who originally worked for whatever client came her way—she was skilled but not necessarily different from other developers. Then a project required her to design a website that was accessible for people with disabilities. Finding the work fascinating, she spent more and more time mastering the best practices for accessible websites. What's more, she realized that few other developers have this specialty. Today, not only can she pick and choose which clients she works with, but she is also paid better and does work she can feel good about because she's helping people. Another example is the tradesman who started off doing regular construction work but took an interest in learning to restore old homes. His new specialty required him to master dozens of lost arts, including complicated woodwork and ornate plastering. Using these skills to transform a house is deeply satisfying to him, but more than that, he gets to work where he wants, when he wants, and how he wants.

By making these changes in your work life, you help minimize burnout and cultivate an environment where you excel. This trajectory doesn't just lead to material success, like recognition and advancement, but meets your personal needs as a sensitive person as well. After all, sensitive people can flourish in almost any profession. Think of the janitors who wrote letters to their patients and hung colorful artwork on the walls. By curating your environment and crafting your job as you go, you can enjoy a career that is meaningful to the sensitive heart—and that doesn't leave you chronically drained. You can be the high performer without the high stress. And you can thrive.

chapter 9

The Sensitive Revolution

> Artists are useful to society because they are so
> sensitive. They are super-sensitive. . . . And when a
> society is in great danger, we're likely to sound the
> alarms.
>
> —Kurt Vonnegut

Today, we think of the Great Depression as a singular era. At the time, however, it was simply the latest in a century-long string of financial calamities. One of the worst, the Panic of 1837, left an entire generation of Americans malnourished and, eventually, measurably shorter for it. Another, the so-called Long Depression, triggered violent gun battles between striking railroad workers and federal troops. One worker told a newspaper that he had nothing left to lose and "might as well die by the bullet as to starve to death by inches." This depression continued for more than twenty years.

The usual answer to financial crises had been to tighten the belt, protect the banks, and wait for the strong to survive. In 1933, however, the country was ready for a different solution. A little-known labor activist named Frances Perkins was appointed secretary of labor, becoming the first woman in U.S. history to hold any cabinet position. Perkins was a wise pick: Her career had begun with volunteering in the settlement houses of Chicago, working side by side with poor and unemployed people. Her cause hit a key turning point on the day of the Triangle Shirtwaist Company fire of 1911, when she watched in horror as workers trapped in the factory jumped to their deaths to escape the flames. No one, it's fair to say, was more committed to helping workers in the United States than Perkins.

But she came with a condition. She would only agree to be secretary if President Franklin D. Roosevelt promised to back her policies: abolishing child labor and instilling a forty-hour workweek, a minimum wage, worker's compensation, federal unemployment relief, social security, and more. Her approach, which we would now call a *social safety net,* was the opposite of the tighten-the-belt philosophy.

President Roosevelt agreed to her terms, and during his presidency, she handed him a raft of policies that would open the fists of the U.S. government at the tightest time in history. Her policies ferried resources to those who needed them most: workers, artists, young people, families, and even those who would never again contribute to the economy, for example, people with disabilities and older adults. The president stuck to his promise and backed all these policies. Suddenly, people found themselves with a minimum wage, a maximum workweek, and funding for schools, roads, and post offices. Roosevelt's only change was to give the policies a snappier name: Frances Perkins had just crafted the New Deal.

Was Perkins a sensitive person? It's impossible to know for sure, because she passed away in 1965, long before there was any awareness of the trait. However, her concern for others certainly embodies one of the greatest gifts of all sensitive people: empathy. Her grandson, Tomlin Perkins Coggeshall, founder of the Frances Perkins Center, told us she wanted to help everyone, so she worked on legislation that would improve the welfare of the largest number of people. We also see this desire to help others in her views on government. Later in life, as she reflected on the impact of the New Deal, she spoke what would become her most famous words: "The people are what matter to government, [and] a government should aim to give all the people under its jurisdiction the best possible life."

We now know that the New Deal not only contributed to ending the Great Depression but also shaped the spirit of the nation for more than a generation. Far from a pie-in-the-sky program, the New Deal put eight million people back to work, injected stimulus money into a badly reeling economy, and protected people's savings in the event of another bank failure. It also broke the cycle of boom and bust. For nearly a century, the United States avoided another crisis on the scale of the Depression. Simply put, sensitive policy is smart policy.

Sensitive People Should Feel Empowered to Lead

Let's return to the Sensitive Way, which we first discussed in Chapter 1. The Sensitive Way is about embracing our sensitivity rather than hiding it. It's about championing our gifts—as Perkins did—instead of being ashamed of the trait that gives us those gifts. More than that, it asks us to slow down and reflect, lead with empathy and compassion, and bravely express the full range of human emotions. In this manner, the Sensitive Way is the antidote to the Toughness Myth. It's exactly what our divided, rushed, and too-much world desperately needs.

Yet for all the lessons that sensitive people have to teach the world, many say they don't feel like teachers or leaders. In fact, without consciously being aware of it, many sensitive people put themselves in a position of low status in their interactions with others. Status is not necessarily determined by how much money you have or your job title (although those things do play a role); it refers to how you carry yourself in the world, including the way you stand, talk, and appear. In this case, status means influence, authority, or power.

Low status versus high status was a concept that originated in improv comedy, of all places. Keith Johnstone, a playwright, realized that actors in a scene communicate unspoken information by signaling their status relative to one another. When he taught them to convey status through their physical actions on the stage, dull scenes came alive. High-status characters, for instance, were instructed to stand with an open body posture, to walk in a straight line, and not to flinch when another actor touched or approached them. Low-status characters were instructed to do the opposite. Some of the most interesting scenes occurred when two characters with large status gaps, like a queen and her butler, interacted. Comedy was born when the characters behaved differently than their inherent status—like if the queen began doing chores for the butler.

The difference between low and high status isn't always as easy to spot in real life. In a group of friends, a high-status person might be the one who stands up from the dinner table first and decides what the group will do next. A low-status person might be the one asking for advice and listening. We all switch our status depending on the situation, and psychologists believe that the healthiest relationships offer opportunities for frequent status reversal. If one person is always stuck in low status, that's not a healthy—or satisfying—relationship.

However, low status isn't necessarily something to avoid. Just as high status comes with certain advantages (like authority and respect), low status has advantages, too. Low-status people appear more trustworthy, approachable, and likable; business coaches often advise people with power—such as the company CEO—to cultivate low-status traits. People who always choose high status may appear arrogant, threatening, and domineering, and they might get lonely because others find relationships with them less enjoyable. We tend to get comfortable playing one role or the other, and the one role becomes our default. Women and introverts, notes bestselling author Susan Cain, tend to communicate in ways associated with low status. So do sensitive people, who usually couldn't care less about dominating or having power over others.

Having high status or low status isn't wrong. However, some sensitive people may feel stuck in low status when they don't want to be. They may have low self-esteem after receiving messages that their sensitivity is a flaw. Sensitive people should feel empowered to step into high status when they want to do so. In reality, lifting our status is exactly what the Sensitive Way asks us to do. It asks us to step up and speak out. It asks us to use our gifts not only in ways that benefit ourselves but also in ways that benefit others. This call to expand our status doesn't mean sensitive people have to change who they are and try to dominate or overpower those around them. It means sensitive people should feel empowered to lead—in their own way.

The Advantage of Sensitive Leadership

To understand how a leader's personality can make a difference, Daniel Goleman and other researchers turned to a hospital in Boston, where two doctors were competing to become the CEO of the corporation that ran the hospital. The researchers called them Dr. Burke and Dr. Humboldt, although those weren't their real names. "Both of them headed up departments, were superb physicians, and had published many widely cited research articles in prestigious medical journals," the researchers explain. "But the two had very different personalities." Burke was described as impersonal, task-focused, and relentlessly perfectionistic. His combative style forced his staff to walk on egg-shells. Humboldt, on the other hand, was equally demanding of his workers, but he was more approachable, friendly, and even playful. The researchers note that people in Humboldt's department seemed much more at ease, smiling and teasing one another in a friendly way. Most important, they felt free to speak their minds. As a result, high-performing employees were often drawn to Humboldt's team but left Burke's department. It should come as no surprise that the hospital board picked Humboldt as the new CEO. Humboldt, exemplifying some of the strengths of the sensitive leader—such as an emotionally intelligent style—created a warm environment for the people who worked with him.

Most of us probably want to work for someone like Humboldt, not Burke. As Goleman and his coauthor, behavioral scientist Richard E. Boyatzis, point out, "Leading effectively is . . . less about mastering situations—or even mastering social skill sets—than about developing a genuine interest in and talent for fostering positive feelings in the people whose cooperation and support you need." In this area, sensitive leaders shine, whether they are leading a corporation, a social movement, or their own friends or family. If you're a sensitive person, you're probably not giving yourself enough credit in the leadership department. You'd probably make a better leader than you think you would be.

Many of the qualities that make a great leader, like empathy, come naturally to sensitive people. As we saw in Chapter 3, sensitive people are the varsity athletes of empathy, which allows them to understand the people around them more deeply. And the ability to "step into" other people's experiences has significant benefits for leaders. According to one study, empathetic leaders encourage higher levels of innovation, engagement, and cooperation in the workplace. When leaders include empathy in the decision-making process, employees are more likely to follow suit—empathy begets more empathy—and are more likely to stick around. Similarly, empathetic leaders help create and maintain more-inclusive workplaces by understanding and supporting different people's experiences.

Along with being more empathetic, sensitive leaders are quick to read a room and tune in to others. These abilities are advantageous in many settings, because understanding other people's emotions is a key to unlocking their potential. An emotionally intuitive boss might quickly pick up on an employee's feelings and struggles and then determine the best course of action to assist this person. An emotionally intuitive parent, teacher, or therapist will do the same. In short, because sensitive people take the time to understand other people's experiences and build strong relationships, sensitive leadership has a powerful effect on their followers' happiness and loyalty.

Euny Hong, a Korean American journalist, offers a word for this capability: *nunchi*. In Korea, she says, nunchi means the art of sensing what people are feeling or thinking—and it's considered the secret to happiness and success. Hong explains, "Kids in Korea know the word by age three. You usually learn it in the negative; if everyone is standing on the right side of an escalator and a kid is lounging on the left, the parent will say, 'Why don't you have any nunchi?' It's partly about not being rude, but it's also partly, 'Why are you not plugged into your environment?'" In practice, nunchi means reading the room, noticing things like who is talking, who is listening, who is frowning, and who isn't paying attention. Those with natural or "quick" nunchi, as Koreans say, are thought to make more connections, appear more competent, negotiate better, and go further in life.

Sensitive people also project warmth, which makes their followers trust them. When Amy Cuddy and her team at Harvard Business School examined the effectiveness of different types of leaders, they found that those who project warmth (like Dr. Humboldt) are more effective than those who appear unapproachable. One reason is trust. Sensitive leaders tend to make it easier for their followers to approach and confide in them, fostering relationships that are more authentic. By being open to a range of perspectives and experiences and actively making space for everyone to share their values and beliefs, these leaders promote a culture of honesty and authenticity. Rather than seeing team members as homogeneous, a sensitive leader is more likely to view them as individuals, understanding their needs and looking out for their best interests.

Finally, sensitive leaders tend to be reflective. They are more likely to analyze every detail to determine what works and doesn't work, adapting and evolving as needed. Moreover, they have a sharpened intuition and can sense when something just doesn't feel right. Being creative and innovative allows them to see problems from many angles and offer fresh insights. Where some leaders only highlight their successes, many sensitive people try to learn from their failures, to avoid making mistakes in the future. Because they take criticism to heart, they will deliver it more constructively to others, holding themselves and their team to a higher standard of self-improvement.

In Their Own Words: What Are Your Strengths as a Sensitive Leader?

"I currently lead a high-profile technology project. I've found that my sensitivity is helpful in several ways. I have a good eye for detail and how all the various pieces of the project fit together—a skill that helps me keep it on track. Because I can understand (or at least try to understand) other people's points of view, I'm able to get along with colleagues in many roles. This ability comes in handy when I need to work with people in other groups, who might have viewpoints or priorities different from my own." —Bruce

"I can sense what my managers need just by the tone of

their voice. I'm able to fill the gaps where they are weak. More important, conflict made me so uncomfortable that I got my master's degree in conflict resolution and then became a certified mediator. Ever since, I've used those skills to teach my teams—and my own children—how to better communicate, listen, and work together." —Wendy

"Being sensitive means I often see team dynamics and staff needs earlier and more accurately than the top execs do. This foresight allows me to better address those issues." —Frankie

"I often find myself the one among friends to take up the lead. Part of it is certainly my sensitive traits; I process things deeply and quickly, which means I can synthesize large amounts of information, whether it's opinions on what game to play or what to do about a problem. Then I turn the conversation from aimless discussion to practical problem-solving." —Julie

Let Your Intuition Lead the Way

Remember, leading doesn't necessarily mean becoming a corporate CEO (although we talked to several CEOs who found their sensitivity to be an asset even in this role). There are many ways to lead, whether you're heading up a sales team or reaching out to your friends or family to plan the next social event. Leadership can be as simple as noticing problems that others overlook and then speaking up about them. For example, at a family birthday party, sensitive leadership might be as simple as saying, "The kids are getting tired, so we should open the gifts now, before they get too drained and spoil the fun." Or at work: "This form might be confusing to prospective clients, who might get frustrated with it and abandon it, so I'll suggest a simpler one." Sensitive people often notice these types of things, but because they have been conditioned to distrust their intuition, they may not say anything even when speaking up would benefit the group.

In this way, being a strong, sensitive leader starts with listening to your intuition. It starts with honoring the voice in your heart and your head that you may have previously silenced, downplayed, or dismissed. This voice notices gaps, red flags, annoyances, or problems—or when something just seems off. It makes predictions—often accurate—about what might happen next or how a certain situation might unfold. As a sensitive person, *you possess secret knowledge. You know things that other people don't know.* You may find that less-sensitive people aren't even aware of these issues, and their lack of awareness is not necessarily because these issues are unimportant or insignificant. When you notice something, speak up with courage and kindness. Anne, the sensitive nurse who we met in Chapter 1, did just that—and her actions saved a life.

You can also lead by example, like by speaking up when you see an injustice. In one small Midwestern town, for example, a school bus driver was harassing Somali students who rode his bus. Other teachers and community members dismissed the young students' complaints of racial discrimination. It took a sensitive teacher to believe them, speak up, and demand the bus company put a stop to it. The teacher did so even when colleagues warned her that her actions might put her own career at risk of backlash from the school administration. "I couldn't *not* do something," the teacher, who wished to remain anonymous, told us. "Kids were being abused and discriminated against, and it was severely affecting their lives and education." Even though she had never thought of herself as a leader, she became one when she listened to her intuition and spoke up on her students' behalf.

Sensitive people are the leaders our world needs. But before they can step into this purpose, they must learn to embrace their sensitivity and end the cycle of shame.

Breaking Free of the Shame Cycle

When we talk to people about what being sensitive means, over and over we hear, "That's me!" Many sensitive people have their own stories to tell, usually related to their childhood: How they wept after discovering a dead bird in their yard or how adults repeatedly told them to shake off their big feelings and "just get over it." When they tell us these stories—at conferences, at parties, and even in public restrooms—they lower their voices to a confidential whisper, as if their experiences were a dirty secret. Many express shame over their sensitivity or feelings of brokenness.

And these expressions of shame are no surprise—as we've seen, the Toughness Myth teaches us sensitive people that our natural state is something that should be changed. As a result, we may question ourselves about how we interact with the world. From needing extra time to write an email or taking a snack break at work to keep our blood sugar stable, we often become conditioned to move through the world carefully. While there's nothing wrong with being cautious, the problem is that we may feel we must warily conceal our true nature from the world.

The antidote is to change how we view ourselves in the context of society. One way to make this change is to stop apologizing for what doesn't warrant an apology. Sensitive people should not apologize for needing downtime or rest, for saying no, for leaving an overstimulating event early, for crying or feeling things deeply, or for other needs related to their sensitive nature. While the decision to stop saying you're sorry might be a long road, it starts here—with you and with the rest of us. All of us can start a collective mindset shift toward normalizing sensitivity. Rather than an embarrassing secret or a stumbling series of explanations, sensitivity should be recognized as what it is: a normal, healthy trait that we all share to some degree. Not only is it normal, but sensitivity can also become a source of pride, something we can love and enjoy about ourselves.

Just as some people are naturally athletic, talkative, or tall, some of us are naturally more sensitive. There's nothing to adjust—it's just who we are. Within this mindset, there's no reason to make excuses or beat yourself up because you supposedly can't handle what other people can. (And when you act this way about your sensitivity, others are more likely to view it as a flaw, too.) Rather, you can choose to see sensitivity as your greatest strength (as it is), and that attitude will help others follow your lead. Remember: Sensitivity is genetic, healthy, and even linked to being gifted.

Now, the natural question becomes, How can you change the way you see your sensitivity? How can you stop thinking of it as bad and shift your perspective to see it as a strength?

Know (and Maybe Even Memorize) the Benefits of Your Strengths

Our workplaces, schools, and other settings have traditionally favored people who don't show sensitive traits. But that's just because our society has overlooked areas where sensitive people shine—such as situations where depth, empathy, understanding, intuition, and attunement to others are needed. Our society has fallen short for everyone in this way. Feelings are—and always have been—important. Even more important is the ability to recognize those feelings as valid, to express them, and to know they are being acknowledged and heard. The scarcity of these supposedly soft skills in society is just one of the gaps that sensitive people can readily fill; it's in our nature to feel others' emotions and use our empathy to connect with them. It's in our nature, too, to go deep and offer new and unexpected solutions.

Make sure you know the strengths you bring to the table. Take a moment to write a list of your sensitivity-related traits that help you or others. Then, keep this list in mind when interacting with others or talking about sensitivity. If you need inspiration, here are some aspects of sensitivity that provide true benefits to the world. (Remember: These statements aren't bragging; they're positive self-talk.)

- "I help those around me feel heard and understood."
- "I catch important details that others might miss, whether in my work, my relationships, or other parts of my life."
- "I can more quickly notice when my energy is low or when I'm getting run down. This awareness helps me avoid the point of burnout that others might reach."
- "My mind doesn't stop at shallow answers. It looks at the big picture as well as the nitty-gritty, and it keeps going until it has breakthroughs. This depth helps me come up with solutions that others don't see."
- "Since I feel things so strongly, anything I do or create carries that intensity, which permeates my values, passion projects, work, art, relationships, and more."
- "I cry easily (or show big emotions in other ways) because I'm so easily moved by life, and not everyone feels the beauty of life in this way."
- "I can see connections between information that seems unrelated to others. When I follow those connections, I can easily see truths that don't occur to other people. It makes me creative and, with practice, it can make me wise."
- "I tend to look ahead and think of all the angles more than other people do. This tendency helps me avoid mistakes, notice small problems before they become big, and overall be better prepared in life."
- "My intuition shows me the path forward. I can often see a unique way to solve a problem or accomplish a goal. Other people benefit from my insights, advice, and leadership because I bring a perspective that less-sensitive people don't have access to."

- "My empathy helps me consider other people's needs and perspectives. It also helps me make more moral, ethical, compassionate, and selfless decisions. I easily sense right from wrong, healthy from unhealthy, true from false."

Elaine Aron, the researcher who coined the term *highly sensitive person*, puts it this way: "You were born to be among the advisors and thinkers, the spiritual and moral leaders of your society. There is every reason for pride."

Practice Embracing Your Sensitivity

Make a point to notice the strengths of your sensitivity throughout the day. Even if you find yourself feeling frustrated about something related to your sensitivity—for example, if you become drained after running errands—make a mental note to pause and reframe. Nudge your brain to notice the positives of the situation, too. You might think, "I'm thankful I have the self-awareness to notice when I'm feeling tired and need to head home," or "Because of my sensitivity, I noticed beauty in my surroundings, such as all the different colors in the sky at sunset."

This change probably won't happen overnight. In fact, it might take months or even years to embrace your sensitivity. But that's okay; a lengthy transition is normal! You've had years and years of practice responding to a society that doesn't get sensitivity in many ways. Give yourself time, starting with small steps that get you comfortable with revealing your sensitivity. In doing so, you'll pave the way for all sensitive people—now and in the future—to embrace who they are and make the changes our world needs.

How to Talk About Sensitivity So Others Will Listen
....

Along with recognizing your strengths as a sensitive person, you'll also need to change how you talk about your sensitivity to others. In a way, you can think of this as doing PR work for sensitivity. But you're also doing something much deeper. You're being authentic and honest about who you are. You're owning your sensitivity. And you're doing it in a way that is confident, clear, and not open for debate. Here are some scripts you can use to explain sensitivity to the people in your life:

- "In psychology, being sensitive means you process both your experiences and your environment very deeply. That's me. It comes with a lot of gifts but also some challenges. I have both sides of it, and I'm proud of it."
- "I'm not looking to change how sensitive I am. It's a good thing, and I would never give it up."
- "You know, I'm a very sensitive person, and I believe it's one of my best qualities. It's why I'm (creative/an idealist/good at my job/so tuned in to people). I wish more people would embrace sensitivity."
- "Nearly one in three people are born a little more sensitive, both emotionally and physically. This is because our brains are wired to process information very deeply. Basically, we think about things longer, we feel things stronger, and we make connections that other people miss. Although it's often misunderstood, it's a healthy trait."

You may find it especially difficult to explain sensitivity to less-sensitive people—those who don't experience life in the same turned-up and tuned-in way that you do. Often, misconceptions about what sensitivity is (and is not) get in the way. Brittany Blount, a mental health writer who is sensitive, wanted her less-sensitive dad to understand what she experiences. "My dad, like most of us, grew up with the idea that sensitivity is a sign of weakness, something to be avoided," she writes on Sensitive Refuge. "One of the biggest challenges in explaining high sensitivity is convincing others, for the very first time, to entertain the possibility that it is a strength, the opposite of what we've been taught." After several failed attempts to explain sensitivity to him, she compared it to his favorite superhero:

> *You know how Superman can hear the tiniest pin drop from far away? It's almost like having superhero senses without the super speed or the ability to fly. . . . When you're highly sensitive, everything you experience is heightened. You notice the tiniest changes. Small sounds such as a clock ticking become loud. A person's cologne or perfume may smell three times as strong and nauseating to you but pleasant to others. And when I talk to people . . . sometimes I know things about people without them telling me. I don't read minds, but I know when I'm being lied to, or if someone pretends to be happy when they're not. I see past the masks people put on. I know their intentions, their hearts, their fears. I have no reason to know; I just do.*

At first, her dad didn't say a word, but Brittany noticed his slight shift in body posture. He was considering what she said. After a few moments, he looked up at her and slowly nodded. "I believe it," he said, finally validating an important part of her that she had waited so long for him to understand.

"You're Too Sensitive" Is Gaslighting

Another important step in embracing your sensitivity is to recognize the accusation "you're too sensitive" for what it is: gaslighting. With this type of manipulation, the other person tries to make you doubt yourself and your reality so that you rely on their own version of events. The term *gaslighting* comes from the 1938 British play *Gas Light*, in which a dishonest husband drives his wife to a mental health crisis by persuading her that she imagined certain things, like sounds in the attic and their house's gaslights growing dimmer. In reality, he did those things in an attempt to steal her family's jewels. Here are some other common statements used to gaslight sensitive people:

- "You're overreacting."
- "You need to toughen up."
- "Grow a thicker skin."
- "Why can't you let things go?"
- "You take everything so personally."

These comments may have been especially damaging if they were said to you in childhood by your parents or another adult caregiver. You may have even come to believe that a right and a wrong level of sensitivity exists. As a result, you may have spent years feeling ashamed about why you're so touchy or easily wounded. These critical statements can hurt just as much, though, when said by a friend, a significant other, or a coworker. Telling you that you're overreacting when you are being victimized is one of the most common forms of gaslighting that narcissists and other abusers do, explains Julie L. Hall, author of *The Narcissist in Your Life*. They say it to discredit you and dismiss your feelings so that they don't have to take responsibility for the hurtful things they said or did. "You're overreacting" allows the narcissist to cast *you* as the irrational or overly emotional one. If they can get you to doubt yourself—"Maybe they're right; maybe the comment wasn't cruel and I'm just being too sensitive"—you will accept their abuse. But narcissists are the ones who are hypersensitive and emotionally dysregulated. When they tell you that you are too sensitive, it's a classic form of projection; they are attributing their own feelings to you.

Not that every person who says these things is a narcissist. Some people may even mistakenly believe they are helping you by pointing out something you didn't know about yourself. Regardless of the person's intentions, these phrases are hurtful, and they should never be used against any sensitive person (or anyone else, for that matter). Here are some things you can do when someone says you're too sensitive:

- **Don't take the bait.** When people say these things, it's tempting to defend yourself or insult them back, especially if you've been actively targeted by them for a long time, says Hall. However, these tactics usually just escalate the conflict rather than calming it, so it's best if you can withhold your emotions. Inject some space into the conversation by reflecting their words back to them: "I hear you. So, what you're saying is, you think I'm too sensitive. Is that right?"
- **Focus on the gifts of sensitivity.** Say something like, "I am learning to like my sensitivity. In fact, I think it's one of my biggest strengths." Or, "I love how sensitive I am. I think I'm just the right level of sensitive." Share some stories or examples of how your sensitivity benefits you in your life or in your relationship with them.
- **Consider limited contact or no contact.** If they don't get the message and continue to judge or disparage you for your sensitivity, then they are probably not someone you want in your life. Over time, gaslighting will erode your self-image and make you question yourself and feel bad about your sensitivity. A healthy relationship, on the other hand, generally leaves you

feeling good about yourself. If possible, spend less time (or no time at all) with this person; if that's not possible (perhaps you work together or are a co-parent), then set boundaries around your interactions with them.

- **Focus on yourself.** Remember, gaslighters want you to doubt your own feelings and experiences so that they can continue to control and abuse you. They tend to target people who are already in the habit of distrusting themselves, whether through compromised boundaries, low self-esteem, or a sense of disconnection from their own body or emotions. Sensitive people have strong intuition, but as we've seen, they are often conditioned to doubt it because the Toughness Myth says emotions are weak. Take a look at your boundaries and see if any need shoring up. Listen to and validate your feelings and intuition. Remember, all feelings are valid; if you're upset, you have reason to be. If you've been the victim of narcissistic abuse, seek support from a therapist, and learn about the trauma that can result from such mistreatment.

- **Cultivate healthy relationships.** When people genuinely care about you, they won't ignore or dismiss your emotions, even when those emotions make them uncomfortable. The right people will not just tolerate your sensitivity but will also embrace and cherish it as an important part of who you are.

The Sensitive Revolution Benefits Everyone

When we embrace our sensitivity—choosing the Sensitive Way over the Toughness Myth—we plant the seeds of revolution at all levels of our society. In our schools, following the Sensitive Way means offering quiet spaces where students can decompress instead of spending every minute bombarded with stimulation. It means training principals and classroom teachers in gentle discipline techniques and empowering parents to advocate in schools for their sensitive kids. It means teaching kids that there's nothing wrong with being sensitive and that it's okay to take extra time to get something done. Instead of "boys don't cry," children would learn that all emotions are normal and healthy and that expressing them is part of being human. It also means getting a curriculum about social and emotional development into every school so that students have models of strong, mentally healthy behavior and can take control of their own well-being. These changes wouldn't just benefit the most sensitive; they would make every kid's future brighter.

In the workplace, the Sensitive Way lifts up those who have been undervalued. It starts with prizing "soft skills" like emotional intelligence when hiring and promoting. Likewise, it's time to train managers to value employees' emotional needs and to lead with compassion. The Sensitive Way means less talk of toughening up, of hustling for the sake of hustling, of getting ahead, or of being more "right" than the person next to you. And for businesses that truly want to thrive, it means investing in long-term results by creating the right physical and emotional environment that is mentally healthy and productive for all workers. Of course, if all these recommendations sound like a lot to ask, companies can take a simple shortcut: Put sensitive people in leadership roles, and watch the problems solve themselves.

This same approach extends to our personal lives. The Sensitive Way puts the focus back on meaningful, healthy interactions between people. It accepts that loud parties, concerts, and networking events are not the only way to socialize and instead embraces quieter venues and more intimate experiences. The Sensitive Way also empowers all people to respect their limits and put their mental and emotional well-being first. It creates a culture where it's socially acceptable to turn down an invitation because you need to stay home and decompress or to leave an event early, no nagging questions asked. It erases any perceived malice or judgment from the phrases "I need some downtime" or "I need some time to think about that."

Picture how our current political system could be transformed through the Sensitive Way. Instead of shouting at the "other" side, name-calling, and demonizing those who don't think like us, we could have more empathy-filled discussions. In a world that embraces being sensitive to others' needs and emotions—even those who are different from us—we could approach political issues with open ears rather than closed hearts. We'd be more apt to view one another as fellow humans instead of opponents. The loudest, most outrage-inducing candidate would no longer eclipse the news.

In our loud, fast, too-much world, we must look to sensitive people, for they have lessons to teach us. They show us the value of slowing down. Of connecting deeply. Of creating meaning in our ordinary lives. More than that, sensitive people are also the compassionate leaders our world needs. They are the ones best positioned to help confront some of society's biggest problems.

Novelist Kurt Vonnegut once said that the world needs sensitive artists because they serve as humanity's canaries—in coal mines filled with poison gas, they keel over "long before more robust types realize that any danger is there." We prefer to see sensitive people differently. Canaries, after all, live in cages, and the way they deliver their message is by sacrificing themselves. Sensitive people have had enough of that job. It's time to break open the cage that has held sensitive people for far too long. Rather than seeing sensitivity as a weakness, we need to start seeing it for what it actually is—a strength. It's time we embrace sensitivity and all it has to offer.

Acknowledgments

To our agent, Todd Shuster, truly the wisest powerhouse of an ally a writer could ask for: Thank you for believing in our book. To Georgia Frances King, Todd's brilliant co-agent, and the entire team at Aevitas: Thank you. You got us through some tough spots and always kept your faith in us.

To Marnie Cochran: A writer couldn't ask for a better editor. You entertained countless ideas, plot twists, and rewrites, always believing that our book would be better for it in the end. Over and over, your insights (and patience) improved what we turned in. Thank you.

To Diana Baroni: We've spoken just once, but it was your words that made us sure that Harmony was our home. You understood our vision for *Sensitive* from the start.

To the entire team at Harmony: We'll never know how many hours you put into making this book perfect. Thank you.

To Lydia Yadi and the team at Penguin Random House UK: Thank you for teaming up to help make *Sensitive* work for an international audience.

To Rachel Livsey and Jeff Leeson: You saw the potential in this book when it was just an idea on the (literal) drawing board. Thank you for your guidance and mentoring.

To Elaine Aron, who has been called the "godmother of highly sensitive people," and rightly so: This book wouldn't even exist if it weren't for your research, vision, and hard work over the years.

To Michael Pluess: Thank you for giving us so much of your time, for always being willing to answer *yet another* question, and for sharing your research and insights. Thank you, also, for the work you do and your commitment to showing the world the positive side of sensitivity.

To Cal Newport, Paul Gilbert, Ron Siegel, Larissa Geleris, Tomlin Perkins Coggeshall, Linda Silverman, Sharon Martin, Julie Bjelland, Brian Johnston, Alicia Davies, Brooke Nielsen, Rachel Horne, Bret Devereaux, Dimitri van der Linden, Suzanne Ouellette, Conrado Silva Miranda, Anindita Balslev, and all the other people who lent us their expertise and insight: We were not able to put all of your words in print, but all of you helped shape and improve this book, in ways big and small. Thank you for sharing your time and wisdom with us.

To BT Newberg: No author has ever had a finer research assistant. Your ability to deep-dive—and sometimes push back—helped take us in new and exciting directions.

To Lauren Valko, our trusted writing assistant: Thank you for helping us outline and figure out so much, on such short timelines.

To Christine Utz: Thank you for being our second set of eyes and helping bring clarity to the confusion.

To our writers' group, Elizabeth, Paul, and John: Whoa, how much of our work have you read? Did you think this book would *ever* be done? Thank you, not only for your feedback and suggestions but also for the tremendous amount of time and encouragement you gave us.

To our team at Sensitive Refuge and Introvert, Dear: Thank you for keeping the ship on course while we were so often absent to focus on the book. You did great.

To the members of the Sensitive Refuge Facebook group: Thank you for being willing to share your personal thoughts and experiences with us, which make up the "In Their Own Words" portions of this book. We believe your words will be a guiding light for other sensitive people. Our only regret is not being able to include more of your responses in the book.

To Amy, Agata, Mathew, Trent, Nancy, Paul, and Elizabeth, who were our beta readers and contributed many helpful insights and suggestions.

To Dawn: Thank you for making a space where writers, editors, and publishers could actually get to know one another. And to David: Thank you for spotting two sensitive, awkward types in that space and deciding we were your friends. This book wouldn't have happened without both of you.

To Daryl: Thank you for your calm and caring voice through stressful times.

To Apollo, who was born on a snowy day in the middle of our writing this book: You endlessly frustrated our attempts to finish it, but the interruptions were worth it. We love you, son.

To Jenn's parents, Marge and Steve Granneman, who cared for baby Apollo when we were sleep-deprived and in need of uninterrupted time to write: Thank you.

Jenn would like to say . . .

To my mom: Thank you for always encouraging my sensitivity and for penning my silly stories even before I could hold a pencil.

To my dad: Thank you for encouraging my interest in science, which has given shape to my writing career. It all began with those petri dishes you brought home from work and then swabbing the mouths of the neighborhood cats and dogs.

To my friends Amber, Amy, Bethany, and Dawn: Thank you for listening to me vent and supporting me through the most difficult moments of completing this book. Now let's go get a glass of wine.

Again, to Elaine Aron: Years ago, after I finished reading your book, *The Highly Sensitive Person,* I cried because I finally understood myself better. Your work changed my life and set me on the course to embrace my sensitivity. Thank you for everything you have done for sensitive people.

To all the teachers and adults who encouraged me to write when I was young: Thank you for believing in this little girl's dream.

To Mattie and Colmes, my cats, who both passed away while I was writing this book: You died within a week of each other, confirming what I've always known: You were meant to be together. I miss you.

To all the sensitive people who shared their stories with me in preparation for writing this book (and often did so in whispered voices): Thank you for being willing to open up and give me a glimpse into your life. I hope for the day when we sensitive people no longer feel the need to whisper.

Andre would like to say . . .
It's a cliché to thank your parents, but you've more than earned it. Dad, you once explained our relationship by saying you are a mechanic and your son is a poet. You did right by this poet, Dad. You may not remember this, but when you found out I wanted to be a writer, you bought me a copy of a book with a bright blue cover titled *If You Want to Write,* by Brenda Ueland. That book was like nothing I'd ever seen, and it tripped every trigger I had. I scribbled it full of notes, rebuilt my head around it, and never once forgot it. Thanks, Dad.

Mom, you taught me to love books, and I'm pretty sure you put the writing bug in me in the first place. You had a policy when I was little that as long as I was reading, it didn't matter if I was still awake after bedtime. Damn good policy, Mom. Thank you for putting your English degree—and your patience—to good use by reading some of the schlockiest, cringiest, embarrassingly bad novels a twelve-year-old could write.

Frederick Dobke, wherever you are, you were more than a teacher. You encouraged and you challenged in the same breath. I'm not sure I would have gotten serious if it weren't for you. And you were right, I do like Simon & Garfunkel.

To the editor who sent me my first (and kindest) rejection letter when I was fourteen: Thank you. I understand now what an acquisition editor's schedule is like, and the message you took the time to write will never be forgotten.

To my sister, Zangmo (Juju): You're the best friend a brother could ask for. How the heck did Mom and Dad get two of us?

To Saumya and Urban: Urban, you're a *rock*. Thank you, brother. Saumya, you're the opposite of a rock—you make me soar. I love you guys.

Brandon, thank you for unconditional friendship, love, and acceptance. Thank you for hearing my rants. Thank you for Monday Notes and so much more. Thank you for being who you are.

To the people who have believed in me and inspired me: Ben, Cole, Beth, Ken, Manda, Arianna, "Good" Andrea, Amber and the ol' Oak Street writers' group in New Orleans, Liz, Cintain, Kevin (we will finish that treehouse, right?), Blake (may you rest in peace), Damien (may you rest in jams), everyone who followed my old blog, Mrs. Burrant, Ms. Lenart, Mrs. Hallenbeck, John Longeway, Aaron Snyder, John Boatman, Matt Langdon, Ari Kohen, the kind-hearted strangers who cared on my journeys, and all the people I'm too silly to remember but who gave me a nudge anyway. (And Jessica, I guess you were right: I always pull it off in the end.)

To all the people who didn't think they were sensitive at all, who paused when I explained what I was writing about, who asked question after question or said nothing and chewed it like a steak—then began to see another side of themselves (and sometimes even admit it): I've been there. You're doing just fine. Just stay true to your (secretly or openly) sensitive self.

And, to the divine, whatever It is: I see you. I see what you did there. Thanks.

To Our Readers

Last, both of us would like to express our gratitude to the readers and fans of Sensitive Refuge and Introvert, Dear. This book wouldn't be what it is without you. Many of you have read our work for years, and your support and enthusiasm have been humbling. Thank you, you quiet and sensitive souls.

Sensitivity Cheat Sheet

- **Sensitivity** means how deeply you perceive and respond to the world, both your physical and your emotional environments. The more deeply your brain processes information, the more sensitive you are. A more accurate word for *sensitive* might be *responsive.*
- **Sensitivity is a fundamental human trait.** Everyone is sensitive to some degree, and some people are more sensitive than others. Roughly 30 percent of people are *highly* sensitive.
- **Sensitivity is both genetic and shaped by your experiences.** If you are sensitive, you were probably born that way. Certain experiences in your early childhood—either lots of support or neglect—may have further increased your sensitivity.
- **If you're sensitive, it's part of who you are.** Sensitive people cannot stop being sensitive, nor should they. Instead, society should recognize that sensitivity comes with many gifts, such as creativity, deep thinking, empathy, and attention to detail. These traits are advantages in science, business, the arts, academia,

leadership, and any other area of life that rewards a keen, careful mind.

- **Sensitive people are attuned to both people and their environment.** They notice subtle sensations, minor details, and shifts or changes that others miss. Because they also pick up more social and emotional cues, they read others well and have a strong sense of empathy, even toward strangers.

- **Sensitivity has a cost: overstimulation.** Sensitive people tend to struggle in chaotic, loud, or busy environments, especially if there is pressure to go faster and accomplish more. Because the sensitive brain processes *all* information deeply, busy environments or schedules overload it.

- **Despite society's misconceptions about sensitivity, it's a healthy personality trait.** Sensitivity is not a disorder, does not require a diagnosis or treatment, and is unrelated to introversion, autism, sensory processing disorder, and trauma.

- **Sensitive people have an advantage—the *Sensitive Boost Effect*.** Because sensitive people are more affected by any kind of experience, they get far more out of support, training, and encouragement than less-sensitive people do. This unlocks a boost effect, which helps sensitive people rocket past others and achieve more, if given the right conditions.

Further Reading and Resources

Elaine Aron's *The Highly Sensitive Person: How to Thrive When the World Overwhelms You* (New York: Carol Publishing Group, 1996)

Tom Falkenstein's *The Highly Sensitive Man: Finding Strength in Sensitivity* (New York: Citadel Press/Kensington Publishing, 2019)

Sharon Martin's *The Better Boundaries Workbook: A CBT-Based Program to Help You Set Limits, Express Your Needs, and Create Healthy Relationships* (Oakland, CA: New Harbinger Publications, 2021)

Our website, Sensitive Refuge, sensitiverefuge.com

Maureen Gaspari's blog, thehighlysensitivechild.com, which offers advice for parenting sensitive children and includes many free resources and printable checklists and worksheets

Michael Pluess's website, sensitivityresearch.com, which is dedicated to bringing academic information about sensitivity to the public

Therapist Julie Bjelland's website, juliebjelland.com, which offers many resources to help sensitive people thrive in life; includes a free blog and podcast as well as paid courses

April Snow's *Find Your Strength: A Workbook for the Highly Sensitive Person* (New York: Wellfleet Press, 2022)

Brian R. Johnston's *It's Okay to Fail: A Story for Highly Sensitive Children*, self-published, 2018

Bill Eddy's *It's All Your Fault! 12 Tips for Managing People Who Blame Others for Everything* (High Conflict Institute Press, 2008) and other resources from the High Conflict Institute, highconflictinstitute.com

Shahida Arabi's *The Highly Sensitive Person's Guide to Dealing with Toxic People: How to Reclaim Your Power from Narcissists and Other Manipulators* (California: New Harbinger Publications, 2020)

Human Improvement Project's Happy Child app, humanimprovement.org/the-happy-child-app, which is not specifically about sensitive people but offers science-backed advice to help any parent create close, healthy bonds with their children

The Healthy Minds Program app, a free meditation and mindfulness app from neuroscientist Richard Davidson's nonprofit organization, Healthy Minds Innovation, hminnovations.org

Daniel J. Siegel and Tina Payne Bryson's *The Whole-Brain Child: 12 Revolutionary Strategies to Nurture Your Child's Developing Mind* (New York: Bantam, 2012), which offers great tips to help parents teach their children emotional regulation

Notes

Chapter 1: Sensitivity: Stigma or Superpower?

Page 10   **Innovation, he suggested:** Georg Simmel's paper "The Metropolis and Mental Life" has been interpreted many ways, and he makes many points we didn't include here. For a scholarly overview, see Dietmar Jazbinsek, "The Metropolis and the Mental Life of Georg Simmel," *Journal of Urban History* 30, no. 1 (2003): 102–25, https://doi.org/10 .1177/0096144203258342. For a general reader, this summary, which was originally published online by Yale University's Modernism Lab, will do nicely: Matthew Wilsey, "The Metropolis and Mental Life," Campuspress, Yale University, n.d., https://campuspress.yale.edu /modernismlab/the-metropolis-and-mental-life/. For Simmel's entire essay, see Georg Simmel, *The Sociology of Georg Simmel,* trans. Kurt Wolff (New York: Free Press, 1950), 409–24.

Page 10   **"external and internal stimuli":** Simmel, *Sociology of Georg Simmel.*

Page 10   **"mental energy":** Simmel, *Sociology of Georg Simmel.*

Page 10   **"blasé" or, simply put:** Simmel, *Sociology of Georg Simmel.*

Page 11   **"being levelled down and swallowed up":** Georg Simmel, "Die Großstädte und das Geistesleben," in *Die Großstadt: Vorträge und*

Aufsätze zur Städteausstellung, vol. 9, ed. T. Petermann, independent translation (Dresden: Zahn & Jaensch, 1903), 186–206.

Page 11   **By some estimates:** Rick Smolan and Jennifer Erwitt, *The Human Face of Big Data* (Sausalito, CA: Against All Odds Productions, 2012); and Susan Karlin, "Earth's Nervous System: Looking at Humanity Through Big Data," *Fast Company,* November 28, 2012, https://www.fastcompany .com/1681986/earth-s-nervous-system-looking-at-humanity-through -big-data.

Page 11   **As of 2020, we produce:** Irfan Ahmad, "How Much Data Is Generated Every Minute? [Infographic]," *Social Media Today,* June 15, 2018, https://www.socialmediatoday.com/news/how-much-data-is-generated -every-minute-infographic-1/525692/.

Page 11   **Researchers who study that instrument:** Leo Goldberger and Shlomo Breznitz, *Handbook of Stress,* 2nd ed. (New York: Free Press, 1993).

Page 13   **"I'm Too Sensitive":** Mariella Frostrup, "I'm Too Sensitive. How Can I Toughen Up?" *Guardian,* January 26, 2014, https://www.theguardian .com/lifeandstyle/2014/jan/26/im-too-sensitive-want-to-toughen-up -mariella-frostrup.

Page 13   **"How to Stop Being":** "How to Stop Being So Sensitive," *JB Coaches,* February 3, 2020, https://jbcoaches.com/how-to-stop-being-so -sensitive/.

Page 14   **It began with a simple:** Robin Marantz-Henig, "Understanding the Anxious Mind," *New York Times Magazine,* September 29, 2009, https:// www.nytimes.com/2009/10/04/magazine/04anxiety-t.html.

Page 14   **"high reactive":** Marantz-Henig, "Understanding the Anxious Mind."

Page 14   **Most earned high grades:** Marantz-Henig, "Understanding the Anxious Mind."

Page 14   **Dozens of researchers have confirmed:** See, for example, Corina U. Greven, Francesca Lionetti, Charlotte Booth, Elaine N. Aron, Elaine Fox, Haline E. Schendan, Michael Pluess, Hilgo Bruining, Bianca Acevedo, Patricia Bijttebier, and Judith Homberg, "Sensory Processing Sensitivity in the Context of Environmental Sensitivity: A Critical Review and Development of Research Agenda," *Neuroscience & Biobehavioral Reviews* 98 (March 2019), 287-305, https://doi.org/10 .1016/j.neubiorev.2019.01.009.

Page 14   **most notably Elaine Aron:** Aron coined the term "highly sensitive person" and introduced it to the general public in her book, *The Highly*

Sensitive Person: How to Thrive When the World Overwhelms You (New York: Broadway Books, 1998).

Page 14   **The fearfulness that Kagan:** Marantz-Henig, "Understanding the Anxious Mind."

Page 16   **Recent research suggests that highly:** In adults, for example, see Francesca Lionetti, Arthur Aron, Elaine N. Aron, G. Leonard Burns, Jadzia Jagiellowicz, and Michael Pluess, "Dandelions, Tulips and Orchids: Evidence for the Existence of Low-Sensitive, Medium-Sensitive and High-Sensitive Individuals," *Translational Psychiatry* 8, no. 24 (2018), https://doi.org/10.1038/s41398-017-0090-6. In children, see Michael Pluess, Elham Assary, Francesca Lionetti, Kathryn J. Lester, Eva Krapohl, Elaine N. Aron, and Arthur Aron, "Environmental Sensitivity in Children: Development of the Highly Sensitive Child Scale and Identification of Sensitivity Groups," *Developmental Psychology* 54, no. 1 (2018), 51–70, doi: https://doi.org/10.1037/dev0000406. And for an integrated overview of a large number of studies, see Michael Pluess, Francesca Lionetti, Elaine Aron, and Arthur Aron, "People Differ in Their Sensitivity to the Environment: An Integrated Theory and Empirical Evidence," (2020). 10.31234/osf.io/w53yc.

Page 22   **For evidence, you need:** Aron, *Highly Sensitive Person.*

Page 22   **What's more, researchers have found:** Emily Deans, "On the Evolution of the Serotonin Transporter Gene," *Psychology Today,* September 4, 2017, https://www.psychologytoday.com/us/blog/evolutionary -psychiatry/201709/the-evolution-the-serotonin-transporter-gene.

Page 22   **Just following around rhesus:** S. J. Suomi, "Early Determinants of Behaviour: Evidence from Primate Studies," *British Medical Bulletin* 53, no. 1 (1997): 170–84, doi:10.1093/oxfordjournals.bmb.a011598; and S. J. Suomi, "Up-Tight and Laid-Back Monkeys: Individual Differences in the Response to Social Challenges," in *Plasticity of Development,* edited by S. Brauth, W. Hall, and R. Dooling (Cambridge, MA: MIT, 1991), 27–56.

Page 23   **The connection between intuition and:** Jonathan P. Roiser, Robert D. Rogers, Lynnette J. Cook, and Barbara J. Sahakian, "The Effect of Polymorphism at the Serotonin Transporter Gene on Decision-Making, Memory and Executive Function in Ecstasy Users and Controls," *Psychopharmacology* 188, no. 2 (2006): 213–27, https://doi.org/10.1007 /s00213-006-0495-z.

Page 23   **Another study, using a computer:** M. Wolf, G. S. van Doorn, and F. J. Weissin, "Evolutionary Emergence of Responsive and Unresponsive

Personalities," *Proceedings of the National Academy of Sciences* 105, no. 41 (2008): 15,825–30, https://doi.org/10.1073/pnas.0805473105.

Page 23   **The nurse didn't like to complain:** Ted Zeff and Elaine Aron, *The Power of Sensitivity: Success Stories by Highly Sensitive People Thriving in a Non-Sensitive World* (San Ramon, CA: Prana Publishing, 2015).

Page 24   **"Although I'm the type":** Zeff, *Power of Sensitivity.*

Page 24   **"If [the patient's] body":** Zeff, *Power of Sensitivity.*

Page 24   **"I knew that I might be":** Zeff, *Power of Sensitivity.*

Page 25   **"I felt honored that I":** Zeff, *Power of Sensitivity.*

Page 26   **In 2010, Jadzia:** Jadzia Jagiellowicz, Xiaomeng Xu, Arthur Aron, Elaine Aron, Guikang Cao, Tingyong Feng, and Xuchu Weng, "The Trait of Sensory Processing Sensitivity and Neural Responses to Changes in Visual Scenes," *Social Cognitive and Affective Neuroscience* 6, no. 1 (2011): 38–47, https://doi.org/10.1093/scan/nsq001.

Page 26   **"they are attending more":** Jagiellowicz et al., "Sensory Processing Sensitivity."

Page 27   **We know this because:** Bianca Acevedo, T. Santander, R. Marhenke, Arthur Aron, and Elaine Aron, "Sensory Processing Sensitivity Predicts Individual Differences in Resting-State Functional Connectivity Associated with Depth of Processing," *Neuropsychobiology* 80 (2021): 185–200, https://doi.org/10.1159/000513527.

Page 27   **"to wash away":** University of California, Santa Barbara, "The Sensitive Brain at Rest: Research Uncovers Patterns in the Resting Brains of Highly Sensitive People," *ScienceDaily*, May 4, 2021, https://www.sciencedaily.com/releases/2021/05/210504135725.htm.

Page 27   **"is a cardinal feature":** University of California, Santa Barbara, "Sensitive Brain at Rest."

Page 28   **"My clinical research":** Linda Silverman, email correspondence with authors, January 7, 2022.

Page 28   **Research on successful musicians:** Scott Barry Kaufman, "After the Show: The Many Faces of the Creative Performer," *Scientific American*, June 10, 2013, https://blogs.scientificamerican.com/beautiful-minds/after-the-show-the-many-faces-of-the-creative-performer/.

Page 28   **Some experts, including Aron:** Elaine Aron, "Time Magazine: 'The Power of (Shyness)' and High Sensitivity," *Psychology Today*, February 2, 2012, https://www.psychologytoday.com/us/blog/attending

-the-undervalued-self/201202/time-magazine-the-power-shyness-and
-high-sensitivity.

Page 29   **Aron estimates that:** Aron, "Time Magazine."

Page 30   **Experts agree that sensitive:** Elaine Aron, "HSPs and Trauma," The
Highly Sensitive Person, November 28, 2007, https://hsperson.com/hsps
-and-trauma/.

Page 30   **However, trauma and sensitivity:** Acevedo et al., "Functional Highly
Sensitive Brain."

Page 32   **"For my entire life":** Fábio Augusto Cunha, "The Challenges of Being a
Highly Sensitive Man," Highly Sensitive Refuge, May 12, 2021, https://
highlysensitiverefuge.com/the-challenges-of-being-a-highly-sensitive
-man/.

Page 32   **"I thought if my male":** Nell Scovell, "For Any Woman Who's Ever Been
Told She's Too 'Emotional' at Work, . . ." Oprah.com, n.d., https://www
.oprah.com/inspiration/for-any-woman-whos-ever-been-told-shes-too
-emotional-at-work.

Page 33   **"It struck me that":** Scovell, "For Any Woman."

Page 33   **"Understanding my HSP":** Michael Parise, "Being Highly Sensitive and
Gay," LGBT Relationship Network, n.d., https://lgbtrelationshipnetwork
.org/highly-sensitive-gay/.

Page 33   **Black people in particular:** Kara Mankel, "Does Being a 'Superwoman'
Protect African American Women's Health?" *Berkeley News,*
September 30, 2019, https://news.berkeley.edu/2019/09/30/does-being-a
-superwoman-protect-african-american-womens-health/.

Page 33   **"unquenchable thirst":** Raneisha Price, "Here's What No One Told Me
About Being a Highly Sensitive Black Woman," Highly Sensitive Refuge,
October 16, 2020, https://highlysensitiverefuge.com/highly-sensitive
-black-woman/.

Page 34   **Simmel spoke of a world:** Simmel, *Sociology of Georg Simmel.*

Chapter 2: The Sensitive Boost Effect

Page 37   **"barn-burning":** Richard Ford, "Richard Ford Reviews Bruce
Springsteen's Memoir," *New York Times,* September 22, 2016, https://
www.nytimes.com/2016/09/25/books/review/bruce-springsteen-born
-to-run-richard-ford.html.

Page 38   **"a pretty sensitive kid":** Bruce Springsteen, "Bruce Springsteen: On
Jersey, Masculinity and Wishing to Be His Stage Persona," interview by
Terry Gross, *Fresh Air,* NPR, October 5, 2016, https://www.npr.org/2016
/10/05/496639696/bruce-springsteen-on-jersey-masculinity-and
-wishing-to-be-his-stage-persona.

Page 38   **"mama's boy":** Bruce Springsteen, *Born to Run* (New York: Simon &
Schuster, 2017).

Page 39   **Multiple studies showed that:** Joan Y. Chiao and Katherine D. Blizinsky,
"Culture-Gene Coevolution of Individualism-Collectivism and the
Serotonin Transporter Gene," *Proceedings Biological Sciences* 277,
no. 1681 (2010): 529–37, https://doi.org/10.1098/rspb.2009.1650.

Page 39   **But this conclusion didn't sit well:** Chiao and Blizinsky, "Culture-Gene
Coevolution."

Page 40   **One study, for example:** Dean G. Kilpatrick, Karestan C. Koenen,
Kenneth J. Ruggiero, Ron Acierno, Sandro Galea, Heidi S. Resnick, John
Roitzsch, John Boyle, and Joel Gelernter, "The Serotonin Transporter
Genotype and Social Support and Moderation of Posttraumatic Stress
Disorder and Depression in Hurricane-Exposed Adults," *American
Journal of Psychiatry* 164, no. 11 (2007): 1693–99, https://doi.org/10
.1176/appi.ajp.2007.06122007.

Page 40   **Another study, this one looking at teenagers:** David Dobbs, "The
Depression Map: Genes, Culture, Serotonin, and a Side of Pathogens,"
Wired, September 14, 2010, https://www.wired.com/2010/09/the
-depression-map-genes-culture-serotonin-and-a-side-of-pathogens/.

Page 41   *social sensitivity gene:* Baldwin M. Way and Matthew D. Lieberman, "Is
There a Genetic Contribution to Cultural Differences? Collectivism,
Individualism and Genetic Markers of Social Sensitivity," *Social
Cognitive and Affective Neuroscience* 2–3 (2010): 203–11, https://doi.org
/10.1093/scan/nsq059.

Page 41   **Today, scientists no longer:** J. Belsky, C. Jonassaint, Michael Pluess, M.
Stanton, B. Brummett, and R. Williams, "Vulnerability Genes or
Plasticity Genes?" *Molecular Psychiatry* 14, no. 8 (2009): 746–54, https://
doi.org/10.1038/mp.2009.44.

Page 42   *plasticity gene:* Belsky et al., "Vulnerability Genes or Plasticity Genes?"

Page 42   **The Three Types of Sensitivity:** Hanne Listou Grimen and Åge Diseth,
"Sensory Processing Sensitivity: Factors of the Highly Sensitive Person
Scale and Their Relationships to Personality and Subjective Health

Complaints," *Comprehensive Psychology* (2016), https://doi.org/10.1177/2165222816660077; Michael Pluess, interview with authors via Zoom, November 23, 2021; and Kathy A. Smolewska, Scott B. McCabe, and Erik Z. Woody, "A Psychometric Evaluation of the Highly Sensitive Person Scale: The Components of Sensory-Processing Sensitivity and Their Relation to the BIS/BAS and 'Big Five,'" *Personality and Individual Differences* (2006), https://doi.org/10.1016/j.paid.2005.09.022.

Page 44   **"Sensitivity may be thought of":** Corina U. Greven and Judith R. Hornberg, "Sensory Processing Sensitivity: For Better or Worse? Theory, Evidence, and Societal Implications," ch. 3 in *The Highly Sensitive Brain: Research, Assessment, and Treatment of Sensory Processing Sensitivity,* ed. Bianca Acevedo (San Diego: Academic Press, 2020).

Page 45   **On the morning of September:** Annie Murphy Paul, "How Did 9/11 and the Holocaust Affect Pregnant Women and Their Children?," *Discover Magazine,* October 14, 2010, https://www.discovermagazine.com/health/how-did-9-11-and-the-holocaust-affect-pregnant-women-and-their-children.

Page 45   **About seventeen hundred of these:** Annie Murphy Paul, *Origins: How the Nine Months Before Birth Shape the Rest of Our Lives* (New York: Free Press, 2011).

Page 45   **About half the women:** Danielle Braff, "Moms Who Were Pregnant During 9/11 Share Their Stories," *Chicago Tribune,* September 7, 2016, https://www.chicagotribune.com/lifestyles/sc-911-moms-family-0906-20160911-story.html.

Page 45   **That same morning:** Rachel Yehuda, Stephanie Mulherin Engel, Sarah R. Brand, Jonathan Seckl, Sue M. Marcus, and Gertrud S. Berkowitz, "Transgenerational Effects of Posttraumatic Stress Disorder in Babies of Mothers Exposed to the World Trade Center Attacks During Pregnancy," *Journal of Clinical Endocrinology & Metabolism* 90, no. 7 (2005): 4115–18, https://doi.org/10.1210/jc.2005-0550.

Page 45   **"Many of these members":** Yehuda et al., "Transgenerational Effects."

Page 46   **A later study added:** Yehuda et al., "Transgenerational Effects." https://www.ncbi.nlm.nih.gov/pmc/articles/PMC2612639/ and https://www.ncbi.nlm.nih.gov/pmc/articles/PMC2612639/.

Page 46   *epigenetics,* **the relatively new study:** Centers for Disease Control and Prevention, "What Is Epigenetics?," U.S. Department of Health & Human Services, August 3, 2020, https://www.cdc.gov/genomics/disease/epigenetics.htm.

Page 47   **recent study on prairie voles:** Sarah Hartman, Sara M. Freeman, Karen
           L. Bales, and Jay Belsky, "Prenatal Stress as a Risk and an Opportunity-
           Factor," *Psychological Science* 29, no. 4 (2018): 572–80, https://doi.org/10
           .1177/0956797617739983.

Page 48   **Your genes are about 47 percent responsible:** Elham Assary, Helena
           M. S. Zavos, Eva Krapohl, Robert Keers, and Michael Pluess, "Genetic
           Architecture of Environmental Sensitivity Reflects Multiple Heritable
           Components: A Twin Study with Adolescents," *Molecular Psychiatry* 26
           (2021): 4896–4904, https://doi.org/10.1038/s41380-020-0783-8.

Page 48   **"This is one of the":** Pluess, interview.

Page 48   **children's sensitivity levels:** Z. Li, M. Sturge-Apple, H. Jones-Gordils,
           and P. Davies, "Sensory Processing Sensitivity Behavior Moderates the
           Association Between Environmental Harshness, Unpredictability, and
           Child Socioemotional Functioning," *Development and Psychopathology*
           (2022): 1–14, https://doi.org/10.1017/S0954579421001188.

Page 51   **But how much do these early:** Pluess, interview.

Page 51   **As Pluess told us:** Pluess, interview.

Page 51   **To test his theory:** Michael Pluess and Ilona Boniwell, "Sensory-
           Processing Sensitivity Predicts Treatment Response to a School-Based
           Depression Prevention Program: Evidence of Vantage Sensitivity,"
           Personality and Individual Differences 82 (2015): 40–45, https://doi.org
           /10.1016/j.paid.2015.03.011.

Page 52   **Sensitive adults on the verge:** Michael Pluess, Galena Rhoades, Rob
           Keers, Kayla Knopp, Jay Belsky, Howard Markman, and Scott Stanley,
           "Genetic Sensitivity Predicts Long-Term Psychological Benefits of a
           Relationship Education Program for Married Couples," *Journal of
           Consulting and Clinical Psychology* 90, no. 2 (2022): 195–207, https://doi
           .org/10.1037/ccp0000715.

Page 52   **Sensitive kids given quality care:** Grazyna Kochanska, Nazan Aksan, and
           Mary E. Joy, "Children's Fearfulness as a Moderator of Parenting in Early
           Socialization: Two Longitudinal Studies," *Developmental Psychology* 43,
           no. 1 (2007): 222–37, https://doi.org/10.1037/0012-1649.43.1.222.

Page 52   **score higher for altruistic behavior:** Paul G. Ramchandani, Marinus
           van IJzendoorn, and Marian J. Bakermans-Kranenburg, "Differential
           Susceptibility to Fathers' Care and Involvement: The Moderating Effect
           of Infant Reactivity," *Family Science* 1, no. 2 (2010): 93–101, https://doi
           .org/10.1080/19424621003599835.

Page 53   **growing up with an angry:** Springsteen, *Born to Run.*

Page 54   **and highest-paid:** "World's Highest-Paid Musicians 2014," *Forbes,*
December 10, 2014, https://www.forbes.com/pictures/eeel45fdddi/5
-bruce-springsteen-81-million/?sh=1f66bd816d71.

Page 54   **"he harbored a gentleness":** Springsteen, *Born to Run.*

Page 54   **"wore on the outside":** Springsteen, *Born to Run.*

Page 54   **"a creation":** Michael Hainey, "Beneath the Surface of Bruce
Springsteen," *Esquire,* November 27, 2018, https://www.esquire.com
/entertainment/a25133821/bruce-springsteen-interview-netflix
-broadway-2018/.

Chapter 3: The Five Gifts of Sensitivity

Page 57   **By the time Jane Goodall:** "Being with Jane Goodall," in *The Secret Life
of Scientists and Engineers,* season 2015, episode 1, January 12, 2015,
PBS, https://www.pbs.org/video/secret-life-scientists-being-jane
-goodall/.

Page 57   **If you've ever seen Koko:** Allen and Beatrix Gardner, the first scientists
to teach a gorilla to use sign language, drew partly on the work of Jane
Goodall. See Roger Fouts and Erin McKenna, "Chimpanzees and Sign
Language: Darwinian Realities Versus Cartesian Delusions," *Pluralist* 6,
no. 3 (2011): 19, https://doi.org/10.5406/pluralist.6.3.0019.

Page 58   **But if you ask:** Maria Popova, "How a Dream Came True: Young Jane
Goodall's Exuberant Letters and Diary Entries from Africa,"
Marginalian, July 14, 2015, https://www.themarginalian.org/2015/07/14
/jane-goodall-africa-in-my-blood-letters/.

Page 58   **"I was told you have to give them numbers":** *The Secret Life of
Scientists,* "Being with Jane Goodall."

Page 59   **"Empathy is really important":** *The Secret Life of Scientists,* "Being with
Jane Goodall."

Page 59   **"vocalized panting":** Frans de Waal, "Sex, Empathy, Jealousy: How
Emotions and Behavior of Other Primates Mirror Our Own," interview
by Terry Gross, *Fresh Air,* NPR, March 19, 2019, https://www.npr.org
/transcripts/704763681.

Page 60   **The word *empathy*:** Karsten Stueber, "Empathy," in *The Stanford
Encyclopedia of Philosophy,* ed. Edward N. Zalta, revised June 27, 2019,

https://plato.stanford.edu/archives/fall2019/entries/empathy/; and Gustav Jahoda, "Theodor Lipps and the Shift from 'Sympathy' to 'Empathy?,'" *Journal of the History of the Behavioral Sciences* 41, no. 2 (2005): 151–63, https://doi.org/10.1002/jhbs.20080.

Page 61   **This is the same trait that:** *The Secret Life of Scientists*, "Being with Jane Goodall."

Page 61   **Empathy, for example, is both genetic:** Helen Riess, "The Science of Empathy," *Journal of Patient Experience* 4, no. 2 (2017): 74–77, https://doi .org/10.1177/2374373517699267; and V. Warrier, R. Toro, B. Chakrabarti, et al., "Genome-Wide Analyses of Self-Reported Empathy: Correlations with Autism, Schizophrenia, and Anorexia Nervosa," *Translational Psychiatry* 8, no. 35 (2018), https://doi.org/10.1038/s41398-017-0082-6.

Page 61   **and teachable (everyone can learn):** Riess, "Science of Empathy"; F. Diane Barth, "Can Empathy Be Taught?," *Psychology Today,* October 18, 2018, https://www.psychologytoday.com/us/blog/the-couch/201810/can -empathy-be-taught; and Vivian Manning-Schaffel, "What Is Empathy and How Do You Cultivate It?," *NBC News,* May 29, 2018, https://www .nbcnews.com/better/pop-culture/can-empathy-be-taught-ncna878211.

Page 61   **a study discussed in Chapter 1:** Bianca Acevedo, T. Santander, R. Marhenke, Arthur Aron, and Elaine Aron, "Sensory Processing Sensitivity Predicts Individual Differences in Resting-State Functional Connectivity Associated with Depth of Processing," *Neuropsychobiology* 80 (2021): 185–200, https://doi.org/ 10.1159/000513527.

Page 61   **one study found that dogs:** Mylene Quervel-Chaumette, Viola Faerber, Tamás Faragó, Sarah Marshall-Pescini, and Friederike Range, "Investigating Empathy-Like Responding to Conspecifics' Distress in Pet Dogs," *PLOS ONE* 11, no. 4 (2016), https://doi.org/10.1371/journal .pone.0152920.

Page 61   **another study found that rats:** Inbal Ben-Ami Bartal, Jean Decety, and Peggy Mason, "Empathy and Pro-Social Behavior in Rats," *Science* 334, no. 6061 (2011): 1427–30, https://doi.org/10.1126/science.1210789.

Page 62   **Psychology professor Abigail Marsh saw:** Abigail Marsh, "Abigail Marsh: Are We Wired to Be Altruistic?" interview by Guy Raz, *TED Radio Hour,* NPR, May 26, 2017, https://www.npr.org/transcripts /529957471; and Abigail Marsh, "Why Some People Are More Altruistic Than Others," video, TEDSummit, June 2016, https://www.ted.com /talks/abigail_marsh_why_some_people_are_more_altruistic_than _others?language=en.

Page 62   **More than twenty years later:** Kristen Milstead, "New Research May
           Support the Existence of Empaths," *PsychCentral,* July 30, 2018, https://
           psychcentral.com/blog/new-research-may-support-the-existence-of
           -empaths#1.

Page 62   **One extreme example of:** Marsh, "Are We Wired to Be Altruistic?"; and
           Marsh, "Why Some People Are More Altruistic."

Page 62   **The absence of empathy drives:** Simon Baron-Cohen, *The Science of
           Evil: On Empathy and the Origins of Cruelty* (New York: Basic Books,
           2012), ch. 3.

Page 62   **Although not all psychopaths:** Tori DeAngelis, "A Broader View of
           Psychopathy: New Findings Show That People with Psychopathy Have
           Varying Degrees and Types of the Condition," *American Psychological
           Association* 53, no. 2 (2022): 46, https://www.apa.org/monitor/2022/03
           /ce-corner-psychopathy.

Page 62   **Court cases back this up:** Kent A. Kiehl and Morris B Hoffman,
           "The Criminal Psychopath: History, Neuroscience, Treatment, and
           Economics," *Jurimetrics* 51 (2011): 355–97; and Wynne Parry, "How to
           Spot Psychopaths: Speech Patterns Give Them Away," *Live Science,*
           October 20, 2011, https://www.livescience.com/16585-psychopaths
           -speech-language.html.

Page 63   **As Stanford professors:** Paul R. Ehrlich and Robert E Ornstein,
           *Humanity on a Tightrope: Thoughts on Empathy, Family and Big Changes
           for a Viable Future* (Lanham, MD: Rowman & Littlefield, 2010).

Page 63   **"empathy deficit":** Claire Cain Miller, "How to Be More Empathetic,"
           New York Times, n.d., https://www.nytimes.com/guides/year-of-living
           -better/how-to-be-more-empathetic.

Page 63   **Smith suggested that the answer:** Adam Smith, *The Theory of Moral
           Sentiments,* ed. D. D. Raphael and A. L. Macfie (Indianapolis: Liberty
           Fund, 1982), part I, section I, chapters III–V, https://www.econlib.org
           /library/Smith/smMS.html?chapter_num=2#book-reader; and Stueber,
           "Empathy."

Page 64   **Smith's contemporary David Hume:** David Hume, *A Treatise of Human
           Nature* (Oxford: Oxford University Press, 1978), 365.

Page 64   **Smith's theory was contentious:** Daniel B. Klein, "Dissing the Theory of
           Moral Sentiments: Twenty-Six Critics, from 1765 to 1949," *Econ Journal
           Watch* 15, no. 2 (2018): 201–54, https://econjwatch.org/articles/dissing
           -the-theory-of-moral-sentiments-twenty-six-critics-from-1765-to-1949.

Page 64   **we now know it's largely right:** Lynne L. Kiesling, "Mirror Neuron Research and Adam Smith's Concept of Sympathy: Three Points of Correspondence," *Review of Austrian Economics* (2012), https://doi.org /10.2139/ssrn.1687343.

Page 64   **Mirror neurons are motor cells:** Kiesling, "Mirror Neuron Research"; and Antonella Corradini and Alessandro Antonietti, "Mirror Neurons and Their Function in Cognitively Understood Empathy," *Consciousness and Cognition* 22, no. 3 (2013): 1152–61, https://doi.org/10.1016/j .concog.2013.03.003.

Page 64   **What is clear from the research:** Valeria Gazzola, Lisa Aziz-Zadeh, and Christian Keysers, "Empathy and the Somatotopic Auditory Mirror System in Humans," *Current Biology* 16, no. 18 (2006): 1824–29, https:// doi.org/10.1016/j.cub.2006.07.072; and Mbema Jabbi, Marte Swart, and Christian Keysers, "Empathy for Positive and Negative Emotions in the Gustatory Cortex," *NeuroImage* 34, no. 4 (2007): 1744–53, https://doi .org/10.1016/j.neuroimage.2006.10.032.

Page 64   **and this includes sensitive people:** Bianca P. Acevedo, Elaine N. Aron, Arthur Aron, Matthew-Donald Sangster, Nancy Collins, and Lucy L. Brown, "The Highly Sensitive Brain: An fMRI Study of Sensory Processing Sensitivity and Response to Others' Emotions," *Brain and Behavior* 4, no. 4 (2014): 580–94, https://doi.org/10.1002/brb3.242.

Page 64   **Much as Smith predicted:** Corradini and Antonietti, "Mirror Neurons."

Page 64   **You can see this connection in experiments:** Paula M. Niedenthal, Lawrence W. Barsalou, Piotr Winkielman, Silvia Krauth-Gruber, and François Ric, "Embodiment in Attitudes, Social Perception, and Emotion," *Personality and Social Psychology Review* 9, no. 3 (2005): 184–211, https://doi.org/10.1207/s15327957pspr0903_1.

Page 64   **Marsh's work has demonstrated:** Abigail Marsh, "Neural, Cognitive, and Evolutionary Foundations of Human Altruism," *Wiley Interdisciplinary Reviews: Cognitive Science* 7, no. 1 (2015): 59–71, https://doi.org/10.1002/wcs.1377; Marsh, "Why Some People Are More Altruistic."

Page 65   **A litany of research:** See, for example, Patricia L. Lockwood, Ana Seara-Cardoso, and Essi Viding, "Emotion Regulation Moderates the Association Between Empathy and Prosocial Behavior," *PLoS ONE* 9, no. 5 (2014): e96555, https://doi.org/10.1371/journal.pone.0096555; Jean Decety and William Ickes, "Empathy, Morality, and Social Convention," in *The Social Neuroscience of Empathy*, ed. Jean Decety and

William Ickes (Cambridge, MA: MIT Press, 2009); Baron-Cohen, *Science of Evil*; and Leigh Hopper, "Mirror Neuron Activity Predicts People's Decision-Making in Moral Dilemmas, UCLA Study Finds," University of California, Los Angeles, January 4, 2018, https://newsroom .ucla.edu/releases/mirror-neurons-in-brain-nature-of-morality -iacoboni.

Page 65   **Even the budding field:** Ari Kohen, Matt Langdon, and Brian R. Riches, "The Making of a Hero: Cultivating Empathy, Altruism, and Heroic Imagination," *Journal of Humanistic Psychology* 59, no. 4 (2017): 617–33, https://doi.org/10.1177/0022167817708064.

Page 65   **To see this effect in action:** Lucio Russo, *The Forgotten Revolution: How Science Was Born in 300 BC and Why It Had to Be Reborn* (New York: Springer, 2004).

Page 66   **"universal solvent":** Baron-Cohen, *Science of Evil*, 194.

Page 66   **Nina Volf, a researcher:** Nina V. Volf, Alexander V. Kulikov, Cyril U. Bortsov, and Nina K. Popova, "Association of Verbal and Figural Creative Achievement with Polymorphism in the Human Serotonin Transporter Gene," *Neuroscience Letters* 463, no. 2 (2009): 154–57, https://doi.org/10.1016/j.neulet.2009.07.070.

Page 67   **One prominent theory among scientists:** Maria Popova, "The Role of 'Ripeness' in Creativity and Discovery: Arthur Koestler's Seminal 1964 Theory of the Creative Process," *Marginalian,* August 8, 2012, https:// www.themarginalian.org/2012/08/08/koestler-the-act-of-creation/; Maria Popova, "How Creativity in Humor, Art, and Science Works: Arthur Koestler's Theory of Bisociation," *Marginalian,* May 20, 2013, https://www.themarginalian.org/2013/05/20/arthur-koestler-creativity -bisociation/; and Brian Birdsell, "Creative Cognition: Conceptual Blending and Expansion in a Generative Exemplar Task," *IAFOR Journal of Psychology & the Behavioral Sciences* 5, SI (2019): 43–62, https://doi .org/10.22492/ijpbs.5.si.03.

Page 67   **"We are made of ":** Carl Sagan, *Carl Sagan's Cosmic Connection: An Extraterrestrial Perspective* (Cambridge: Cambridge University Press, 2000), 190.

Page 67   **Born in Budapest:** Wikipedia, s.v. "Arthur Koestler," updated June 21, 2020, https://en.wikipedia.org/wiki/Arthur_Koestler.

Page 70   **Sometimes, this level of sensitivity:** Kawter, "Heroic Wife Brings Husband back to Life One Hour after His 'Death,' " *Goalcast,* August 5,

2020, https://www.goalcast.com/wife-brings-husband-back-to-life-one
-hour-after-his-death/.

Page 70   **In the military, for example:** National Research Council, *Tactical Display for Soldiers: Human Factors Considerations* (Washington, DC: National Academies Press, 1997).

Page 71   **It's a major part of why airplanes:** Mica R. Endsley, "Situation Awareness and Human Error: Designing to Support Human Performance," paper presented at the Proceedings of the High Consequence Systems Surety Conference, Albuquerque, NM, 1999. https://www.researchgate.net/publication/252848339_Situation _Awareness_and_Human_Error_Designing_to_Support_Human _Performance.

Page 71   **why nuclear plants don't melt:** Maggie Kirkwood, "Designing for Situation Awareness in the Main Control Room of a Small Modular Reactor," *Proceedings of the Human Factors and Ergonomics Society Annual Meeting* 63, no. 1 (2019): 2185–89, https://doi.org/10.1177 /1071181319631154.

Page 71   **why crimes get solved:** T. F. Sanquist, B. R. Brisbois, and M. P. Baucum, "Attention and Situational Awareness in First Responder Operations Guidance for the Design and Use of Wearable and Mobile Technologies," report prepared for the U.S. Department of Energy, Richland, WA, 2016.

Page 71   **A lack of situational awareness:** Endsley, "Situation Awareness and Human Error."

Page 71   **such as a hospital injecting:** Jeanne M. Farnan, "Situational Awareness and Patient Safety," Patient Safety Network, April 1, 2016, https://psnet .ahrq.gov/web-mm/situational-awareness-and-patient-safety.

Page 71   **Meanwhile, in sports, sensory intelligence:** Craig Pulling, Philip Kearney, David Eldridge, and Matt Dicks, "Football Coaches' Perceptions of the Introduction, Delivery and Evaluation of Visual Exploratory Activity," *Psychology of Sport and Exercise* 39 (2018): 81–89, https://doi.org/10.1016/j.psychsport.2018.08.001.

Page 71   **You've seen field vision:** Wikipedia, s.v. "Wayne Gretzky," updated March 19, 2019, https://en.wikipedia.org/wiki/Wayne_Gretzky.

Page 71   **"the Great One":** Wikipedia, s.v. "Wayne Gretzky."

Page 71   **"I get a feeling about":** Wikipedia, s.v. "Wayne Gretzky."

Page 72   **NFL quarterback:** Wikipedia, s.v. "Tom Brady," updated February 25, 2019, https://en.wikipedia.org/wiki/Tom_Brady.

Page 72 **Sensitive enough that he cries:** TeaMoe Oliver, "Tom Brady Cried on
National Television, and That's Why He's Great," *Bleacher Report,*
April 12, 2011, https://bleacherreport.com/articles/659535-tom-brady
-cried-on-national-television-and-thats-why-hes-great.

Page 73 **In both humans and monkeys:** H. P. Jedema, P. J. Gianaros, P. J. Greer,
D. D. Kerr, S. Liu, J. D. Higley, S. J. Suomi, A. S. Olsen, J. N. Porter,
B. J. Lopresti, A. R. Hariri, and C. W. Bradberry, "Cognitive Impact of
Genetic Variation of the Serotonin Transporter in Primates Is
Associated with Differences in Brain Morphology Rather Than
Serotonin Neurotransmission," *Molecular Psychiatry* 15, no. 5 (2009):
512–22, https://doi.org/10.1038/mp.2009.90.

Page 74 **The source of this gift:** R. M. Todd, M. R. Ehlers, D. J. Muller, A.
Robertson, D. J. Palombo, N. Freeman, B. Levine, and A. K. Anderson,
"Neurogenetic Variations in Norepinephrine Availability Enhance
Perceptual Vividness," *Journal of Neuroscience* 35, no. 16 (2015):
6506–16, https://doi.org/10.1523/jneurosci.4489-14.2015.

Page 74 **As far back as the 1960s:** Sharon Lind, "Overexcitability and the Gifted,"
SENG—Supporting Emotional Needs of the Gifted, September 14, 2011,
https://www.sengifted.org/post/overexcitability-and-the-gifted.

Page 75 **Educators who work with:** Lind, "Overexcitability and the Gifted"; D. R.
Gere, S. C. Capps, D. W. Mitchell, and E. Grubbs, "Sensory Sensitivities
of Gifted Children," *American Journal of Occupational Therapy* 63, no. 3
(2009): 288–95, https://doi.org/10.5014/ajot.63.3.288; and Linda
Silverman, "What We Have Learned About Gifted Children 1979–2009,"
report prepared by the Gifted Development Center, 2009, https://www
.gifteddevelopment.org/s/What-We-Have-Learned-2009.pdf.

Page 75 **One possible explanation:** Jennifer M. Talarico, Kevin S. LaBar, and
David C. Rubin, "Emotional Intensity Predicts Autobiographical
Memory Experience," *Memory & Cognition* 32, no. 7 (2004): 1118–32,
https://doi.org/10.3758/bf03196886; and Olga Megalakaki, Ugo
Ballenghein, and Thierry Baccino, "Effects of Valence and Emotional
Intensity on the Comprehension and Memorization of Texts," *Frontiers
in Psychology* 10 (2019), https://doi.org/10.3389/fpsyg.2019.00179.

Page 75 **Today, though, we tend:** Heather Craig, "The Theories of Emotional
Intelligence Explained," PositivePsychology.com, August 2019, https://
positivepsychology.com/emotional-intelligence-theories/.

Page 75 **That's because emotional intelligence has:** John D. Mayer, Richard D.
Roberts, and Sigal G. Barsade, "Human Abilities: Emotional

Intelligence," *Annual Review of Psychology* 59, no. 1 (2008): 507–36, https://doi.org/10.1146/annurev.psych.59.103006.093646.

Page 75   **For example, sensitive people tend:** J. D. Mayer, P. Salovey, and D. R. Caruso, "Emotional Intelligence: New Ability or Eclectic Traits?," *American Psychologist* 63, no. 6 (2008): 503–17, https://doi.org/10.1037 /0003-066x.63.6.503.

Page 76   **improved mental health:** Hassan Farrahi, Seyed Mousa Kafi, Tamjid Karimi, and Robabeh Delazar, "Emotional Intelligence and Its Relationship with General Health Among the Students of University of Guilan, Iran," *Iranian Journal of Psychiatry and Behavioral Sciences* 9, no. 3 (2015), https://doi.org/10.17795/ijpbs-1582.

Page 76   **better job performance:** Dana L. Joseph, Jing Jin, Daniel A. Newman, and Ernest H. O'Boyle, "Why Does Self-Reported Emotional Intelligence Predict Job Performance? A Meta-Analytic Investigation of Mixed EI," *Journal of Applied Psychology* 100, no. 2 (2015): 298–342, https://doi.org/10.1037/a0037681.

Page 76   **leadership ability:** Robert Kerr, John Garvin, Norma Heaton, and Emily Boyle, "Emotional Intelligence and Leadership Effectiveness," *Leadership & Organization Development Journal* 27, no. 4 (2006): 265–79, https:// doi.org/10.1108/01437730610666028.

Page 76   **Martin Luther King Jr.:** Kelly C. Bass, "Was Dr. Martin Luther King Jr. a Highly Sensitive Person?" Highly Sensitive Refuge, February 4, 2022, https://highlysensitiverefuge.com/was-dr-martin-luther-king-jr-a -highly-sensitive-person/.

Page 77   **"This music was filled with":** Bruce Springsteen, *Born to Run* (New York: Simon & Schuster, 2017).

Page 77   **"The secret ingredients":** Springsteen, *Born to Run.*

Page 78   **"I liked who I was":** Bruce Springsteen, "Bruce Springsteen: On Jersey, Masculinity and Wishing to Be His Stage Persona," interview by Terry Gross, *Fresh Air,* NPR, October 5, 2016, https://www.npr.org/2016/10/05 /496639696/bruce-springsteen-on-jersey-masculinity-and-wishing-to -be-his-stage-persona.

Chapter 4: Too Much, Too Loud, Too Fast

Page 80   **Alicia Davies:** Alicia Davies, email correspondence with authors, March 13, 2022.

Page 80   **"one riddled with":** Alicia Davies, "This Is What Overstimulation Feels Like for HSPs," Highly Sensitive Refuge, October 14, 2019, https://highlysensitiverefuge.com/what-overstimulation-feels-like/.

Page 80   **"lovely little bedroom":** Davies, "What Overstimulation Feels Like."

Page 80   **"drilling, sawing,":** Davies, "What Overstimulation Feels Like."

Page 81   **"Any sort of conversation":** Davies, "What Overstimulation Feels Like."

Page 81   **"I wanted to wail":** Davies, "What Overstimulation Feels Like."

Page 84   **Yet no matter:** Larissa Geleris, interview with authors via Zoom, June 28, 2021.

Page 85   **"Once the bucket":** Geleris, interview.

Page 85   **"My therapist says":** Geleris, interview.

Page 85   **"I could feel that":** Geleris, interview.

Page 85   **"I turned around":** Geleris, interview.

Page 86   **Although we think:** Geleris, interview.

Page 87   **"Throughout our day":** Geleris, interview.

Page 87   **sensitive people have a nervous system:** Geleris, interview.

Page 88   **Threat mode:** Paul Gilbert, interview with authors via Zoom, July 14, 2021.

Page 88   **"amygdala hijack":** Daniel Goleman, *Emotional Intelligence* (New York: Bantam Books, 2005).

Page 89   **"gives you these buzzes":** Gilbert, interview.

Page 89   **"people become absolutely obsessed":** Gilbert, interview.

Page 90   **"Thankfully for me":** Davies, email correspondence.

Page 92   **"a feeling of lightning":** Lama Lodro Zangmo, email correspondence with authors, April 15, 2022.

Page 92   **"If I kept silent":** Zangmo, email correspondence.

Page 92   **"The tendency to become":** Tom Falkenstein, Elaine Aron, and Ben Fergusson, *The Highly Sensitive Man: Finding Strength in Sensitivity* (New York: Citadel Press, 2019).

Page 94   **"In the moment":** Geleris, interview.

Page 94   **Proprioceptive input:** Geleris, interview.

Page 95   **"You wouldn't have calmed":** Falkenstein, Aron, and Fergusson, *Highly Sensitive Man.*

Page 96   **"When your emotional brain":** Julie Bjelland, "This Simple Mental Trick Has Helped Thousands of HSPs Stop Emotional Overload," Highly Sensitive Refuge, December 12, 2018, https://highlysensitiverefuge.com /highly-sensitive-people-trick-bypass-emotional-overload/.

Page 96   **Write down at least three:** Bjelland, "This Simple Mental Trick."

Page 98   **When you're overwhelmed:** Stephen C. Hayes and Spencer Xavier Smith, *Get Out of Your Mind and Into Your Life: The New Acceptance & Commitment Therapy* (Oakland, CA: New Harbinger Publications, 2005).

Page 99   **"They are meant to come":** Steven C. Hayes, "The Shortest Guide to Dealing with Emotions: People Often Avoid Emotions Instead of Confronting Them," *Psychology Today,* April 13, 2021, https://www .psychologytoday.com/us/blog/get-out-your-mind/202104/the-shortest -guide-dealing-emotions.

Page 99   **Psychologists call this focus on play:** Carolyn Cole, "How to Embrace Your 'Play Ethic' as a Highly Sensitive Person," Highly Sensitive Refuge, June 14, 2021, https://highlysensitiverefuge.com/how-to-embrace-your -play-ethic-as-a-highly-sensitive-person/.

Page 99   **"gets covered up":** Cole, "Embrace Your 'Play Ethic.'"

Page 100   **"If you can, ride the wave":** Geleris, interview.

Chapter 5: The Pain of Empathy

Page 101   **Rachel Horne was:** Rachel Horne, "Sensitive and Burned Out? You Might Be Ready for the Nomad Life," Highly Sensitive Refuge, October 19, 2020, https://highlysensitiverefuge.com/ready-for-the -nomad-life/.

Page 102   **"It was impossible":** Rachel Horne, interview with authors via Zoom, June 11, 2021.

Page 102   **"I could hold it together":** Horne, interview.

Page 103   **That was when she:** Rachel Horne, "As an HSP, the Hermit's Life Is the Best Life for Me," Highly Sensitive Refuge, July 26, 2021, https:// highlysensitiverefuge.com/as-an-hsp-the-hermits-life-is-the-best-life -for-me/.

Page 104   **Case in point: In 2021:** Qing Yang and Kevin Parker, "Health Matters: Turnover in the Health Care Workforce and Its Effects on Patients," *State Journal-Register,* March 14, 2022, https://www.sj-r.com/story/news

/healthcare/2022/03/14/turnover-health-care-workforce-and-its-effects
-patients/7001765001/.

Page 106 **the *chameleon effect*:** T. L. Chartrand and J. A. Bargh, "The Chameleon
Effect: The Perception-Behavior Link and Social Interaction," *Journal of
Personality and Social Psychology* 76, no. 6 (1999): 893–910, https://doi
.org/ 10.1037//0022-3514.76.6.893.

Page 106 **This biological process:** Gary W. Lewandowski Jr., "Is a Bad Mood
Contagious?," *Scientific American Mind* 23, no. 3 (2012): 72, https://doi
.org/10.1038/scientificamericanmind0712-72a.

Page 108 **spouses deeply influence:** Sherrie Bourg Carter, "Emotions Are
Contagious: Choose Your Company Wisely," *Psychology Today,*
October 20, 2012, https://www.psychologytoday.com/us/blog/high
-octane-women/201210/emotions-are-contagious-choose-your
-company-wisely.

Page 108 **women are more susceptible:** Elaine Hatfield, John T. Cacioppo, and
Richard L. Rapson, *Emotional Contagion* (Cambridge: Cambridge
University Press, 2003).

Page 108 **depression in a spouse:** Bourg Carter, "Emotions Are Contagious."

Page 108 **watch an unfortunate test subject:** Bourg Carter, "Emotions Are
Contagious."

Page 108 **the world's emotional super-spreaders:** Hatfield, Cacioppo, and
Rapson, *Emotional Contagion.*

Page 109 **it can also lead to:** Kelly McGonigal, "How to Overcome Stress by
Seeing Other People's Joy," *Greater Good,* July 15, 2017, https://
greatergood.berkeley.edu/article/item/how_to_overcome_stress_by
_seeing_other_peoples_joy.

Page 109 **"happiest man in the world":** Ronald Siegel, interview with authors via
Zoom, June 3, 2021.

Page 110 **"Can I please switch":** Ronald Siegel, "Overcoming Burnout: Moving
from Empathy to Compassion," *Praxis,* July 3, 2019, https://www
.praxiscet.com/posts/overcoming-burnout-moving-from-empathy-to
-compassion/.

Page 110 **That's the magic of:** Siegel, "Overcoming Burnout."

Page 110 **leading compassion researcher:** Tania Singer and Olga M. Klimecki,
"Empathy and Compassion," *Current Biology* 24, no. 18 (2014):
R875–78, https://doi.org/10.1016/j.cub.2014.06.054.

Page 112 **We see the impact:** Denise Lavoie, "Two 9/11 Widows Raise Funds to Help Bereaved Afghan Women," Boston.com, August 4, 2010, http:// archive.boston.com/news/local/massachusetts/articles/2010/08/04/two _911_widows_raise_funds_to_help_bereaved_afghan_women/.

Page 114 **One proven way to:** Antoine Lutz, Julie Brefczynski-Lewis, Tom Johnstone, and Richard J. Davidson, "Regulation of the Neural Circuitry of Emotion by Compassion Meditation: Effects of Meditative Expertise," *PLoS ONE* 3, no. 3 (2008): e1897, https://doi.org/10.1371/journal.pone .0001897.

Page 113 **"Empathy, without care":** Richard Davidson, "Tuesday Tip: Shift from Empathy to Compassion," Healthy Minds Innovations, December 8, 2020, https://hminnovations.org/blog/learn-practice/tuesday-tip-shift -from-empathy-to-compassion.

Page 113 **shift your attitude or "orientation":** Davidson, "Tuesday Tip."

Page 114 **"Wishing Your Loved Ones":** Richard Davidson, Healthy Minds Program app, Healthy Minds Innovations, https://hminnovations.org /meditation-app.

Page 114 **a free track:** Healthy Minds Innovations, "Wishing Your Loved Ones Well: Seated Practice," SoundCloud, 2021, https://soundcloud.com/user -984650879/wishing-your-loved-ones-well-seated-practice.

Page 114 **"May you experience":** Healthy Minds Innovations, "Wishing Your Loved Ones Well."

Page 114 **Ricard, the so-called happiest man:** Matthieu Ricard, "Interview with Matthieu Ricard," interview by Taking Charge of Your Health & Wellbeing, University of Minnesota, 2016, https://www.takingcharge.csh.umn.edu /interview-matthieu-ricard.

Page 114 **"then I think we should":** Ricard, "Interview."

Page 114 **"not center too much":** Ricard, "Interview."

Page 115 **Some researchers have suggested that empathic:** Dorian Peters and Rafael Calvo, "Compassion vs. Empathy," *Interactions* 21, no. 5 (2014): 48–53, https://doi.org/10.1145/2647087; and Jennifer L. Goetz, Dacher Keltner, and Emiliana Simon-Thomas, "Compassion: An Evolutionary Analysis and Empirical Review," *Psychological Bulletin* 136, no. 3 (2010): 351–74, https://doi.org/10.1037/a0018807.

Page 115 **people are less likely to move to compassion:** Peters and Calvo, "Compassion vs. Empathy"; and Goetz et al., "Compassion."

Page 116 **Research shows that when:** McGonigal, "Seeing Other People's Joy."

Page 116   **"Is this feeling mine"**: Brooke Nielsen, interview with authors via Zoom, June 4, 2021.

Page 118   **"I hope you packed"**: Horne, interview.

Page 118   **"For the first time"**: Horne, interview.

Page 119   **"stop running"**: Horne, interview.

Page 119   **"Highly sensitive people process everything"**: Horne, "Sensitive and Burned Out?"

Chapter 6: Full-Hearted Love

Page 121   **"I was that annoying kid"**: Brian R. Johnston and Sarah Johnston, interview with authors via Zoom, August 12, 2021.

Page 121   **Although they knew:** Brian R. Johnston, "My High Sensitivity Saved My Marriage. But First, It Almost Ruined It," Highly Sensitive Refuge, November 4, 2020, https://highlysensitiverefuge.com/my-high -sensitivity-saved-my-marriage/.

Page 122   **"I may not be"**: Johnston and Johnston, interview.

Page 122   **"instant family"**: Johnston and Johnston, interview.

Page 122   **"She's the kind of"**: Johnston and Johnston, interview.

Page 122   **"completely different"**: Johnston and Johnston, interview.

Page 124   **"Being sensitive is something"**: Johnston and Johnston, interview.

Page 124   **Sensitivity expert Elaine Aron:** Elain Aron, *The Highly Sensitive Person in Love: Understanding and Managing Relationships When the World Overwhelms You* (New York: Harmony Books, 2016).

Page 124   **"bored" and "stuck"**: Aron, *Highly Sensitive Person in Love.*

Page 124   **"When you are bored"**: Aron, *Highly Sensitive Person in Love.*

Page 127   **American Perspectives Survey:** Daniel A. Cox, "The State of American Friendship: Change, Challenges, and Loss," Survey Center on American Life, June 8, 2021, https://www.americansurveycenter.org/research/the -state-of-american-friendship-change-challenges-and-loss/.

Page 127   **from helping you live longer:** Julianne Holt-Lunstad, Timothy B. Smith, and J. Bradley Layton, "Social Relationships and Mortality Risk: A Meta-Analytic Review," *PLoS Medicine* 7, no. 7 (2010), https://doi.org /10.1371/journal.pmed.1000316.

Page 127   **recover from illness:** Office of Public Affairs, "Seven Reasons Why
Loving Relationships Are Good for You," University of Utah,
February 14, 2017, https://healthcare.utah.edu/healthfeed/postings/2017
/02/relationships.php.

Page 127   **making you happier:** Johnny Wood, "Why Workplace Friendships Can
Make You Happier and More Productive," World Economic Forum,
November 22, 2019, https://www.weforum.org/agenda/2019/11/friends
-relationships-work-productivity-career/.

Page 127   **Harvard Medical School goes:** "The Health Benefits of Strong
Relationships," Harvard Health Publishing, November 22, 2010, https://
www.health.harvard.edu/staying-healthy/the-health-benefits-of-strong
-relationships.

Page 128   **valuable things in our lives:** Margaret S. Clark, Aaron Greenberg, Emily
Hill, Edward P. Lemay, Elizabeth Clark-Polner, and David Roosth,
"Heightened Interpersonal Security Diminishes the Monetary Value of
Possessions," *Journal of Experimental Social Psychology* 47, no. 2 (2011):
359–64, https://doi.org/10.1016/j.jesp.2010.08.001.

Page 128   **In South Sudan:** "War and Peace and Cows," presented by Noel King
and Gregory Warner, *Planet Money*, NPR, November 15, 2017, https://
www.npr.org/transcripts/563787988.

Page 128   **But according to:** Eli J. Finkel. *The All-or-Nothing Marriage: How the Best
Marriages Work* (New York: Dutton, 2017); and Eli J. Finkel, "The All-or-
Nothing Marriage," *New York Times*, February 14, 2014, https://www
.nytimes.com/2014/02/15/opinion/sunday/the-all-or-nothing-marriage
.html.

Page 129   **"It's thin-skinned":** *Sideways,* directed by Alexander Payne (Fox
Searchlight Pictures, 2004), DVD.

Page 132   **Researchers have found that couples' conflicts:** John Gottman, *The
Marriage Clinic: A Scientifically-Based Marital Therapy* (New York:
Norton, 1999); and B. J. Atkinson, *Emotional Intelligence in Couples
Therapy: Advances in Neurobiology and the Science of Intimate
Relationships* (New York: Norton, 2005).

Page 132   **"When my husband":** Megan Griffith, "How to Survive a Fight with
Your Partner When You're the Sensitive One," Highly Sensitive Refuge,
February 19, 2020, https://highlysensitiverefuge.com/how-to-survive-a
-fight-with-your-partner-when-youre-the-sensitive-one/.

Page 132   **However, avoiding conflict:** April Snow, email correspondence with authors, September 1, 2021.

Page 132   **"the other person":** Snow, email correspondence.

Page 132   **"You learn how to":** Snow, email correspondence.

Page 133   **Bill Eddy of the:** William A. Eddy, *It's All Your Fault!: 12 Tips for Managing People Who Blame Others for Everything* (San Diego: High Conflict Institute Press, 2008).

Page 134   **In light of her thirty years:** Lisa Firestone, "4 Ways to Say (and Get) What You Want in Your Relationship," *Psychology Today,* December 11, 2015, https://www.psychologytoday.com/us/blog/compassion-matters /201512/4-ways-say-and-get-what-you-want-in-your-relationship.

Page 134   **"When you speak":** Firestone, "4 Ways to Say."

Page 135   **Your words should be:** Firestone, "4 Ways to Say."

Page 135   **Vulnerability has been:** Brené Brown, *Daring Greatly: How the Courage to Be Vulnerable Transforms the Way We Live, Love, Parent, and Lead* (New York: Gotham Books, 2012).

Page 136   **"rough edges":** Robert Glover, *No More Mr. Nice Guy: A Proven Plan for Getting What You Want in Love, Sex, and Life* (Philadelphia: Running Press, 2017).

Page 136   **"Vulnerable is the only":** Seth Godin and Hugh MacLeod, *V Is for Vulnerable: Life Outside the Comfort Zone* (New York: Penguin, 2012).

Page 137   **"Ask anyone who":** Deborah Ward, "The HSP Relationship Dilemma: Are You Too Sensitive or Are You Neglecting Yourself?" *Psychology Today,* February 2, 2018, https://www.psychologytoday.com/us/blog /sense-and-sensitivity/201802/the-hsp-relationship-dilemma.

Page 138   **First, you must get:** Sharon Martin, "How to Set Boundaries with Toxic People," Live Well with Sharon Martin, December 14, 2017, https://www.livewellwithsharonmartin.com/set-boundaries-toxic -people/.

Page 138   **"I've seen people":** Sharon Martin, email correspondence with authors, April 3, 2022.

Page 139   **That's where a:** Martin, "Boundaries with Toxic People."

Page 139   **"Narcissistic and 'toxic' people":** Martin, email correspondence.

Page 140   **"extreme end":** Johnston and Johnston, interview.

Page 140   **"I don't need to change":** Johnston and Johnston, interview.

Page 141   **"It's not a character defect":** Johnston and Johnston, interview.

Chapter 7: Raising a Sensitive Generation

Page 150   **"It is so difficult":** Elaine Aron, "For Highly Sensitive Teenagers," part 1, "Feeling Different," The Highly Sensitive Person, February 28, 2008, https://hsperson.com/for-highly-sensitive-teenagers-feeling-different/.

Page 151   **sensitive people suffer more:** Bianca Acevedo, *The Highly Sensitive Brain: Research, Assessment, and Treatment of Sensory Processing Sensitivity* (San Diego: Academic Press, 2020).

Page 151   **To take just one example:** Barak Morgan, Robert Kumsta, Pasco Fearon, Dirk Moser, Sarah Skeen, Peter Cooper, Lynne Murray, Greg Moran, and Mark Tomlinson, "Serotonin Transporter Gene (*SLC6A4*) Polymorphism and Susceptibility to a Home-Visiting Maternal-Infant Attachment Intervention Delivered by Community Health Workers in South Africa: Reanalysis of a Randomized Controlled Trial," *PLOS Medicine* 14, no. 2 (2017): e1002237, https://doi.org/10.1371/journal.pmed.1002237.

Page 152   **Michael Pluess found:** Michael Pluess, Stephanie A. De Brito, Alice Jones Bartoli, Eamon McCrory, Essi Viding, "Individual Differences in Sensitivity to the Early Environment as a Function of Amygdala and Hippocampus Volumes: An Exploratory Analysis in 12-Year-Old Boys," *Development and Psychopathology* (2020): 1–10, https://doi.org/10.1017/S0954579420001698.

Page 153   **A study from the:** Brandi Stupica, Laura J. Sherman, and Jude Cassidy, "Newborn Irritability Moderates the Association Between Infant Attachment Security and Toddler Exploration and Sociability," *Child Development* 82, no. 5 (2011): 1381–89, https://doi.org/10.1111/j.1467-8624.2011.01638.x.

Page 153   **Pediatrician W. Thomas Boyce:** W. Thomas Boyce, *The Orchid and the Dandelion: Why Some Children Struggle and How All Can Thrive* (New York: Alfred A. Knopf, 2019).

Page 156   **"They would have trouble":** Maureen Gaspari, "Discipline Strategies for the Sensitive Child," The Highly Sensitive Child, August 28, 2018, https://www.thehighlysensitivechild.com/discipline-strategies-for-the-sensitive-child/.

Page 156   **In a review of studies:** Monika Baryła-Matejczuk, Małgorzata
Artymiak, Rosario Ferrer-Cascales, and Moises Betancort, "The Highly
Sensitive Child as a Challenge for Education: Introduction to the
Concept," *Problemy Wczesnej Edukacji* 48, no. 1 (2020): 51–62, https://
doi.org/10.26881/pwe.2020.48.05.

Page 157   **"They tend to act as":** Amanda Van Mulligen, "Why Gentle Discipline
Works Best with the Highly Sensitive Child," Highly Sensitive Refuge,
March 27, 2019, https://highlysensitiverefuge.com/highly-sensitive
-child-gentle-discipline/.

Page 157   **That's why Baryła-Matejczuk:** Baryła-Matejczuk, "Challenge for
Education."

Page 159   **"I am not perfect":** Gaspari, "Discipline Strategies."

Page 163   **One study even found that:** Kimberley Brindle, Richard Moulding,
Kaitlyn Bakker, and Maja Nedeljkovic, "Is the Relationship Between
Sensory-Processing Sensitivity and Negative Affect Mediated by
Emotional Regulation?," *Australian Journal of Psychology* 67, no. 4
(2015): 214–21, https://doi.org/10.1111/ajpy.12084.

Page 163   **According to psychologist:** John Gottman, Lynn Fainsilber Katz, and
Carole Hooven, *Meta-Emotion: How Families Communicate Emotionally*
(New York: Routledge, 2013).

Page 165   **Girls tend to learn:** G. Young, and J. Zeman, "Emotional Expression
Management and Social Acceptance in Childhood," poster presented at
Society for Research in Child Development, Tampa, FL, April 2003.

Page 165   **According to the data, parents:** Susan Adams, Janet Kuebli, Patricia A.
Boyle, and Robyn Fivush, "Gender Differences in Parent-Child
Conversations About Past Emotions: A Longitudinal Investigation," *Sex
Roles* 33 (1995): 309–23, https://link.springer.com/article/10.1007
/BF01954572.

Page 165   **particularly comfortable sharing:** Robyn Fivush, "Exploring Sex
Differences in the Emotional Context of Mother-Child Conversations
About the Past," *Sex Roles* 20 (1989): 675–91, https://link.springer.com
/article/10.1007/BF00288079.

Page 165   **Sons are more likely:** Susanne A. Denham, Susan Renwick-DeBardi,
and Susan Hewes, "Affective Communication Between Mothers
and Preschoolers: Relations with Social Emotional Competence,"
Merrill-Palmer Quarterly 40 (1994): 488–508, www.jstor.org/stable
/23087919.

Page 166   **All children are damaged by:** Young and Zeman, "Emotional
Expression Management"; Adams et al., "Gender Differences in Parent-
Child Conversations"; Fivush, "Exploring Sex Differences"; and
Denham et al., "Mothers and Preschoolers."

Page 166   **Researchers have identified:** Peter A. Wyman, Wendi Cross,
C. Hendricks Brown, Qin Yu, Xin Tu, and Shirley Eberly, "Intervention
to Strengthen Emotional Self-Regulation in Children with Emerging
Mental Health Problems: Proximal Impact on School Behavior," *Journal
of Abnormal Child Psychology* 38, no. 5 (2010): 707–20, https://doi.org
/10.1007/s10802-010-9398-x.

Chapter 8: More Than Just a Paycheck

Page 171   **One survey even found:** Bhavini Shrivastava, "Identify and Unleash
Your Talent," BCS, The Chartered Institute for IT, July 24, 2019, https://
www.bcs.org/articles-opinion-and-research/identify-and-unleash-your
-talent/.

Page 176   **In fact, if you believe:** Linda Binns, "Why Your Workplace Doesn't
Value HSPs—and How to Change That," Highly Sensitive Refuge,
October 11, 2021, https://highlysensitiverefuge.com/why-your
-workplace-doesnt-value-hsps-and-how-to-change-that/.

Page 176   **"When you see yourself":** Binns, "Workplace Doesn't Value HSPs."

Page 177   **"They are often driven":** Anne Marie Crosthwaite, "I Am a Highly
Sensitive Person. Here's What I Wish More People Knew About HSPs,"
MindBodyGreen, August 4, 2017, https://www.mindbodygreen.com
/articles/i-am-a-highly-sensitive-person-heres-what-i-wish-more
-people-knew-about-hsps/.

Page 177   **According to research by management consulting:** Naina Dhingra,
Andrew Samo, Bill Schaninger, and Matt Schrimper, "Help Your
Employees Find Purpose—or Watch Them Leave," McKinsey &
Company, April 5, 2021, https://www.mckinsey.com/business-functions
/people-and-organizational-performance/our-insights/help-your
-employees-find-purpose-or-watch-them-leave.

Page 177   **by one estimate:** Shawn Achor, Andrew Reece, Gabriella Kellerman, and
Alexi Robichaux, "9 out of 10 People Are Willing to Earn Less Money to
Do More-Meaningful Work," *Harvard Business Review,* November 6,

2018, https://hbr.org/2018/11/9-out-of-10-people-are-willing-to-earn -less-money-to-do-more-meaningful-work.

Page 177   **Companies also retain:** Reece, "Meaning and Purpose at Work."

Page 179   **"most actors are":** Jennifer Aniston, "Nicole Kidman Steps into Spring," *Harper's Bazaar,* January 5, 2011, https://www.harpersbazaar.com /celebrity/latest/news/a643/nicole-kidman-interview-0211/.

Page 179   **Dolly Parton:** Lauren Effron, "Dolly Parton Opens Up About Song Inspirations, Being 'Aunt Dolly' to Female Country Artists and Those Tattoos," *ABC News,* November 11, 2019, https://abcnews.go.com /Entertainment/dolly-parton-opens-song-inspirations-aunt-dolly -female/story?id=66801989.

Page 179   **Lorde:** Rob Haskell, "Good Lorde! Behind the Blissed-Out Comeback of a Pop Iconoclast," *Vogue,* September 8, 2021, https://www.vogue.com /article/lorde-cover-october-2021.

Page 179   **Elton John:** Tatiana Siegel, " 'Rocketman' Takes Flight: Inside Taron Egerton's Transformation into Elton John (and, He Hopes, a Major Star)," *Hollywood Reporter,* May 6, 2019, https://www.hollywoodreporter .com/movies/movie-features/rocketman-takes-taron-egertons -transformation-elton-john-1207544/.

Page 179   **Yo-Yo Ma:** Carolyn Gregoire, "Why So Many Artists Are Highly Sensitive People," *HuffPost,* December 28, 2015, https://www.huffpost .com/entry/artists-sensitive-creative_n_567f02dee4b0b958f6598764 ?u4ohia4i=.

Page 179   **Alanis Morissette:** *Sensitive: The Untold Story,* directed by Will Harper (Global Touch Group, Inc., 2015), DVD.

Page 179   **Bruce Springsteen:** Bruce Springsteen, "Bruce Springsteen: On Jersey, Masculinity and Wishing to Be His Stage Persona," interview by Terry Gross, *Fresh Air,* NPR, October 5, 2016, https://www.npr.org/2016/10/05 /496639696/bruce-springsteen-on-jersey-masculinity-and-wishing-to -be-his-stage-persona.

Page 179   **Creative people tend to:** Scott Barry and Carolyn Gregoire, *Wired to Create: Unraveling the Mysteries of the Creative Mind* (New York: TarcherPerigee, 2016).

Page 179   **"Creative people's openness":** Barry and Gregoire, *Wired to Create.*

Page 179   **Barrie Jaeger, author of:** Barrie Jaeger, *Making Work Work for the Highly Sensitive Person* (New York: McGraw-Hill, 2004).

Page 181   **The reason, according to:** Cal Newport, interview with authors via Zoom, April 29, 2021.

Page 182   **Your hunter-gatherer brain:** Newport, interview.

Page 182   *hyperactive hive mind:* Newport, interview.

Page 182   **"It's a disaster":** Newport, interview.

Page 182   **"It's extra bad":** Newport, interview.

Page 184   **"These things would happen":** Newport, interview.

Page 185   **When researcher Amy Wrzesniewski:** David Zax, "Want to Be Happier at Work? Learn How from These 'Job Crafters,'" *Fast Company,* June 3, 2013, https://www.fastcompany.com/3011081/want-to-be-happier-at -work-learn-how-from-these-job-crafters.

Page 185   **Wrzesniewski developed what she calls:** Amy Wrzesniewski and Jane E. Dutton, "Crafting a Job: Revisioning Employees as Active Crafters of Their Work," *Academy of Management Review* 26, no. 2 (2001): 179–201, https://doi.org/10.5465/amr.2001.4378011; and Justin M. Berg, Jane E. Dutton, and Amy Wrzesniewski, "Job Crafting and Meaningful Work," in *Purpose and Meaning in the Workplace*, ed. Bryan J. Dik, Zinta S. Byrne, and Michael F. Steger (Washington, DC: American Psychological Association, 2013).

Page 185   **Since then, countless studies:** Rebecca Fraser-Thill, "The 5 Biggest Myths About Meaningful Work," *Forbes,* August 7, 2019, https://www .forbes.com/sites/rebeccafraserthill/2019/08/07/the-5-biggest-myths -about-meaningful-work/?sh=7cda524770b8; Catherine Bailey, "What Makes Work Meaningful—or Meaningless," *MIT Sloan Management Review,* June 1, 2016, https://sloanreview.mit.edu/article /what-makes-work-meaningful-or-meaningless/; Amy Wrzesniewski, Nicholas LoBuglio, Jane E. Dutton, and Justin M. Berg, "Job Crafting and Cultivating Positive Meaning and Identity in Work," *Advances in Positive Organizational Psychology* (2013): 281–302, https://doi.org/10 .1108/s2046-410x(2013)0000001015; Wrzesniewski and Dutton, "Crafting a Job"; and Justin M. Berg, Amy Wrzesniewski, and Jane E. Dutton, "Perceiving and Responding to Challenges in Job Crafting at Different Ranks: When Proactivity Requires Adaptivity," *Journal of Organizational Behavior* 31, no. 2–3 (2010): 158–86, https://doi.org/10 .1002/job.645.

Page 185   **everything from blue-collar jobs:** Berg et al., "Challenges in Job Crafting."

Page 185   **Job crafting is effective:** Tom Rath, "Job Crafting from the Outside In,"
           Harvard Business Review, March 24, 2020, https://hbr.org/2020/03/job
           -crafting-from-the-outside-in; and Wrzesniewski and Dutton, "Crafting
           a Job," 187, 193–194.

Page 186   **In fact, since job crafting tends:** Cort W. Rudolph, Ian M. Katz,
           Kristi N. Lavigne, and Hannes Zacher, "Job Crafting: A Meta-Analysis
           of Relationships with Individual Differences, Job Characteristics, and
           Work Outcomes," *Journal of Vocational Behavior* 102 (2017): 112–38,
           https://doi.org/10.1016/j.jvb.2017.05.008.

Page 186   **When researchers compared:** Alessio Gori, Alessandro Arcioni,
           Eleonora Topino, Letizia Palazzeschi, and Annamaria Di Fabio,
           "Constructing Well-Being in Organizations: First Empirical Results on
           Job Crafting, Personality Traits, and Insight," *International Journal of
           Environmental Research and Public Health* 18, no. 12 (2021): 6661,
           https://doi.org/10.3390/ijerph18126661.

Page 186   **Part of job crafting means:** Wrzesniewski and Dutton, "Crafting a Job";
           and Berg et al., "Job Crafting and Meaningful Work."

Page 186   **This aspect of job crafting:** Wrzesniewski and Dutton, "Crafting a Job";
           and Berg et al., "Job Crafting and Meaningful Work," pp. 89–92.

Page 187   **For example, a nurse's job:** Wrzesniewski and Dutton, "Crafting a Job,"
           185–86.

Page 187   *task crafting:* Wrzesniewski and Dutton, "Crafting a Job"; and Berg et
           al., "Job Crafting and Meaningful Work," 86–87.

Page 188   **Research shows that having meaningful:** L. Meyers, "Social
           Relationships Matter in Job Satisfaction," *American Psychological
           Association* 38, no. 4 (2007), https://www.apa.org/monitor/apr07/social.

Page 188   *relational crafting:* Wrzesniewski and Dutton, "Crafting a Job"; and
           Berg et al., "Job Crafting and Meaningful Work," 87–89.

Page 189   **tailor your approach:** Berg et al., "Challenges in Job Crafting."

Page 189   **According to Cal Newport:** Newport, interview.

Chapter 9: The Sensitive Revolution

Page 191   **One of the worst:** "The Bank War," presented by Jacob Goldstein and
           Robert Smith, *Planet Money,* NPR, March 24, 2017, https://www.npr.org
           /transcripts/521436839; and Martin A. Armstrong, "Panic of 1837,"

Armstrong Economics, Princeton Economic Institute, n.d., https://www
.armstrongeconomics.com/panic-of-1837/.

Page 191 **Another, the so-called Long Depression:** Wikipedia, s.v. "Long
Depression," updated December 13, 2020, https://en.wikipedia.org/wiki
/Long_Depression.

Page 191 **"might as well die":** U.S. Department of the Interior, National Park
Service, "The Baltimore and Ohio Railroad Martinsburg Shops,"
National Historical Landmark Nomination document, July 31, 2003, 41,
https://npgallery.nps.gov/pdfhost/docs/NHLS/Text/03001045.pdf.

Page 192 **A little-known labor activist:** "Her Life: The Woman Behind the New
Deal," Frances Perkins Center, 2022, http://francesperkinscenter.org/life
-new/.

Page 192 **But she came with a condition:** "Her Life."

Page 192 **President Roosevelt agreed:** "Her Life."

Page 193 **Her grandson, Tomlin:** Tomlin Perkins Coggeshall, founder of the
Frances Perkins Center, interview with authors via Zoom, September 16,
2021.

Page 193 **"The people are what matter":** Frances Perkins and J. Paul St. Sure, *Two
Views of American Labor* (Los Angeles: Institute of Industrial Relations,
University of California, 1965), 2.

Page 193 **We now know that the New Deal:** Brian Dunleavy, "Did New Deal
Programs Help End the Great Depression?," *History*, September 10,
2018, https://www.history.com/.amp/news/new-deal-effects-great
-depression.

Page 194 **Low status versus high:** Keith Johnstone and Irving Wardle, *Impro:
Improvisation and the Theatre* (New York: Bloomsbury Academic, 2019).

Page 194 **Keith Johnstone, a playwright:** Johnstone, *Impro.*

Page 194 **We all switch our status:** Assael Romanelli, "The Key to Unlocking the
Power Dynamic in Your Life," *Psychology Today,* November 27, 2019,
https://www.psychologytoday.com/us/blog/the-other-side-relationships
/201911/the-key-unlocking-the-power-dynamic-in-your-life.

Page 195 **Women and introverts:** Susan Cain, "7 Tips to Improve Communication
Skills," April 20, 2015, https://susancain.net/7-ways-to-use-powerless
-communication/#.

Page 195 **researchers turned to a hospital in Boston:** Daniel Goleman and
Richard E. Boyatzis, "Social Intelligence and the Biology of Leadership,"

Harvard Business Review, October 31, 2016, https://hbr.org/2008/09/social-intelligence-and-the-biology-of-leadership.

Page 195 **"Both of them headed":** Goleman and Boyatzis, "Social Intelligence."

Page 196 **"Leading effectively is":** Goleman and Boyatzis, "Social Intelligence."

Page 196 **According to one study:** Tracy Brower, "Empathy Is the Most Important Leadership Skill According to Research," *Forbes,* September 19, 2021, https://www.forbes.com/sites/tracybrower/2021/09/19/empathy-is-the-most-important-leadership-skill-according-to-research/?sh=15d7a3453dc5.

Page 197 **Along with being:** Eric Owens, "Why Highly Sensitive People Make the Best Leaders," Highly Sensitive Refuge, March 4, 2020, https://highlysensitiverefuge.com/why-highly-sensitive-people-make-the-best-leaders/.

Page 197 **Euny Hong, a Korean American journalist:** Adrienne Matei, "What Is 'Nunchi,' the Korean Secret to Happiness?," *Guardian,* November 11, 2019, https://www.theguardian.com/lifeandstyle/2019/nov/11/what-is-nunchi-the-korean-secret-to-happiness.

Page 197 **"Kids in Korea":** Matei, "What Is 'Nunchi'?"

Page 197 **When Amy Cuddy:** Emma Seppälä, "The Hard Data on Being a Nice Boss," *Harvard Business Review,* November 24, 2014, https://hbr.org/2014/11/the-hard-data-on-being-a-nice-boss.

Page 198 **They are more likely to analyze:** Owens, "Make the Best Leaders."

Page 204 **"You were born to be":** Elaine Aron, *The Highly Sensitive Person: How to Thrive When the World Overwhelms You* (New York: Broadway Books, 1998).

Page 206 **"My dad, like most of us":** Brittany Blount, "Being an HSP Is a Superpower—but It's Almost Impossible to Explain It," Highly Sensitive Refuge, March 4, 2019, https://highlysensitiverefuge.com/highly-sensitive-person-hsp-superpower/.

Page 206 **"You know how Superman":** Blount, "Being an HSP Is a Superpower."

Page 206 **"I believe it":** Blount, "Being an HSP Is a Superpower."

Page 207 **The term** *gaslighting:* Brian Duignan, "Gaslighting," *Encyclopedia Britannica,* n.d., https://www.britannica.com/topic/gaslighting.

Page 207 **Telling you that you're overreacting:** Julie L. Hall, "When Narcissists and Enablers Say You're Too Sensitive," *Psychology Today,* February 21,

2021, https://www.psychologytoday.com/us/blog/the-narcissist-in-your
-life/202102/when-narcissists-and-enablers-say-youre-too-sensitive.

Page 208 **When people say these things:** Hall, "Narcissists and Enablers."

Page 211 **"long before more robust":** Kurt Vonnegut, "Physicist, Heal Thyself,"
Chicago Tribune, June 22, 1969.

Index

sensitive

....

Jenn Granneman and Andre Sólo

A BOOK CLUB GUIDE

Dear readers,

Both of us—Jenn and Andre—grew up as sensitive kids, and neither of us knew what that meant. We only knew that we saw the world a little differently than other people and didn't always fit in. In fact, the message we got was to "fix" our sensitivity (or at least hide it). "Stop being so sensitive!" and "it's not a big deal" were phrases we heard time and time again. We wondered why we couldn't handle common things that other people seemed to handle easily, like a busy day at school or a loud party with friends. We found ourselves needing to slow down, to pause, to build downtime into our lives—all while the others around us seemed ready to go, go, go. Because of our sensitivity, we thought something was wrong with us.

Like us, if you're also a sensitive person, you may have been shamed for your sensitivity or made to feel like you had to toughen up and power through. Or maybe you are turning to our book not because you consider yourself to be a sensitive person but because you have a sensitive person in your life: a spouse, child, or coworker. If so, there is one message that we hope you take away from our book, for yourself and for others: Being sensitive is a strength, not a drawback. It comes with many gifts, such as increased creativity, empathy, and attention to detail. Sensitivity is more than just a "normal" and healthy trait—when harnessed correctly, it's an advantage in an often loud, rushed, and insensitive world.

Perhaps you see the gifts of sensitivity in your own life. You see how your need to slow down and reflect leads to deeper insights and unique solutions. Or how your "people radar" and heightened attention to detail make you the ultimate human lie detector and body language decoder. Perhaps you are the friend or colleague who everyone seeks out for your advice and wisdom. Or, like other famous sensitive people—Nicole Kidman, Dolly Parton, Yo-Yo Ma, and others—your sensitivity

264 A Book Club Guide

fuels your creativity. Could you really do these things without your sensitivity? Probably not.

As you read *Sensitive*, you may discover that you are—or are not—a highly sensitive person. The questions that follow are designed with both kinds of reader in mind. Sure, you can answer them in a journal, but we gently encourage you to discuss them with others (and not to be afraid to go deep—something sensitive people do best!). By talking about your own experiences of sensitivity, you help normalize the trait for others. And when you do that, you help to end the stigma that being sensitive is a flaw or a weakness.

Ultimately, this is the mission of *Sensitive*: to show the world that sensitive is strong. We wish our younger selves could have lived in a world where sensitivity was celebrated, not ridiculed or punished. We can't go back in time and change the past, but we can work to change the future for sensitive people today.

By picking up this book, you have become a part of that shift: You are helping to change what it means to be sensitive.

Welcome to the sensitive revolution.

Peacefully yours,
Jenn and Andre

Set the Sensitive Vibe

Both of us have cozy reading nooks of our own, and we use our environment to avoid overstimulation. Here's our dream environment for reading *Sensitive*—which in many ways matches the environment where it was written!

Sip: Rooibos or chamomile tea to soothe the mind without caffeine. A rich, velvety Zinfandel for wine lovers.

Listen: Anything gentle and dreamy—try Chopin's nocturnes. A white noise app to let the world fall away.

Breathe: A cedar-scented or amber candle. A slightly open window on a breezy night.

Soothe: A soft lamp, no overhead light. Fuzzy things. Always fuzzy things.

Ask: Family or roommates to give you an hour of quiet. To be patient with yourself when you pause and think, write, hum, daydream.

Questions and Topics for Discussion

1. How did you define "sensitive" before reading this book? How do you define it now?

2. Do you identify as a sensitive or highly sensitive person? Does the book help you understand anyone else you know?

3. Why do you think society at large looks down on sensitivity and rewards "toughness"? What might we look like if we listened to the Sensitive Way instead of buying into the Toughness Myth?

4. Either through examples in the book or your own experience, why is sensitivity a "gift"? Or what are the gifts that come with being sensitive?

5. What are some of the costs of being a sensitive person?

6. What makes you feel overstimulated? The book offers several tools to deal with overstimulation. What have you tried? What would you like to try?

7. Talk about empathy—both the positives and drawbacks. How do the emotions of others affect you? Why do negative emotions spread more quickly than positive ones?

8. What are some strengths of being sensitive when it comes to relationships? What are some of the challenges?

9. Talk about the importance of boundaries for sensitive people. What purpose do they serve? Are they difficult or easy for you to establish?

10. What are some healthy, mindful ways to parent a sensitive child?

11. What might be some benefits of hiring sensitive employees? What can companies do to accommodate them so that they can offer their best?

12. Do you think sensitive people make good leaders? Why or why not?

13. Are there people in your life with whom you'd share this book? Why do you think they would enjoy or relate?

What to Do When You Feel Overstimulated – a Checklist

The sensitive mind processes everything deeply. This deep processing is the source of our gifts, but it can also lead to overstimulation. Here's what to do when overstimulation rears its head:

1. Take a break.

   - "I need a few minutes to sort out my thoughts."
   - "I'm feeling overstimulated. I'm going to take a short walk to calm my body down."
   - "Let me think about your question and get back to you."

2. Bring your awareness to your body.

   - What emotions am I feeling right now?
   - What thoughts or images come to mind?
   - Where in my body am I experiencing these emotions?
   - How does my body feel, physically?

3. Overstimulation is, at its root, a threat response.

   - Remind yourself that you're not actually in danger, despite what your nervous system is telling you.
   - When you feel overstimulated, it is simply your highly sensitive brain doing what it does best—going deep.

4. Give yourself calming sensory input.

   - A hug.
   - Gentle exercise—stretch, take a short walk, or do mini desk push-ups.
   - Put your back against a wall and push against it.
   - Turn down the lights or take a few minutes in a darker, calmer space.

5. Imagine yourself as a child and speak comforting words to yourself.

   - "I know this isn't easy for you."
   - "I can feel your pain."
   - "You're not alone, I'm here with you."
   - "Tell me what's wrong."

6. Introduce lightheartedness and play.

   - Find something funny to laugh about.
   - Play with your child.
   - Sing along to the car radio.

7. Spend time relaxing in a place that feels safe, calm, and comfortable to you—your personal sanctuary.

8. Consider whether you need to set some boundaries to prevent the overstimulation from happening again.

9. Above all, give yourself time.

   - In this moment, it might feel like the overstimulation will never end and your feelings will never change—but they will.
   - Even a few minutes from now, you will feel differently.
   - In a few hours or days, this moment will be nothing but a memory.

How to Explain Being Sensitive to Others

What to say, in a nutshell:

"I'm a sensitive person. Being sensitive means you're wired to process information deeply. That deep processing helps me a lot, because it means I often pick up on things that others miss. But it also means I can get overstimulated easily."

Your sensitive talking points:

1. **Keep it simple.** Being a sensitive person means . . .

   - Your brain is wired to process information deeply.
   - You respond strongly to your environment.
   - You think deeply, feel strongly, and notice subtle details that others miss.

2. **Keep it relatable.** Being sensitive is normal.

   - Sensitivity is a continuum. Everyone is sensitive to a degree.
   - Thirty percent of people score high for sensitivity—that's nearly one in three people in the world.
   - Being highly sensitive is a healthy personality trait that comes with many gifts.

3. **Keep it positive.** Your sensitivity is one of the best things about you.

   - Talk about the gifts. Sensitive gifts include deep thinking, creativity, empathy, understanding emotions, and being attuned to our physical surroundings.

- Use an example. Remy from the movie *Ratatouille* is a good example of a sensitive person. His sensitive nose could detect poison and his creativity made him an amazing chef.

4. When it really counts . . .

- **At work:** "I do my best work when I can schedule periods of uninterrupted time to focus. I'd like to talk to you about the best times for me to schedule those blocks."
- **At school:** "My child is a sensitive person, and we're trying to encourage that. Are you familiar with sensitivity as a personality trait?"
- **With friends:** "I'm sensitive, so I can get overstimulated sometimes. Can we meet somewhere a little quieter for drinks this time? I know a great place . . ."
- **On a date:** "I think of myself as a sensitive person. It's something a lot of people try to hide but I try to be open about it. It's something I like about myself."

Remember: The most powerful thing you can do as a sensitive person is accept and embrace your sensitivity. The more we normalize being sensitive, the more our sensitive gifts can help the world.

Meaningful Conversation Starters

Sensitive people are wired to go deep—and we struggle with shallow, superficial chitchat. Here are fifty prompts to start richer, more meaningful conversations.

Explain something you have learned recently, either about yourself or the world around you.

Name something you have recently struggled with. How are you coping with it?

Talk about an experience or a person who left a mark on you. How has this event or relationship stuck with you or changed you?

Talk about your spiritual beliefs—or your lack of spiritual beliefs—and how you came to believe these things.

Talk about a time when you felt scared. Why did you feel this way? Does thinking about the event still scare you today?

Read a scene or passage from your favorite book.

Play (or name) the last song you chose to listen to. Why did you choose this song?

Describe a kind act that someone recently did for you. What made it feel especially kind?

Describe a childhood memory—either a positive or negative experience.

Everyone has daily routines. Describe one of your routines and why it's important to you.

When you're feeling stressed or down, what is something that comforts you? What do you find comforting about it?

Would you enjoy being famous? Why or why not? And what would you choose to be famous for?

If you didn't have to worry about fashion or practicality, what outfit would you always wear because of how it makes you feel?

If you were going to spend a day completely alone, where would you spend it and what would you do?

Describe a person or a place that makes you feel happy.

Describe a childhood memory that still makes you laugh.

What did you dream about last night? Why do you think you dreamed this?

Tell the story (to the best of your knowledge) of how your parents met.

What three songs would be on your "happy" playlist? Your "sad" playlist? Why?

What's your favorite way to "waste time"? Why?

Name an object or place (not a person) that you instantly fell in love with. What made you love it so much?

Tell the story of a moment in your life that you wish the news had covered.

Name something that amazes you.

Say it's a typical day. What are three things that you can always count on happening?

Describe what you would consider a "perfect" day.

If you could choose anyone in the world as a dinner guest, who would you choose and why?

If you were given the chance to change one thing about your childhood, what would you change?

Is there something that you dream of doing but haven't done yet? What stops you from doing it?

If you could wake up tomorrow with a certain skill or ability, what would it be?

How do you feel about your relationship with your mother? Your father? Your siblings?

Share an embarrassing moment from any point in your life.

Describe a problem that you are currently experiencing and ask for advice on how to solve it.

Name a goal that you are working toward. What are you doing to reach this goal? Why do you want to achieve it?

Name something that has recently given you a surprising amount of inspiration.

Answer the question, "How are you?" but instead of saying, "fine" or "good," name a word or phrase that describes how you really feel.

What is one life lesson that you learned the hard way?

Everyone is creative on some level. Name a creative hobby, interest, or task that you do—and why you are drawn to it.

What is an idea, experience, or problem that recently kept you awake at night because you were thinking about it?

What is something that you don't usually tell people about yourself when you first meet them? Why do you hold it back?

What is something that you have done recently to better yourself as a person? Why did you choose to work on that thing?

Talk about an event, experience, or relationship that changed the trajectory of your life.

Talk about a good movie, show, or book you stumbled upon. In your opinion, what made it so good?

Name one thing that you miss about being a child. Why do you miss it?

If you had one chance—and only one—to travel back in time, when would you go and why?

If you had $100,000 to give away to any cause, which cause would you donate to and why?

If you magically gained an extra hour every day, what would you do more of and why?

If someone gave you all the money you needed to start a business, what business would you start and why?

Name a person or thing that you are grateful for today.

Name something that stresses you out when you're traveling.

What is something that most people enjoy but you dislike?

Resources, Advice, and Inspiration for Sensitive People

SensitiveRefuge.com

IntrovertDear.com

Join the sensitive refuge Facebook group to connect with other sensitive people:

Facebook.com/groups/sensitiverefuge

Get to know us:

@sensitiverefuge

@introvertdear

@jenngranneman

@justandresolo

ABOUT THE AUTHORS

Jenn Granneman and Andre Sólo are the creators of Sensitive Refuge, the world's largest website for sensitive people. Both are regular contributors to *Psychology Today* and *Forbes*.

Granneman is the founder and editor in chief of the world's largest online community for introverts, Introvert, Dear. An educator, journalist, and the author of *The Secret Lives of Introverts*, she has been featured in *HuffPost*, *The Washington Post*, the BBC, *Oprah Daily*, *BuzzFeed*, *Glamour*, and more, as well as numerous podcasts. Since embracing her own sensitivity, she reads too many self-help books and lives a pleasantly boring life in Saint Paul, Minnesota.

Sólo is the cofounder and editor in chief of Sensitive Refuge. He is an author, researcher, and international speaker, and serves as Chief Make-It-Happen Officer of Introvert, Dear. He has been interviewed by or featured in *HuffPost*, *The Washington Post*, MSNBC, *The Telegraph*, *Vogue*, and more, as well as numerous podcasts. He divides his time between New Orleans and Saint Paul, Minnesota, where he makes friends with misfits, over-waters his houseplants, and has a bad habit of taking on the impossible.

Sensitiverefuge.com
@sensitiverefuge

Introvertdear.com
@introvertdear